DATE DUE

LESSON 101:
Perfect Happiness

A Path to Joy
from
A COURSE IN MIRACLES

JON MUNDY, PhD

STERLING ETHOS

New York

STERLING ETHOS
New York

An Imprint of Sterling Publishing
387 Park Avenue South
New York, NY 10016

© 2014 by Jon Mundy

ISBN 978-1-4549-0818-0

Mundy, Jon.
  Lesson 101 : perfect happiness : a path to joy from a Course in miracles / Jon Mundy,
Ph.D.
     pages cm
Includes index.
ISBN 978-1-4549-0818-0
1. Course in Miracles. 2. Happiness--Religious aspects. I. Title.
BP605.C68M867 2014
299'.93--dc23
                    2013038768

Distributed in Canada by Sterling Publishing
c/o Canadian Manda Group, 165 Dufferin Street
Toronto, Ontario, Canada M6K 3H6
Distributed in the United Kingdom by GMC Distribution Services
Castle Place, 166 High Street, Lewes, East Sussex, England BN7 1XU
Distributed in Australia by Capricorn Link (Australia) Pty. Ltd.
P.O. Box 704, Windsor, NSW 2756, Australia

For information about custom editions, special sales, and
premium and corporate purchases, please contact Sterling Special Sales
at 800-805-5489 or specialsales@sterlingpublishing.com.

Manufactured in the United States

2 4 6 8 10 9 7 5 3 1

www.sterlingpublishing.com

This is a book about
Hope, Home, Happiness, and Heaven
It's about Light, Life, Laughter, and Love
It's about Truth, Trust, and Timelessness
It's about God, Goodness, and Grace

If Real Love is possible, if God, Heaven, Truth and Eternity are
Real then Perfect Happiness is not only possible,
it is the only thing there is.

MARIANNE WILLIAMSON,
AUTHOR OF *A RETURN TO LOVE*

✳

CONTENTS

PART III

Basic Principles in *A Course in Miracles*

PART IV

The Laws of Happiness

About the Course

A Course in Miracles was copyrighted in 1975 and published on June 26, 1976 by the Foundation for Inner Peace. It was scribed (through inner dictation) by Dr. Helen Schucman (1909–1981). Helen took down the Course in shorthand. She then read the notes to Dr. Bill Thetford (1923–1988), who typed up what she had taken down. The process began in October 1965 and ended in September 1972. Helen and Bill were both professors at Columbia University School of Physicians and Surgeons in New York City.

The Course consists of a *Textbook,* a *Workbook,* and a *Manual for Teachers,* plus two pamphlets that came from the same source as the Course. They are *Psychotherapy: Purpose, Process & Practice* and *The Song of Prayer.*

More than 2.5 million copies of the Course have been distributed in English. It has been translated into twenty-two different languages and there are several more translations in the works. Adding up the various translations, total sales are now in excess of 3 million. Respect for the Course has grown consistently since its publication. Having passed the test of time, it is now regarded by many as a modern spiritual classic.

Referencing *A Course in Miracles*

Quotations and paraphrasing from *A Course in Miracles,* unless otherwise designated, come from the third edition, published by the Foundation for Inner Peace. The location of the various quotes and paraphrases appears immediately after the reference with a listing of the chapter, section, paragraph, and sentence as in T-4.III.5:7. "T" means *Text,* "4" is the chapter, "III" is the section, "5" is the paragraph, and "7" is the sentence.

T: is for *Textbook*

W: is for *Workbook*

M: is for *Manual for Teachers*

C: is for "Clarification of Terms"

P: is for *Psychology: Purpose, Process and Practice*

S: is for *The Song of Prayer*

In: is for "Introduction"

R: is for "Review"

Other than in the Introduction, *A Course in Miracles* is referred to throughout as the "Course."

I often put lines from the Course in bold for emphasis.

Only rarely does the Course boldface a word or phrase within a sentence.

Bracketed words sometimes appear inside quotes from the Course (added so the reader will understand what the word *it* or *here* or he, etc., refers to).

Quotations from the Bible are from the King James version, the version referenced within the Course and Dr. Helen Schucman's favorite translation.

If no source is given after a centered poem, rhyme, aphorism, or alliteration, it's mine.

PART I

INTRODUCTION

If God created you perfect,
*you **are** perfect.*

T-10.IV.1:4

You do not live here.
We are trying to reach your real home.
We are trying to reach the place where you
are truly welcome. We are trying to reach God.

W-49.5–8

The Path to Happiness

What would it be like to have no worries, no anxieties, no problems, no major concerns? What would it be like to hold no grievances, no hurt feelings—make no judgments? What would it be like to be consistently calm, patient, and serene? What if it were possible to experience the love of God flowing from our hearts to everyone we meet, all the time? What if we had no fear of death—no sense of limitation? What if we knew we were not a body? What would it be like to know eternity? What would it be like to know God?

No snowflake ever falls in the wrong place. Everything happens *as* it should, *when* it should, and *as* it can. Finding *A Course in Miracles* is not an accident, a stumble, a mistake, or a fall. No one is where they are by accident, and chance plays no part in God's universe. Discovering *A Course in Miracles* is an auspicious, propitious part of being on the path of Self-discovery. Having found the Course, we are asked to maintain focus with consistency. We are being asked to do what we've always wanted to do, to be who we were meant to be—who we always have been—awake, alive, free of illusions and dreams.

There is "something" about this book called *A Course in Miracles*. It has about it a diamond-like quality of clarity, brilliance, durability, and a literary excellence found in only the world's most inspired works. There is a "dignity," "presence," and "spirit" in the Course. It is poetic and profound. It is also uncompromising in its instance that Heaven is our Home and God's will for us is perfect happiness. The Course offers a whole new way of seeing outside the insane perspective of the ego. It holds for each of us tremendous hope.

Open the Course, turn to any page, read a paragraph or two, and you will soon ask, "Who wrote this?" No "body," no "ego" wrote it. It came though the mind and hands of Dr. Helen Schucman. Helen was the scribe. She was not the author. We could say that Jesus, as a manifestation of the Holy Spirit, wrote it. We might say that the Enlightened Mind wrote it or the Right Mind wrote it. Or, since "God creates only mind awake" (W-167.8:1), "you" wrote it back before time began, before we all fell asleep and drifted off into fantasyland.

> *This is a manual for a special curriculum, intended*
> *for teachers of a special form of the universal course.*
> *There are many thousands of other forms,*
> *all with the same outcome. They merely save time.*

M-1.4:1–3

One of the things you have to love about the Course is that you don't have to do it. There are *many thousands* of pathways back to God. *Many thousands* is a really big number. *Many thousands* means thousands upon thousands, which means trillions and trillions. There are as many pathways back to God as there are split-offs from the Mind of God, each seeking their way Home. Having different egos, the undoing of the ego takes a different "form" for everyone. The more clearly we approach the center, the clearer the light becomes and the more the different paths begin to look like one and the same path, all bringing us home again to God.

A host of mystics, masters, saints, and sages from different faiths and different ages have said what the Course says. Read the Gnostic teachings, the Buddhist Sutras, or the Kabbalah, and you'll find some of the same imagery. Study the Vedanta system of Hinduism and you'll see many similarities. All these works were, however, written hundreds, if not thousands, of years ago for a different time and a different era in human development.

What is exciting about the Course is that it is truly a document of the twenty-first century. It has about it a level of psychological sophistication that both incorporates and transcends the findings of Sigmund Freud (1856–1939) and other depth psychologies. What is most exciting about the Course is that it "works." It has, in a very subtle way, changed for the better the lives of millions and it will, no doubt, very subtly change for the better, the lives of millions more.

> *This course has explicitly stated that*
> *its goal for you is happiness and peace.*
>
> T-13.II.7:1

Happiness is a state of mind, and *perfect happiness* is perfectly possible *because it already is.* Nothing is difficult that is *wholly* desired (T-6.V.B.8:7). Heaven is an awareness of perfect oneness (T-18.VI.1:6) and perfect oneness = perfect happiness.

> *Happiness is your nature. It is not wrong to desire it.*
> *What is wrong is seeking it outside when it is inside.*
>
> INDIAN SAGE, RAMANA MAHARSHI (1875–1941)

Self-Improvement or Self-Discovery

When I shared the idea for this book with my publisher, he expressed skepticism, saying, "There are a lot of books out there on happiness, and I'm not sure any of them are helping to make anyone any happier." Many of the books on happiness are about becoming happier by getting a better body, a more secure job, more money in the bank, and/or better relationships. There is nothing wrong with having money in the bank, good relationships, and a healthy body. However:

> *You must have noticed an outstanding characteristic*

of every end that the ego has accepted as its own.
When you have achieved it, "it has not satisfied you."

T-8.VIII.2:5–6

The world you see is merciless indeed,
unstable, cruel, unconcerned with you,
quick to avenge and pitiless with hate.
It gives but to rescind, and takes away all things
that you have cherished for a while.
No lasting love is found, for none is here.
This is the world of time, where all things end.

W-129.2:3–6

Let's begin with a few basic premises.
1. There is no perfection in this world.
2. If you have a body, you have an ego.
3. If you have a mind, you have a spirit.
4. Heaven is a state of perfection. We never left.
5. The kingdom of Heaven is in you.
6. It *is not* in the body. It *is* in the mind.
7. The body is physical. It will die.
8. The Mind is formless and eternal. Having always been, it cannot die.
9. God's function is ours, and happiness cannot be found apart from our joint Will (T-11.V.12:4).

Nearly all mankind is more or less unhappy
because nearly all do not know the true Self.
Real happiness abides in Self-knowledge alone....
To know one's Self is to be blissful always.

RAMANA MAHARSHI

Lesson 101: God's Will for Me Is Perfect Happiness

Lesson 101 is the numerical system used to designate a basic class, such as English 101, Philosophy 101, or Sociology 101. Lesson 101 from the workbook of *A Course in Miracles* is "God's will for me is perfect happiness."

> *God's Will for you is perfect happiness because there is no sin,*
> *and suffering is causeless. Joy is just, and pain is but the sign*
> *you have misunderstood yourself. Fear not the Will of God.*
> *But turn to it in confidence that it will set you free from all the*
> *consequences sin has wrought in feverish imagination. Say:*
> *God's Will for me is perfect happiness.*
> *There is no sin; it has no consequence.*

> W-101.6:1–7

> *The Atonement is therefore the perfect lesson.*

> T 3.1.7:8

The Perfect Lesson

In the next several pages, we're going to explore a "process" called the *atonement*. It is a process by which we cancel out error, "remove the blocks to an awareness of Love's presence," and restore to our awareness the truth of our being and thus, attain perfect happiness. The awareness of Love's presence is the awareness of God's presence. God is life. Holiness created life and you are life.

> *. . . your life is not a part of anything you see.*
> *It stands beyond the body and the world,*
> *past every witness for unholiness,*
> *within the Holy, holy as Itself.*

In everyone and everything His Voice would speak to you
of nothing but your Self and your Creator,
Who is One with Him.

W-151.12:1–3

This world is a school. The body is a *learning device* and this is a *course* in miracles. We are here to learn a lesson. I may have cancer. I may be going through bankruptcy and a divorce. I may be dealing with a screaming child or a car accident. I brought these experiences to myself, not because I am bad and need to be punished. I gave these assignments to myself so I might learn to be free of sin, guilt, fear, pain, suffering, and all the things that make for unhappiness. Lesson 337 from the Course asks us to say to ourselves,

. . . only happiness can be my state,
for only happiness is given me.
What must I do to know all this is mine?
I must accept Atonement for myself and nothing more.

W-337.1:2–4

The body is a learning device; it is also the ego's *chosen home* (T-20.II.4:6) and we easily fall into the trap of seeing ourselves restricted to a body. It's an easy illusion to come by. Seeing ourselves as bodies only is a hard addiction to break. A wide range of pleasures and pains present themselves and the temptation to overindulge in food, in drink, in drugs abounds. The Course is trying to help us get out of the illusory story of the ego/body; out of time and back into eternity and thus, to perfect happiness. *Perfection* means "going all the way"—home again to God—the only place we can be completely safe and totally free.

Why wait for Heaven?
Those who seek the light are merely covering their eyes.
The light is in them now.
Enlightenment is but a recognition, not a change at all.

W 188.1.1–4

Perfect happiness — enlightenment. Enlightenment is awareness of perfect oneness. What is absent in enlightenment is duality. There is no twoness in oneness. It is for this reason that *all things must be first forgiven* (T-30.V.1:6). I cannot be happy and at the same time harbor angry, aggressive, attack thoughts. If I hold such thoughts, I place a block between myself and the door of Heaven.

Each of us is the light of the world,
and by joining our minds in this light we
proclaim the Kingdom of God together and as one.

T-6-II.13:5

Umeuswe

There is no *you and me*. There is no subject and object in perfect oneness. I started to write a children's story about an African boy named Umeuswe. *Umeuswe* is all of us combined. *Umeuswe* is You, Me, Us, and We. There is only one of us here. There is only one Mind. We are called upon to be willing to give our little minds back to the Mind, back to the Thinking of the Universe (W-52). Joining again with the mind of God leads to perfect happiness, and the joyous "re-cognition," or "re-membering" of oneness and thus, the experiencing of perfect.

Happy dreams come true, not because they are dreams,
but only because they are happy. And so they must be loving.

Their message is, "Thy Will be done," and not,
"I want it otherwise."

T-18.V.4:1–3

The Happy Dream

The goal of the Course is to transform our unhappy and sometimes nightmare lives—"dreams of pain and suffering"—into happy dreams. The happy dream is still a dream, but it is a dream in which we begin to awaken and thus, let go of an illusory world. The happy dream leads beyond illusion to truth. The happy dream is the dream of forgiveness. As we let go of the projections we place upon the world, we see things the way they are. We can then be happy in knowing that we are moving further and further away from an artificial (that is, made-up), insane "reality" and deeper and deeper into awareness of the truth of our perfect being.

Salvation, perfect and complete,
asks but a little wish that what is true be true;
a little willingness to overlook what is not there;
a little sigh that speaks for Heaven as a preference to
this world that death and desolation seem to rule.
In joyous answer will creation rise within you, to replace
the world you see with Heaven, wholly perfect and complete.
What is forgiveness but a willingness that truth be true?

T-26.VII.10:1–3

We are embarking on a journey of transcendence. The ideas we are about to explore are revolutionary, but not because they are new. They are revolutionary because they are the opposite of everything the world has taught and continues to teach.

CHAPTER 1

Who Wants to Know?

Who is the "you" who are living in this world?
Spirit is immortal and immortality is a constant state.
It is as true now as it ever was or ever will be,
because it implies no change at all.

T-4.II.11:8–10

I wonder if I've been changed in the night?
Let me think. Was I the same when I got up this morning?
I almost think I can remember feeling a little different.
But if I'm not the same, the next question is
"Who in the world am I?"

ALICE, FROM *ALICE IN WONDERLAND* (1865),
BY LEWIS CARROLL (1832–1898)

This body called "Jon" grew up on a farm in central Missouri during the 1940s and '50s, an only son with a younger sister, Ann. Ann and I were exceedingly fortunate. We had loving parents, grandparents, and several great-aunts and -uncles who lived on nearby farms. World War II had just ended, but we knew nothing about that. It was a simple time. We had a beautiful 1950s, nearly self-sufficient farm. Mother and Daddy bought the farm in 1941, two years after they were married. They were not, however, able to start working the farm until Daddy came home from the army at the end of World War II. Our house had no electricity, no indoor plumbing, and no central heating. Each of these features Daddy added later on.

You could stand in the front yard; look north, south, east, or west; and behold a bucolic view of nothing but land, hills, and trees for miles. You could just make out the smokestack on the power plant in Mexico, Missouri seven miles due south.

Farm boys were expected to be available to work all the time. If, however, for some reason, you were free, the thing to do was to go hunting. The woods were right behind the barn and I could be in the woods within minutes. There was a quiet aliveness in the trees, serenity in the soil, the moss, the ponds, and the nearby Salt River. There were lots of red squirrels. Brush piles all around made secure homes for rabbits and quail. The ponds and the river were filled with catfish and frogs. Rabbits, quail, fish, frogs, and sometimes the more exotic pheasants found their way to our dinner table.

On the top of the hill out behind the barn stood a grove of walnut trees where I could sit with my back against a tree and look out through a clearing for miles to the south, past the river and Paul West's cornfields in the valley below. There were other children a year or two older or younger on each of five nearby farms. However, there were no children my age and I was the only student in my class in grades 1 through 8. Our one-room, country schoolhouse sat in the corner of a cow pasture. Weather permitting; we usually rode horses to school. If, after school, there was no work to do, I would put my books in the house, take my 410 "over and under" combination shotgun/rifle, and head for the woods for an hour or more of hunting before doing the evening chores.

Freezing

There is a thing you do when you hunt, which we called "freezing." You walk into the woods, stop, stand perfectly still, and just look and listen.

If you are not tromping through the woods (so the animals cannot hear you) and if they are not downwind of you (so they can't smell you), they may just walk right out as though you were not there, because, as far as they know—you're *not* there.

One sunny fall day in 1957, when I was fourteen, I was hunting in the ten-acre woods on the hill behind the barn. I was still a kid; so while "frozen," I decided to play a game. I pretended that I did not exist. I stood perfectly still for a long, quiet moment and unexpectedly slipped into a nonanalytical state. Suddenly, it was as though. . .

There was "no one" there—no hunter hunting, no thinker thinking.

There were just eyes staring, like a video camera, mindlessly recording a scene in the woods.

There was observing without commentary or analysis.

There was awareness and surprising transcendence.

What brought me back was the thought, "What is having this experience?"

And an inner voice said, "Who wants to know?"

That was it! It was simple. It was profound.

Sooner or later
something seems to call us onto a particular path.
You may remember this "something" as a signal moment in childhood
when an urge out of nowhere, a fascination,
a peculiar turn of events struck like an annunciation:
This is what I must do,
this is what I've got to have. This is who I am.

FROM *THE SOUL'S CODE*,
BY DR. JAMES HILLMAN (1926–2011)

I knew then that I would spend the rest of my life trying to answer that question. Anyone can make money, have a career, and raise a family. Albert Einstein (1879–1955) said that all he wanted was to know the "thoughts of God." Einstein was a mathematical genius. I was a Missouri farm boy, a "would-be" country preacher and philosophy teacher. Einstein and I were asking the same question. *A Course in Miracles* answers that question.

Fifty years later, in June 2007, I was bitten by a bunch of mosquitoes while facilitating a retreat on a lake in New Hampshire. The bites swelled. They got ugly-looking and I started to feel as though I were coming down with the flu. I was feeling so bad that I went to the emergency room of the local hospital where the doctor said that, indeed, I was coming down with the flu and I should go home and go to bed. The next day I struggled to get up and go to my home office. I was just standing in my office when my assistant, Fran, said, "What are you doing?" I said, "I'm sleeping." She said, "Standing up?" That is the last thing I remembered for over a week. What happened next is what I was told.

Fran called my wife, Dolores, at work and told her, "There is something wrong with your husband. You should come home right away." Dolores and Fran asked me some more questions, to which I gave nonsense answers. Realizing that I had a high fever, they called an ambulance. My temperature was up to 106—Dolores said 107. The same doctor who refused to admit me the day before refused once again, saying it was just the flu. The ambulance attendant insisted that it was more than the flu and while they were arguing I had a grand mal seizure and went into a coma. My body was immediately packed in ice to bring down the fever and, thinking I might have a case of deadly and contagious meningitis, the hospital staff put me into quarantine.

The local hospital could not determine what was wrong. Finally, after performing a spinal tap and after sending my "vitals" to a national laboratory, they came up with a diagnosis—Viral La Cross Encephalitis (LACV), a virus transmitted to humans through the bite of an infected mosquito. Only seventy cases a year are reported in the United States. How lucky can you get? The chances of winning the lottery are better. La Cross Encephalitis produces seizures and coma and often leads to paralysis and permanent brain damage. There is no treatment for it. You come out of it or you don't; many remain in a vegetative state and in need of round-the-clock treatment for the rest of their lives.

> *Did you ... learn that secret from the river: that there is no time?*
>
> SIDDHARTHA, SPEAKING TO THE FERRYMAN,
>
> IN *SIDDHARTHA*, BY HERMANN HESSE (1877–1962)

There is no time in a coma. There are no people and no things. There are no responsibilities. There is no awareness of bodily life. There are no thoughts about eating or anything worldly or physical. It was dark and "dazzling." I quietly floated through black, empty space, looking at white lights tinged with gold—like the stars at night —each connected by luminescent rays that ran from the center of one to the center of another. The intricacy of the patterns was awe-inspiring, an endless kaleidoscopic pattern moving further out and deeper in. It was peaceful. It was quiet. There was so much more. There was Love—but not of this world.

> *... and in the silent darkness watch the lights that are not of*
> *this world light one by one,*
> *until where one begins another ends ...*
>
> W-126.7:5

Bodies are a lot of work and it was a relief to be body-free, pain-free. I was not bound by a body. There was no place of beginning and end. It was silent and immediate. It took many days to come back to this misnomer, this dream we call a body, and to "reality." It took a while for "brain chatter" to renew itself. In deep wonder, there is nothing for the mind to chatter about.

I went away, I think, to learn something, to have a talk with the "powers that be." I think everyone who goes into a coma has something of this experience, only few remember anything at all. Dr. Eben Alexander (1953–present) in his book *Proof of Heaven* provides us with a wonderful example of what can happen in a coma. There were images but no words. I actually forgot about the everyday world, as happens when we are in a dream. This is, I think, what happens to all of us when we let our body go, which is proof of the fact that we are not bodies.

You are at home in God, dreaming of exile
but perfectly capable of awakening to reality.

T-10.I.2:1

Let's not feel bad for loved ones who leave their often frail and damaged bodies. There is no permanence in any body. Bodies are temporary, dream characters. Bodies are "learning devices," and our mission is simple. We are asked to live so as to demonstrate that we are not an ego (body) (T-4. IV.6:2). We are not slaves to time. We are part of the eternal.

After a week or so, I came out of the coma, but I was in no sense really "back." It happened late one night. There was a little red light over my bed. No one was around. I picked up my right hand and brought it around in front of my face. Thirty years earlier, I had the same experience of slowly bringing my hand around in front of my face after returning from a powerful journey into inner space, brought on by the use of powerful psychotropic drugs during a shamanic journey in the jungles of Chiapas, in southern Mexico. Coming out of that experience, I had also stared at my hand. Talking was impossible then and now, once again, I could not talk. If you have ever seen the face of someone who has come out of a coma, perhaps on television, he just stares. You may talk to him and he will look at you as though he does not understand you because he doesn't.

That Is a Hand!

I looked at my right hand and thought, "That is a hand!" That may not seem profound, but it was quite profound at that moment. I wiggled my fingers—what an incredible experience! What was wiggling these fingers? A thought? Where did the thought come from? What was thinking this thought? "I" (whatever that was) was somehow connected to that thought. I wiggled my fingers some more. "Wow! This is so cool!"

The ego, then, raised the first question
that was ever asked, but one it can never answer.
That question, "What are you?"
was the beginning of doubt. The ego has never answered
any questions since, although it has raised a great many.

T-6:IV.2:6–8

I looked at my hand and wondered how I knew what that object was called? And for the second time in fifty years, I heard an inner voice say, "Who wants to know?" Dolores said that for many days thereafter I played with my hands, holding them out in front of my face as if they were toys. A pediatric nurse told me that at about the age of three months, babies become fascinated looking at, playing with, and learning to develop control over these wonderful appendages we call fingers and their attachment to something we call a hand.

The ego always speaks first. And the ego says, "I want to know." Words are labels we use to define "things." There are no words in a coma. I had been for some time without words and could only slowly adjust to the world around me. It was a long, slow awakening. It took several weeks to come back to ordinary, or worldly, thinking. For a time, there was awareness without an object, no real sense of self. There was no memory of particularity or individuality. What if there was no past, no guilt to hold you there? What if there was no future to think about and nothing was needed? There was sensing. There was seeing. There was "what was"—a watcher, witnessing. I rather suspect that animals live in this state much of the time.

I came back slowly, and slowly was fine because slowly was fast enough. There was much to see, including a three-dimensional painting of a pastoral landscape across from my bed. There were people wearing caps, gloves, and masks all around me, taking care of me, turning me over and cleaning my body. Even their feet were inside plastic booties. I thought at first that they were angels, because I realized that they were trying to help me and I felt the deepest love for them. I tried to talk to them, even to joke with them. I later realized that I was experiencing what in medical language is called "ICU psychosis."

Dolores came to see me but all I could do was stare at her face, her eyes, and her incredible red hair. It was some time before I was able to talk. Lots of things seemed funny, as though I were looking at life from the outside. I lost some thirty pounds. I was very weak and my muscles had atrophied significantly. Reaching out to take Dolores's hand in mine, I said my first comprehensive statement: "Will you marry me?"

I awoke only to see [that] the rest of the world was still asleep!

ITALIAN RENAISSANCE ARTIST

LEONARDO DA VINCI (1452–1519)

A newborn child is language-free. She does not analyze, compare, judge, or self-reference. The child simply sees, feels, smells, hears, and tastes. Life for the next few days was filled with new adventures and discoveries, along with a profound, peaceful continuity. *Tranquility* would be a good word for it. I was happy just being and I could see the interconnectedness of all things. I merely "watched the world." Then after another week or so had passed, there came the thought that brought me back to the world: "You have bills to pay!"

Dolores said, "One of the strangest parts of that experience was that you stopped planning."

Back home I could only eat slowly, if at all. I sat at the table and watched Dolores and our daughter, Sarah, eating. If you don't eat for a long time, you lose your appetite. Eating is a very gross "unconscious" act. Teeth are strange things—they masticate food—often eating other bodies. I played with my food and tried to eat because I was supposed to. It took time to get back into the habit.

> *To be alive and not to know yourself is to believe that you*
> *are really dead. For what is life except to be yourself,*
> *and what but you can be alive instead?*
> *Who is the doubter? What is it he doubts?*
> *Whom does he question? Who can answer him?*
>
> W-139.3:2–7

Who is the seeker? Who wants to know? Who is reading or listening to this book, studying this Course? Who would we be without our neuroses, our problems, our insanity? A body is an object, a limitation in form. It is not who we are. When asked a question, the Indian sage Ramana Maharshi would often say, "Who wants to know?" Who is asking the question? That is the question. The things we say we are—our name, where we live, our history, our resume, the stuff that seems to make us "something"—are all projections. "Who is the projector, and who wants to know?"

> *. . . only the mind is real, because only the mind can be shared.*
> *The body is separate, and therefore cannot be part of you.*
> *To be of one mind is meaningful,*
> *but to be one body is meaningless.*
> *By the laws of mind, then, the body is meaningless.*
>
> T-6.V.A. 3:2–5

PART II

PERFECTION IS
AND CANNOT BE DENIED

There is no fear in perfect love.
We will but be making perfect to you
what is already perfect in you.
You do not fear the unknown but the known.
You will not fail in your mission because I did not fail in mine.
Give me but a little trust in the name of the complete trust I
have in you, and we will easily accomplish the goal of
perfection together. **For perfection "is," and cannot be denied.**
To deny the denial of perfection is not so difficult as to deny
truth, and what we can accomplish together
will be believed when you see it as accomplished.

T-12.II.8.1–7

A Perfect B

INTRODUCTION TO *A COURSE IN I.*

There Must Be Another Way

In June 1965, during a particularly contentious day at work, Dr. William Thetford, head of the Department of Psychology at Columbia University's College of Physicians and Surgeons in New York City, was frustrated with the back-biting, ego games, and fighting in his own department. He turned to his associate, Dr. Helen Schucman, and said in exasperation, "There must be another way!" Meaning, there had to be some way they could all get along. A miraculous moment of sanity prevailed and Helen said, "You're right! I'll help you find it!" The willingness of Bill and Helen to "see things differently" was a turning point in their lives and the stimulus for *A Course in Miracles*.

Helen was subject to vivid dreams and visionary experiences. As a friend and a psychologist, Bill encouraged Helen to write down her dreams and images and in October 1965, while recording one of her experiences, there came the line, "This is *A Course in Miracles*, please take notes." Imagine that you are a poet and you begin to hear the words of a poem or you are a musician and you begin to hear the notes of a song.

I met Helen and Bill in 1973, when they came to a lecture I was giving at a conference sponsored by Spiritual Frontiers Fellowship in Chicago.

e (1907–1982), Edgar Cayce's son, was the keynote
the Course was being given to Helen as its scribe, Helen
to explore similar "gifts," like the works of Edgar Cayce
and the Seth material, by Jane Roberts (1929–1984). My first
rning to Die, had just been released, and I was giving a talk on
m and near-death experiences at the conference.

len was living on East 17th Street in New York City. I was doing
oral studies while living in the General Theological Seminary,
ween West 20th and 21st Streets, within easy walking distance
f Helen's home. In April 1975, Helen called and told me she had
something for me. I had no idea what she was talking about but agreed
to meet with her, Bill, Dr. Ken Wapnick (1942–present), and Father
Benedict Groeschel (1933–present) in Ken's little studio apartment, also
on East 17th Street, across the street from Helen's.

Helen sat on Ken's daybed and told me about the Course, how it
came to be, and how it affected those in the room. She then gave me the
newly scribed pamphlet, *Psychotherapy: Purpose, Process & Practice*,
which came from the same source as the Course. I walked home that
night thinking that "probably" the most important thing that had ever
happened to me had just happened. I had no idea what it was.

I was impressed with Helen, Bill, and Ken's credentials and Helen's
presentation about the Course. I was, however, skeptical. Four years earlier,
in 1971, I'd done a "guru backpack trek" through India, spending time with
Muktananda (1908–1982), Osho (1931–1990), and Sai Baba (1926–2011).
Osho was by far the most impressive. He was a great storyteller, and he
loved to laugh—always the sign of a good teacher. I enjoyed my time with
Osho, but I became disenchanted with "guru worship."

> *You are a perfect creation, and should experience awe*
> *only in the Presence of the Creator of perfection.*
>
> T-1.II.3:3

Older brothers and sisters are entitled to respect for their greater experience and obedience for their wisdom (T-1.II.3:7). Bowing down, however, and worshipping at someone's feet struck me as a misperception. Fortunately, Helen's "self-worth" was never defined by her being the scribe of the Course and I admired the way Helen, Bill, and Ken kept themselves out of the limelight when it came to the Course. Helen simply did what she was asked to do. Would that all of us did the same.

The Philosopher's Stone

Six weeks after Helen introduced me to the Course, she met Judy Whitson. Judy and I were both on the faculty at the New York University School of Continuing Education, and we were both members of the American Society for Psychical Research. At the time, I was dating Vera Feldman, secretary to the president of the society and one of Judy's best friends. When Judy discovered the Course, she "took fire" with it, thinking it was what she had been looking for all her life. Encouraged by Judy's enthusiasm, Ken's deep commitment, and more than anything just reading the Course itself, I soon realized that the Course was what is referred to in mystical literature as the "Philosopher's Stone," a clear path to perfect oneness and thus to perfect happiness.

Like all of us, Helen moved back and forth between two minds. Helen, however, moved in extremes. She could set her ego-mind aside so completely that she could hear the Holy Spirit, the Voice for God. When she was not in her right-mind, she could slip into the wrong-mind and become alarmingly judgmental. We can all sympathize with her humanity. Helen "knew" the Course. She never claimed to have mastered it, though she clearly understood the "process" of the Course and she knew how to teach it. You don't have to be enlightened to understand the goal and the process.

Helen's name did not appear on the first (1976) edition of the
Course, being added later to the second (1992) edition, published some
eleven years after Helen's passing. Helen sometimes referred to herself
as a "militant atheist," a wonderful oxymoron (how can you be angry
with someone you don't believe in?). I was present at Helen's funeral
in February 1981. Ken Wapnick gave the eulogy. The whole of that
eulogy was about Helen's devotion to God. Despite her resistance, Helen
developed a dynamic relationship with God and she got into a dialogue
with Jesus. A similar dialogue goes on inside each of us. For Helen, that
dialogue got "writ out loud" for the world to see.

Helen and Ken worked together almost daily. Ken was always the
"number-one son." Judy Whitson was the "daughter." Helen called Judy
by the endearing term "Kitten," and she called Judy's daughter "Kitty."
Judy, in turn, called Helen "Mama." Judy tells a wonderful story about
being with Helen before she died. Helen said, "You know why I'm going,
don't you, Kitten?" Judy said, "No, Mama. Why?" And Helen said, "I
have to get out of its way." By "it" she meant the Course. Helen would
not speak at public gatherings. She refused to do interviews on radio or
television. That task fell to Judy, Ken, or Bill.

Three Whom Helen Helped

I was among those Helen helped in this life-journey process. There was
also Joe Janis, who passed in 1991. Joe trained to be a Jesuit, but never
became a full-fledged member of the order. He started one of the first
Miracles groups. The Joe Janis Foundation in North Carolina continues
his work. Then there was the Indian, Tara Singh (1909–2006), a yogi
who saw the truth of the Course reflected in the teaching of Eastern
philosophy. His work continues as the Joseph Plan Foundation. Helen
was offering counsel to a "would-be" Catholic priest, an Indian yogi, and
a Protestant minister.

Helen "held my hand" through the last five years of her life, helping me to understand this strange world. I had not yet met Dolores and, during these years, I went through an emotional roller-coaster ride, including three heart-wrenching relationships. There were too many choices, and it seems I was either breaking someone's heart or having my own heart broken. I was often overwhelmed with guilt; I was not a good student, and I fell frequently.

The Church

Helen also helped see me through my struggles with the Church. On the parish level, things were working well. On the hierarchical level, however, my inability to settle down as a married man and my interests in mysticism, parapsychology, esoteric philosophies, metaphysics, humanistic psychology, interspiritual and interfaith matters, and new age philosophies were all getting in the way. More than anything, I wanted to answer the question that arose on the farm in Missouri.

Ministry can be a rewarding profession. Much of ministry is just being nice to people. That is easy, fun, and satisfying. Sermon preparation is a wonderful weekly discipline, funerals are a time for deep connection, and weddings are always a joy . While I enjoyed the "pastoral" aspects of ministry, I was not a "churchman." I was not growing *in* the church—I was slowly growing *out* of it. Eventually, the split grew too wide, and in 1989, after sixteen years of trying to bring the Course into the Church, I quit. Reverend Diane Berke and I then founded Interfaith Fellowship, with Sunday services in Cami Hall, across from Carnegie Hall in New York City. Thirteen years later, in early 2002, I left the parish ministry altogether, finding it more rewarding to be a "guest minister" than a church administrator.

I experienced Helen when she was in her "helping mode," or her social mode. The only picture I have taken with Helen was at a wedding Helen recruited me to perform for two of her friends. I knew from Judy and others about Helen's more cantankerous side. That was not my experience. Helen was just a little older than my mother, and I was fortunate to know her loving, motherly side. Like my own mother, Milly, she never judged me. She was simply a very wise and gentle guide, always available.

GIFTS FROM GOD

Muhammad (570–632) said that the Quran was dictated to him by the archangel Gabriel. As with the Course, the Quran says that only by doing God's will can one know true happiness.

Saint Hildegard of Bingen (1098–1179), the renowned Catholic seer who was subject to lifelong visions, felt commanded to "Write what you hear." She said that each of her revelations and her many songs were received "in an instant."

Saint Bridget of Sweden (1303–1373), founder of the Bridgettine Religious Order, said that an entire book was given to her "in a flash." Other authors have said the same thing; sometimes even a detailed story appears quite suddenly.

Saint Teresa of Ávila (1515–1582), the foremost female Catholic mystic of the sixteenth century, said that she did not write her book; it was "given" to her.

Wolfgang Amadeus Mozart (1756–1791), the brilliant and prolific Austrian composer, said he did not write his sonatas; they were "given" to him. Of course, Mozart knew how to write music.

Srinivasa Ramanujan (1887–1920), a famous Indian mathematician and a deeply religious man, said that the nearly 3,900 theorems he produced during his short life were all "given" to him. Keep in mind that Ramanujan knew how to formulate math. In fact, he could only think in math.

Edgar Cayce (1877–1945), known as the "sleeping prophet," had only a ninth-grade education. He made it clear that the words he spoke in his "sleeplike state" were given to him and were not of his making.

Richard Bach (1936–present), an American aviator and the author of the 1970 classic *Jonathan Livingston Seagull*, which sold more than forty million copies, said that he did not write his book; instead, it was "given" to him. Much of the book describes detailed and rather intricate aerobatic moves and Richard Bach is an accomplished aviator and stunt pilot.

Helen Schucman (1909–1981) did not write *A Course in Miracles*. It was given to her. While Helen did not "write" the Course, she knew the language of psychology, in particular the work of Sigmund Freud. She understood how the ego worked. She understood denial, repression, and projection. She was a perfect choice to scribe this profound psychospiritual document.

Thy Will Be Done

The God of resurrection demands nothing,
for He does not will to take away.
He does not require obedience,
for obedience implies submission.
He would only have you learn your will and follow it,
not in the spirit of sacrifice and submission,
but in the gladness of freedom.

T-11.VI.5:6–8

When Jesus tells his disciples that they should go out and preach, the disciples point out to him that he has taught them nothing about preaching. He tells them not to worry: All they have to do is to open their mouths and what they are to say will be given to them. When the truth is spoken words flow forth in simple continuity. The ego, is cunning and clever, knowing how to lie.

> *You cannot be happy unless you do what you will truly,*
> *and you cannot change this because it is immutable.*
> *It is immutable by God's Will and yours,*
> *for otherwise His Will would not be extended.*
> *You are afraid to know God's Will,*
> *because you believe it is not yours.*
> *This belief is your whole sickness and your whole fear.*
>
> T-11.I.10:1–4

> *You do not have to know that Heaven is yours to make it so.*
> *It "is" so.*
> *Yet to know it, the Will of God must be accepted as your will.*
>
> T-13.XI.10:5–7

> *God wills you perfect happiness now.*
>
> T-9.VII.1:8

God has willed us to be happy. God's will is unchangeable. The sooner we accept our fortunate destiny, the happier we can be. Deep inside, all of us know what God would have us do with our lives. It's not a matter of not knowing; it's a matter of *doing* what we are being asked to do so we can hear His Voice even better. Just as believing in the "thought" of separation leads to the dream we call the ego, choosing to believe in oneness leads to Oneness. The only catch is: We must be *willing* to give our mind back to The Mind.

It is possible to reach a state in which you bring your mind
under my guidance without conscious effort, but this
implies a willingness that you have not developed as yet.

T-2.VI.6:1

Salvation, perfect and complete,
asks but a little wish that what is true be true;
a little willingness to overlook what is not there;
a little sigh that speaks for Heaven as a preference to
this world that death and desolation seem to rule.
In joyous answer will creation rise within you, to replace
the world you see with Heaven, wholly perfect and complete.
What is forgiveness but a willingness that truth be true?

T-26.VII.10:1–3

The Bible says that a deep sleep fell on Adam. Nowhere does it say that he woke up. All dreams seem real while we are dreaming them. No reawakening or rebirth is possible as long as we continue to dream and to thus miscreate (T-2.I.3:6–7).

It still remains within you, however, to extend as God extended
his spirit to you. In reality this is your only choice, because
your free will was given you for your joy in creating the perfect.

T-2.I.3:8–9

Knowing why this dream world was created, we then begin to reverse the process by which the world was made in order to return home. What makes the process seem difficult is our desire to "fix" the dream rather than awakening from dreaming. Trying to "fix" the dream, we become identified "with" the dream.

Awareness of dreaming is the real function of God's teachers.
They watch the dream figures come and go,
shift and change, suffer and die.
Yet they are not deceived by what they see.

T-12.6:6–8

There Is a Way Out!

To the end of his life, Sigmund Freud (1856–1939), the Austrian neurologist and the father of psychoanalysis, remained an atheist, going as far as to describe belief in God as collective neurosis. Collective neurosis is the "dreaming of the world." Everything is an ego prop to persuade us that this world is real. What we see on the news each evening or read about in our magazines is a reporting on the current state of the global dream. In private we have our dreams to ourselves; in society we dream in concert. This dreaming is so pervasive that we do not see it. Revelation, or enlightenment, means awakening from the dream.

Freud understood how unhappy the ego made us. He also thought we were damned with it; that is, stuck with it. According to Freud, the ego got stronger as we got older, and we died with it—end of story. If Freud had studied Eastern philosophy, he might have taken a longer, deeper view. In truth, in reality, in perfection we cannot be damned. There is a way out. It is possible to be free. It's possible to be happy. It is possible right now.

If you cannot hear the Voice for God,
it is because you do not choose to listen

T-4.IV.1:1

There are no regulations, dogmas, creeds, doctrines, canons, or codes of belief in the Course. There are, however, lots of positive propositions as to how we should live if we want to be happy.

The only rule in the entire Course is its request that we not do more than one workbook lesson per day. Go slower if you like, but not faster.

There is no central organization or hierarchy for the Course. Thank God! Let's keep the ego out of it. The Course is a book. It is a course of study. It is a spiritual process by which we can remember Home. We don't have to die to remember Heaven. God never left us, and we never left Heaven.

Take a good look at the selfish, self-centered, self-seeking side of separation. Exposing the ego leads to resistance and fear. One man told me he took a knife to the Course, stabbing it many times; another tore out the pages and tried to flush them down the toilet. More than one person has thrown the book off a bridge. Many a book has been hurled onto the floor, across the room, or into a fire. Burn it if you wish. Reduce it to ashes—it does not matter. Truth is not found in matter but in Mind and choosing the truth sets us free.

The subtitle of *Thus Spoke Zarathustra,* a book by German philosopher Friedrich Nietzsche (1844–1900), is *A Book for All and for None.* Ken Wapnick has suggested that this subtitle might also serve as a subtitle for *A Course in Miracles.* The Course is a book for *all* because of its universality, and it is a book for *none* because of the tremendous resistance we have to doing what it asks us to do.

Story Time

There was once a bright young man whose parents were so proud that he was graduating from Harvard that before he went off to law school they rewarded him with a free trip to India. There he met a guru who convinced him to give up his worldly ways and his pursuit of prestige, money, and fame, telling him that in these things he would lose himself rather than find himself. He was so impressed with the guru that he wrote a letter home to his parents and told them that he would not be returning to Harvard Law School; rather, he planned on staying in India where he could devote himself to a simple, contemplative life.

A year passed and his parents received another letter telling them how happy he was. There was no rivalry and competition in the ashram, no scrambling to see who could make the most money. Why, in only one year he had become the number-two disciple, and he thought that, if he played his cards right, by next year, he would probably be number one. Nobody wants to look at or admit to the subtle hold the ego has on our psyche, and yet, every time the ego is recognized for what it is, it is weakened.

> *The Kingdom of Heaven is like a merchant seeking beautiful*
> *pearls, who, when he had found one pearl of great price,*
> *went and sold all that he had and bought it.*
>
> MATTHEW 13:45–46

I have referred to the Course as a diamond. We might also think of it as a pearl of great price because it clearly shows us how to return to the Mind and thus, awaken from dreaming, a dream that is, for many, a nightmare.

Living the Course means *recognizing* a dimension of Mind that transcends space/time and "reality" as we know it. The Course is slow and gentle. We begin our journey by spending a few minutes at the beginning of our day reading or listening to the gentle message. We thereby set our feet on the trail that brings us home, trusting God as our guide. We turn to God again before we sleep, seeking gentle dreams.

> *We waken hearing Him, and let Him*
> *speak to us five minutes as the day begins,*
> *and end the day by listening again five minutes more*

before we go to sleep. Our only preparation is to
let our interfering thoughts be laid aside,
not separately, but all of them as one.

W-140.11.1-2

We begin by letting go of *all* projections, *all* interfering thoughts, *all* judgment, *all* fears, and anxieties. There is nothing like the Course. Those who study the Course see it as a gift. The truth is inviolate, and thank God it's inescapable: The truth is "You are love."

You "will" undertake a journey because
you are not at home in this world.
And you "will" search for your home whether
you realize where it is or not.
If you believe it is outside you the search will be futile,
for you will be seeking it where it is not.
You do not remember how to look within
for you do not believe your home is there.
Yet the Holy Spirit remembers it for you,
and He will guide you to your home
because that is His mission.
As He fulfills His mission He will teach you yours,
for your mission is the same as His.
By guiding your brothers home you are but following Him.

T-12.IV.5:1–7

CHAPTER 3

A Perfect Path

GOD'S PLAN FOR SALVATION (GPS)

And God wills you perfect happiness now.
Is it possible that this is not also your will?
And is it possible that this is not also the will of your brothers?

T-9.VII.1:8–10

My doctor insisted that I come to see you," the patient told the psychiatrist. "Goodness knows why. I'm healthy, happily married, and secure in my job, lots of money in the bank, lots of friends, no worries . . ."

"Hmm," said the psychiatrist, reaching for his notebook, "and how long have you been like this?"

Each day, each hour and minute, even each second,
you are deciding between the crucifixion and the resurrection;
between the ego and the Holy Spirit.
The ego is the choice for guilt;
the Holy Spirit the choice for guiltlessness.
The power of decision is all that is yours.

. . .

You are guilty or guiltless, bound or free, unhappy or happy.

T-14.III.1-3&6

Happiness is a subjective experience. It is a feeling. It is a thought. It is a choice. My body might be limited to the confines of a wheelchair or a prison cell, while my mind is perfectly ordered. I might be driving an expensive car and living in a mansion while my mind is racked with guilt and fear. It's where the mind (not the body) is that matters. When the mind is aligned with The Mind, peace and happiness prevail, regardless of external circumstances.

God gives me only happiness.
He has given my function to me.
Therefore my function must be happiness.

W-66.5:2-4

Within the framework of this world perfection is impossible. Ultimately, however—which means now—there is no ego and this leads us to perfect happiness.

The Holy Spirit begins by perceiving you as perfect.

. . .

To perceive yourself this way is the only way
in which you can find happiness in the world.
That is because it is the acknowledgment that
you are not in this world, for the world "is" unhappy.

T-6.II.5:1&6-7

This is a world of war, disease, and death. It is a world where women are brutalized, children abused, and young men go about killing and maiming innocent people. The whole world has bought the ego's game.

We are all *egoholics,* addicted to our dreams. It is hard to break an addiction if you don't know you have one. Still, for many people there is an underlying suspicion that the world—as presented on television, through all forms of media, through our various religions and social mores—is not the way "it is." Something is amiss.

> *Once upon a tiny tick in time,*
> *There came a thought into the mind.*
> *There came a supposition.*
> *Nothing more than a minuscule cognition.*
> *A rumor rolled around inside the mind,*
> *Like many a myth, it made us blind.*
> *A fantasy, a wisp of wit,*
> *Led to a most incredible split.*
> *What if it were possible to pull off a fantastic fraud?*
> *What if I could think a thought*
> *outside of the Mind of God?*

The story of Adam and Eve from the Bible is a helpful tool in understanding how so much unhappiness came into the world. Adam's experience is described as a "fall." We "fell" into space—as bodies—and into time. Those who experience near-death experiences often speak of the return to the body as "falling back" into form.

> **The separation was not a loss of perfection,**
> *but a failure in communication. A harsh and strident*
> *form of communication arose as the ego's voice.*
>
> T-6.IV.12:5–6

Depending on how we view historical time, for the past several hundred thousand, if not million, years, several billion of us have been trying to do what Adam and Eve tried to do—to think a thought outside of the Mind of God. It can't be done! It is, however, the thing that gave rise to this whole world and every aspect of it.

> *Until the "separation," which is the meaning of the "fall,"*
> *nothing was lacking. There were no needs at all.*
> *Needs arise only when you deprive yourself.*
> *You act according to the particular order*
> *of needs you establish.*
> *This, in turn, depends on your perception of what you are.*

> *A sense of separation from God is the only lack you really*
> *need correct. This sense of separation would never have arisen*
> *if you had not distorted your perception of truth,*
> *and had thus perceived yourself as lacking.*

T-1.VI.2:1-2

What Makes Us Unhappy?
THE FOUR PASSING SIGHTS
According to Buddhist teaching, after the birth of Prince Siddhartha (who became the Buddha), the prince's father asked eight Brahmins to predict his son's future. Seven of the Brahmins said he would either become a great raja (king) or a Buddha, an enlightened being. Only one Brahmin predicted that he would become a Buddha and not a raja. Siddhartha's father wanted his son to become a great king. He also knew that in order for Siddhartha to become a Buddha, he would first have to become a *sadhu*, a renunciate and a seeker of truth. He would have to give up all worldly pursuits and pleasures.

A first step in that journey would mean becoming dissatisfied with the ways of the world. Siddhartha's father, therefore, sought to keep him from any suffering or disappointments that would cause him to question the nature of what we call reality. His father confined the young prince within the palace and provided for his every need, concealing from him the realities of life in the world.

Inevitably, Siddhartha grew restless. Finally, at the age of twenty-nine, he broke free and set forth in a chariot accompanied by Channa, his charioteer and guide. In so doing, he was exposed to the veracity of the world and the brevity of bodily life. In his travels, he experienced the four "passing sights":

1. First, Siddhartha sees an old man, revealing to him the effects of aging and the illusion of time.

2. Second, he sees a sick person suffering from a disease. Channa explains that all beings are subject to disease and pain.

3. Third, Siddhartha sees a corpse and Channa explains that death is an inevitable fate that befalls everyone.

4. Finally, Siddhartha sees a sadhu who is peaceful and serene. Siddhartha then resolves to follow the sadhu's example and seek enlightenment.

While *A Course in Miracles* is Christian in context, it bears a number of striking similarities to Buddhism. The goal of both is enlightenment, or God realization. God is perfect. Heaven is perfect and *you are a perfect creation* (T-1.II.3:3). What God creates is Spirit and, as Spirit, you are perfect. Our bodies, which are part of the world, will never be perfect. All bodies have built-in implodes. They all age, become diseased, and they all die. Following the guidance of the ego, we'll never be happy. God has, however, set up a plan for our salvation and provided us with a guide to help us along the path to salvation.

Wide is the gate and broad is the way that leads
to destruction and many there are that go there in.

Straight is the gate and narrow is the way that leads
unto Life and few there are that find it.

MATTHEW 7:13–14

But ask yourself if it is possible that God would have a plan
for your salvation that does not work. Once you accept His
plan as the one function that you would fulfill,
there will be nothing else
the Holy Spirit will not arrange for you without your effort.
He will go before you making straight your path,
and leaving in your way no stones to trip on,
and no obstacles to bar your way.

T-20.IV.8:3–5

GPS: God's Plan for Salvation

A Course in Miracles makes forty-eight references to God's Plan for Salvation (GPS). This process can be compared to a GPS (Global Positioning System). It's remarkable how GPS works. You take a "little black box." You punch into it your intended destination. There is a button on the box called HOME. If you are in Anchorage, Alaska, and your home is in Miami, Florida, when you push that button called HOME, *instantaneously* (at the speed of light), this little black box makes contact with three different silver and gold angelic beings (satellites), flying around the earth at twelve thousand miles per hour, their arms stretched out to catch the energizing golden beams of the sun.

What could you not accept, if you but knew that everything
that happens, all events, past, present and to come, are
gently planned by One Whose only purpose is your good?
Perhaps you have misunderstood His plan,

for He would never offer pain to you.
But your defenses did not let you see His loving
blessing shine in every step you ever took.
While you made plans for death,
He led you gently to eternal life.

W-135.18:1–4

The word *satellite* comes from the Latin *satelles,* meaning an "attendant." The word *angel* comes from the Greek *angelos,* meaning a "celestial attendant," "messenger," or "envoy." The Course, thus, speaks symbolically of angels (messengers) who "light the way." Principle 4 from the "Fifty Miracle Principles," on the opening page of the Course, reads:

All miracles mean life, and God is the Giver of life.
His Voice will direct you very specifically.
You will be told all you need to know.

T-1.I.4

GPS is established through a process of triangulation. One gets your latitude; one gets your longitude; one gets your altitude. When it comes to GPS (God's Plan for Salvation), one gets your attitude. They have a little conference (again at the speed of light). They put all this information together and, within seconds, they send the directions to you, telling you where to go, foot-by-foot, step-by-step, to your chosen destination.

The ego-mind looking out for itself, and not focusing on God's plan, wanders along the road, making it difficult to stay on track. Whenever we go off track, GPS consistently and without complaint or malice simply "recalculates" our position and tells us what we need to do to find our way back to the "straight way," leading to the "narrow gate." Practicing the Course facilitates the process of helping us repeatedly adjust our position, so we can more perfectly focus specifically on home.

A choice made with the power of Heaven to uphold it
cannot be undone. Your way is decided.
There will be nothing you will not be told,
if you acknowledge this.

T-22.IV.2:3–5

Do what GPS asks and you'll get home by the shortest and straightest possible route. Rather than following God's guidance, however, we say instead, "I would rather do it myself." In the Introduction to the Course, we read, "Free will does not mean that you can establish the curriculum. It means only that you can elect what you want to take at a given time" (T-In.1:4). All willful attempts to write the curriculum for ourselves—that is, create our own world— make us unhappy.

If I intervened between your thoughts and their results,
I would be tampering with a basic law of cause and effect;
the most fundamental law there is.
I would hardly help you, if I depreciated the power of your
own thinking. This would be in direct opposition
to the purpose of this course.

T-2.VII.1:4–6

In Jesus's parable of the Prodigal Son (Luke 15:11–32), when the son asks for his inheritance, the father (clearly referring to God) does not deny him what he asks. The father *does not say*, "Now, let's talk this over. Is this really a good idea?" The third line from the parable says, ". . . and the father divided up his property and gave it to him and the young man took his journey into a far country, and there wasted his substance on wanton living." Similarly, in John Bunyan's classic, *Pilgrim's Progress* from 1678, a temptress, named Wanton (*wanton* means "willful," "loose," or "extravagant"), tries to distract Pilgrim and take him off his course. The thing that animates the body is the Spirit. In the "dreaming of the world," the ego preempts Spirit and makes the body its home. In this sense, we are all addicted to or "possessed" by the ego.

> *As long as any mind remains **possessed***
> *of evil dreams, the thought of hell is real.*

> M-28.6:2

> *Your mind can be **possessed** by illusions,*
> *but spirit is eternally free.*

> T-1.IV.2:8

Perfect Communication

The Course persistently reminds us of the power of our minds and our ability to choose. Happiness is learning how to turn decision making back over to Spirit, the only part of us that can take direction from the Holy Spirit, and thus, remember God. The only Voice that Jesus hears is that of the Holy Spirit. In this sense Jesus and the Holy Spirit are one. Just as Jesus and the Holy Spirit are one, so is your Spirit one with that of the Holy Spirit. As Jesus says in John 15:5, "I am the vine, you are the branches." We abide in him; he abides in us.

A Holy Instant is a time when "perfect communication" is established. Perfect communication occurs when we are in our right-mind, when our tuner is turned on and we are following God's Plan for Salvation. When people love each other and wish only the best for each other, perfect communication occurs. When the ego is running the show, when anger, hostility, and resentment predominate, communication breaks down.

Prayer is then the medium of miracles. It is the means
of communication of the created with the Creator.
Through prayer love is received,
and through miracles love is expressed

T-1.I.11:1-3

The Perfect Teacher

Helen Schucman, the scribe of the Course, said that the purpose of the Course was to help us become increasingly aware of the presence of the Inner Teacher.

The Holy Spirit is the Perfect Teacher.
He uses only what your mind already understands to teach you
that you do not understand it. The Holy Spirit can deal with a
reluctant learner without going counter to his mind,
because part of it is still for God.
Despite the ego's attempts to conceal this part, it is still much
stronger than the ego, although the ego does not recognize it.
The Holy Spirit recognizes it perfectly because it is His Own
dwelling place; the place in the mind where He is at home.

T-5.III.10:1–5

The Holy Spirit is "in" us in a literal sense—not in the body, but in the mind—mediating always in favor of the spirit (T-7.IX.1:5). The Holy Spirit thus functions in our right-mind, serving as the translator or the communication link between God and ourselves, transforming perception to knowledge.

. . . you must choose to hear one of two voices within you.
One you made yourself, and that one is not of God.

But the other is given you by God,
Who asks you only to listen to it.
The Holy Spirit is in you in a very literal sense.
His is the Voice that calls you back to where
you were before and will be again.
It is possible even in this world to hear only
that Voice and no other.
It takes effort and great willingness to learn.

T-5.II.3:6—10

I call the voice on the GPS system in my car Rhoda. We might think of the Holy Spirit as the Voice of our internal GPS. This Voice is our pilot, escort, chaperone, or the One Who directs us in our journey through this foreign land. Remember, "We do not live here." Our real Home is Heaven. Like Jiminy Cricket in the story of Pinocchio, the Holy Spirit's goal is to see us safely home. Similarly, the boy hero in the book and movie *The Polar Express* has a train conductor as his guide on his journey. Seeing that we are unconscious (asleep), as is the boy in the *Polar Express,* our guide's task is to help us awaken from dreaming.

Good can withstand any form of evil,
as light abolishes forms of darkness.
The Atonement is therefore the perfect lesson.
It is the final demonstration that all the other lessons I taught
are true. If you can accept this one generalization now,
there will be no need to learn from many smaller lessons.
You are released from all errors if you believe this.

T-3.I.7:7—11

The Perfect Lesson

Think of the Holy Spirit as the master computer that connects all the satellites (angels) together and works perfectly through each one. While the ego emphasizes separation, the Holy Spirit is leading us to Oneness. The Holy Spirit is the *mechanism of miracles*, Who is aware of both God's Plan for our salvation and our illusions. The atonement is the process of "undoing" the illusion of separation and recognition of our perfect state. It is the "recalculating" methodology by which GPS gets us back on track. *Atoning* means "undoing. What we're undoing is the ego and the perpetual process of wrong-mindedness. The Course is a course in mind training. The atonement reinstates Spirit, not the ego, as the guide for the mind.

> *Here is the real basis for your escape from fear.*
> *The escape is brought about by your acceptance of the*
> *Atonement,* **which enables you to realize**
> **that your errors never really occurred.**
>
> T-2.I.4:3–4

> *A miracle is a correction introduced into false thinking*
> *which acts as a catalyst, breaking up false perception.*
>
> T-1.I.37:1–3

The Holy Spirit separates the true from the false by perceiving *perfectly* rather than partially. We are constantly being given the exact information we need to find our way home. We must, however, pay attention to what it asks us to do. We can always do it our own way if we want. But how are we going to find our way home if we are unwilling to follow direction? On several different occasions in the Gospels, Jesus says, "Let those who have ears hear." The ego cannot follow direction, being itself the director and often the dictator.

Do you prefer that you be right or happy?

T-29.VII.1:9

I love it when you are reading a book other than the Course and you come across a line from the Course. For example, in *The Hitchhiker's Guide to the Universe* (1979) by English author and humorist Douglas Adams (1952–2001), the captain of a spaceship yells out, "I would rather be right than happy!" So it is in the ego's world. Only spirit can communicate with the Holy Spirit and, thus, lead us to perfect happiness. Following the guidance of the ego, we are led steadily into a hellish state of mind.

It is possible to reach a state in which you bring your mind
under my guidance without conscious effort, **but this implies**
a willingness that you have not developed as yet.
The Holy Spirit cannot ask more than you are willing to do.
The strength to do comes from your undivided decision.
There is no strain in doing God's Will
as soon as you recognize that it is also your own.

T-2.VI.6:1–4

The point of greatest despair is often the point at which we realize that *only* God's Plan for Salvation will work. Only the arrogant ego could think it knows more than God. Shall I follow the path of trial and error and fail over and over again until I'm so miserable I have no choice but to do it God's way? Or should I go ahead and trust that God's plan for my awakening is as perfect as the ego is fallible (T-14.V.2:5).

When the Prodigal Son returns home and says, "Father, I have sinned against you and before Heaven. I am no longer worthy to be called your son," the father does *not* say, "That's right. You've been a naughty boy but I, a good man, will forgive you." The father doesn't say a word about where the Prodigal Son went or what he did. The only thing the father says is this: "Get a gold ring and put it on his finger, get a cloak and put it on him, get some sandals and put them on his feet." In other words, his status is being returned to him. "Kill the fatted calf, call in the musicians, we're going to have a party because my son was lost and he has been found; he was dead and he has come back to life again and that is the only thing that matters."

And, that *is* the only thing that matters. Where "you" went, what "you" did, the level of illusion any one of us gets caught in (an illusion is an illusion is an illusion)—none of that matters. The only thing that matters is that, at some point, we awaken, remember home, and turn in the direction that leads eventually to perfect happiness.

When you have given up this voluntary dis-spiriting, you will
see how your mind can focus and rise above fatigue and heal.

T-4.IV.6:3

When it comes to GPS, Holy Spirit never says, "What are you doing!? I told you to go right and you went left!" Instead, GPS patiently and consistently continues to "recalculate" and offer us the "right guidance." It is up to each of us to decide if we are going to follow that guidance or if we will continue to try to do it our own way, in our own time, until time runs out.

Perfect Correction

Without a proper GPS, the ego wanders around lost until it finally fails. Each step of the path is clearly marked and the destination assured; yet we must be willing to *choose* to take each step that leads us home.

A guide does not control but he does direct,
leaving it up to you to follow. "Lead us not into temptation"
means "Recognize your errors and choose to abandon
them by following my guidance."

T-1.III.4:6–7

God Himself gave you the perfect correction for everything
you made that is not in accord with His holy Will.
I am making His plan perfectly explicit to you,
and will also tell you of your part in it.

T-5.VII.4:3–4

God's plan for our awakening is as perfect as the ego's plan is fallible.
Once you accept His plan as the one function that you would
fulfill, there will be nothing else the Holy Spirit
will not arrange for you without your effort.
He will go before you making straight your path, and leaving in
your way no stones to trip on, and no obstacles to bar your way.
Nothing you need will be denied you.
Not one seeming difficulty but will melt away
before you reach it.
You need take thought for nothing, careless of everything
except the only purpose that you would fulfill.

T-20.IV.8:4–8

CHAPTER 4

A Perfect You

Be you therefore perfect, even as
your Father which is in Heaven is perfect.

MATTHEW 5:48

Who could ask of Perfection that He be imperfect?

P-3.I.1:10

An imperfect world is not God's world
and what is not of God is not.

The Parable of the King's Son

A story is told of a king and queen, in ancient times, who had a much-loved three-year old son with a distinctive, heart-shaped birthmark on his right shoulder. One night, thieves broke into the palace, killed the king and the queen, stole their possessions, and abducted the young prince. The thieves traveled for many days before giving the young prince to a couple of peasant farmers.

The king's minister discovered the bodies of the king and the queen, but not that of the prince. Assuming the child had been abducted, they searched for many years for the Kingdom's rightful heir. Finally, the prince was found in a remote village. The child had no memory of his father and mother. Hoping to refresh the boy's memory, the minister told him the story of a Kingdom in which there had lived a king, a queen, and their young child, who was heir to a throne. The minister recounted how thieves had broken in, killed the king and queen, and kidnapped the prince. Once the prince was found, he said, it was believed that he would restore the Kingdom to its former glory and he would relieve his people of their suffering and pain.

The boy was intrigued by the minister's story. "I am a farmer, and someday I am going to meet this prince!" he declared. "He will solve all the problems of the people in our village." "But," said the minister, "you are that prince!" When the boy heard this, he looked left and right before deciding that there must be something wrong with the minister. "I am nothing!" he replied, "I am just a farm boy." The minister said, "I have irrefutable proof and absolute knowledge that you are this prince."

Then the minister told the boy about the distinctive, heart-shaped birthmark on his right shoulder, and he described what it looked like. Offering further proof, the minister asked the boy's parents, "Did you give birth to this boy?" "No," they said. "He was given to us many years ago by travelers passing through our village." Hearing that, the prince's doubts began to fade. However, despite reassurance that he was a king, the boy continued to awaken each morning thinking he was a peasant.

. . . the Atonement belongs at the center
of the inner altar, where it undoes the separation
and restores the wholeness of the mind.

T-2.III.2:1–2

Every morning, the young prince had to remind himself that he was a king and not a peasant. Every morning he had to remind himself about the truth of his being. He had to practice daily being aware of the extent of the erroneous thinking that kept him from the truth. He kept saying to himself, "Nothing I see is as it was."

> *You are a child of God,*
> *a priceless part of His Kingdom,*
> *which He created as part of Him.*
> *Nothing else exists and only this is real.*

T-6.IV.6:1–2

Meditative work like the daily lessons in the Course slowly reawakens the memory of spirit. The ego was not created in a day, and it's not going to go away quickly. It takes time to dispel erroneous notions and end confusion. There never was a time in which the farm boy was not a prince. There never was a time in which you were not a perfect child of God—never! And yet, we cling fast to the dreaming of the world and the notion that we are something other than who we are in truth.

God and the Ego

The word *God* appears 2,207 times in the Course. The word *ego* appears 475 times. Each word is three letters long. Each contains the word *go*. One word begins with *go,* and one ends with *go. Ego* gets this world going. *Ego* ends in *o* (zero). Out of nothing there comes nothing. The ego never existed and can never exist as anything except a thought that has no eternity (that is, reality) to it. It can only temporarily possess the mind. It is at best a fleeting fantasy, like last night's dream, soon gone.

> *We say "God is" and then we cease to speak.*

W-169.5:5

O is the central letter in the word *God*. God is nothingness and everything. God is the wholeness and oneness of which *O* is also the symbol. God is so far beyond words that words don't work in describing God. Every one of the world's religions describes God as love, but we can't really say what love is. I look at my wife Dolores, and I say, "I love you." I want to say more, but "I love you very much" or "I love you a lot" doesn't cut it. I write a poem, but poems are not enough. Words don't work in describing God and they don't work in describing love. "Words are symbols of symbols, twice removed from reality" (M-21.1:9). Words, at best, can only point the way. As limiting as words are, they are the primary tools we have to help us find our way through this amazing maze and thus, back home again.

Mistaken Nonidentity: There Is No Ego

If God exists, perfection exists; and if God exists, the ego never existed. How could a fantasy, which is a distortion of reality, be true? Fantasies are unrealities and not the truth. Living within the ego's tyranny means living in a dream. The ego is a misnomer—nothingness in a form that seems like something, a case of mistaken nonentity. The ego is the "dreamer of the dream" we call "life." Collective belief in the ego makes it appear real. Remove the belief and the ego ceases to be. The ego is a dream, a sleep in which we often have bad dreams.

Within the dream, the ego knows how to "Go for it—and get it!" The ego is out there in the world: it is obvious, it is involved, it is aggressive, it does not look inside. To the ego, God is scary. "If God wins, I lose," or so thinks the ego. If I turn my individuality over to God, I lose my entire identity. The ego always disappears in the face of God. What is left, however, is not nothing, but everything. Those who achieve this state find it much more satisfying than isolated individuality.

Right-, Wrong-, and One-Mindedness

Let's explore some basic terminology in the Course. The Course distinguishes between right- and wrong-mindedness. As we go through the Course, we become progressively aware of when we are in our *wrong* mind and when we are in our *right* mind. Stepping away from the wrong mind—from anger, projection, and judgment—and consistently choosing the right mind—the part of our separated mind that contains the Voice of forgiveness and reason, we come to know One-mindedness.

> *God's perfect Son remembers his creation.*
> *But in guilt he has forgotten what he really is.*

> T-31.I.9:6

Why Aren't We Happy?

As we look at the things that bring us pain, the one thing we overlook is guilt. The ego is the symbol of our separation from God and the teacher of guilt. Guilt says, "I have sinned"; "I have separated myself off from God", "I have done something wrong." Guilt makes us sick. It is the last thing we want to look at so we keep it buried and yet, only by looking at it can we be set free of it. By refusing to look at guilt, we are unaware of our miscreations. We choose to believe that our illusions are real and our projections justified. Understanding (seeing) this is crucial. If we do not see that we are the perpetuators of illusion (dreamers of a dream), how can we stop dreaming? As long as we project our thoughts onto the world, we will be unhappy and we will feel guilty.

Not wanting to look at guilt within ourselves, we displace (project) it onto the world. The mind can project the source of guilt wherever it wants, so it hides guilt in the body—in sickness, in drugs, in food, liquor, and a variety of physical stimulations and overindulgences. Keeping ourselves distracted by the outside world in this way, we never look within.

Wrong-mindedness is the part of our split mind that includes the ego and, thus, believes in sin, guilt, fear, anger, attack, and the like. It's easy to see when we are wrong-minded. The wrong mind is unbalanced. It is insane. It attacks and denies. It is jealous, boastful, upset, projective, and judgmental. If we're honest, we know when we're in our wrong mind. To be wrong-minded is to be unhappy. We are learning how to become progressively more right-minded, aware, more and more conscious, and thus, happier in all that we do.

Right-mindedness contains the Holy Spirit—the communication link between ourselves and God. Right-mindedness restores the mind to sanity. It heals misperceptions. If we are honest, it is easy to see when we are in our wrong mind. It is also easy to see when we are in our right mind. When we are in our right mind, we are kind, gentle, patient, loving, truthful, and joyful.

No matter what your spiritual condition is,
no matter where you find yourself in the universe,
your choice is always the same:
to expand your awareness or contract it.

FROM *THE LAZY MAN'S GUIDE TO ENLIGHTENMENT*,
BY AMERICAN AUTHOR THADDEUS GOLAS (1924–1997)

Wrong-mindedness perceives sin, justifies anger, and seeks to make illusions real. It contracts rather than expands. Until we are fully enlightened, we move back and forth between these two minds. The task is learning how to stay in the right mind and progressively let go of insanity, or wrong-mindedness.

Right-mindedness = higher mind = sanity = awareness = reason = spirit = freedom (liberty, sovereignty, openness) = love.

Wrong-mindedness = lower mind = insanity = unconsciousness = unreasonableness = ego = addiction (compulsions, obsessions, cravings) = fear.

The Decision Maker

We need a way to speak about the part of the mind that makes the choice about which voice we will listen to. A third mind, thus, stands between right-mindedness and wrong-mindedness. Ken Wapnick has identified this mind as the "decision maker." The phrase *decision maker* appears only once in the Course in the *Manual for Teachers* (M-5.II.1:7).

> *Both miracles and fear come from thoughts.*
> *If you are not free to choose one,*
> *you would also not be free to choose the other.*
> *By choosing the miracle you "have" rejected fear,*
> *if only temporarily.*

T-2.VII.3:1–3

Choosing right-mindedness means listening to the Voice for God. It means following GPS (God's Plan for Salvation) down a straight and narrow path that happily leads us home to Heaven. Choosing wrong-mindedness, we listen to the ego, and in so doing, we go down a broad and often crooked path.

> *The ego is the part of the mind that believes in division.*

T-5.V.3:1

Arrogance

At almost every workshop I offer, someone will ask, "How did this ego thing get started in the first place?" In some ways this is not a good question because the "split" (or fall) actually never got started, though it certainly looks as though it did. It appears as though the split did get started, so we want an answer.

I once said to a lady at a workshop, "I can answer the question for you, but you will not be happy with my answer because once I answer it you will say, 'Well, yes, but why's that?'" The Why? question leads into an infinite regression. There is always a why behind the why. The "answer" is that the ego thinks it is possible to think a thought outside the mind of God. It is not possible to think a thought outside the mind of God, but just for a moment that thought is entertained. The thought of separation could, thus, be said to come from arrogance. But, why arrogance?

> *To accept yourself as God created you cannot*
> *be arrogance because it is the denial of arrogance.*
> *To accept your littleness "is" arrogant, because it means*
> *that you believe your evaluation of yourself is truer than God's.*
>
> T-9.VIII.10:8–9

Hubris

Another more "psychological" word we might use instead of arrogance is *hubris*. *Hubris* means "excessive arrogance." British historian Sir Ian Kershaw (1943–present), regarded by many as the world's leading expert on Adolf Hitler, wrote two books on the life of Hitler: The first is titled *Hubris*; the second, *Nemesis*. Our nemesis is the one thing we cannot overcome. Hubris makes us blind and in that blindness lies our nemesis. The one opponent that cannot be defeated is our own arrogance or hubris.

Pride

Another more "theological" word is pride. As the saying goes, "Pride cometh before the fall." Pride looks down, and if you are looking down, you can get dizzy and fall. Adam's experience is described as the *fall of humankind*. Still, nothing happened. It is all mythology.

We can leave God only in nightmare dreams and all dreams end when we awaken. Pride is considered the *original* and the most serious of the seven deadly sins, as it is the source of all the other vices. The Italian poet Dante (1265–1321) spoke of pride as a "perverted love of self."

Along with arrogance, there also often comes aggression. Attack thoughts make us unhappy. Attack thoughts do not serve us. Lesson 23 from the workbook says: "I can escape from the world I see by giving up attack thoughts."

One-mindedness, which is perfect happiness, is our ultimate goal. Right-mindedness must be achieved before One-mindedness can be restored. One-mindedness is eternally whole and cannot be split. The more we choose for the right mind, the more we progressively move toward One-mindedness. One-mindedness (our natural home) is the mind of God, or Unified Mind. *Ultimately* (which includes *now*), only One-mindedness exists. *Ultimately,* only Heaven exists. *Ultimately,* there is nothing outside of Heaven. Within an illusory dream world we can, however, "think" it is possible to live outside of Heaven.

Perfect Oneness

Perfection is a state of knowing the truth from a point of absolute wholeness. Perfection comes first. It has to. There is no way around it. In the beginning and the end, in the alpha and the omega, we have perfection. Everything that is not of God is not. A split mind cannot, therefore, know perfection.

Either God or the ego is insane.

T-11.II.IN.1:1

Either perfect oneness is true or separation and illusion are true. Both cannot be true. In each moment of "now," the choice is "given": Choose the right mind (Holy Spirit's vision of love) and awaken to perfect oneness or choose the wrong mind (the projection of fear/ separation) and remain asleep.

Moment by moment in choosing right-mindedness, we awaken from the illusion of division. English author and humorist Douglas Adams, in *The Hitchhiker's Guide to the Galaxy*, describes a series of human-made, dream planets, spread throughout the universe, where humans and other beings could go to make their dreams come true.

> *Maybe this world is another planet's hell.*
>
> ENGLISH AUTHOR ALDOUS HUXLEY (1894–1963)

Choosing Illusion: The Outer Mask and the Inner Self

The craftiness of the ego seems unlimited. Even when advances in choosing for the right mind are made, it is easy to slip back to wrong-mindedness. To each temptation the devil put before Jesus, he responded, "Get thee hence, Satan" (Matthew 4:10). Surrendering to the illusion of the ego leads to a fall. Surrendering to the love of God leads us to perfect happiness.

Going for Perfection: Thy Kingdom Come

English author John Milton (1608–1674), in his epic poem *Paradise Lost,* described the devil breaking away from God in an effort to establish his own Kingdom. Darth Vader, in the movie *Star Wars,* tries to make his own world on the "dark side." We create isolated Kingdoms in our minds, our bodies, our homes, at work, at church, in our communities, and in the world.

It is impossible to forgive another,
for it is only your sins you see in him.

S-2.I.4:2

Where is happiness and unhappiness? Where is guilt? Where is shame? Where is forgiveness or unforgiveness? Whenever I forgive anyone, I must forgive myself for having an ego reaction. External circumstances matter not at all when the mind is attuned to God. Jesus went to the cross without fear and with peace of mind, knowing that "going for perfection" was the right thing to do.

How can you tell when you are seeing wrong,
or someone else is failing to perceive
the lesson he should learn?
Does pain seem real in the perception?
If it does, be sure the lesson is not learned.
And there remains an unforgiveness hiding in the mind
that sees the pain through eyes the mind directs.

W-193.7:1–4

Jesus came out of the wilderness clear about his identity. He refused the outer and chose his identity as Christ. He remembered the truth of his identity, chose perfection over imperfection, and, in so choosing, remembered Eternity.

What a distraction the body can be.
It takes so much time away from me.

The body dominates our lives, and yet, we know the day is coming when our bodies will be turned into ashes and scattered to the wind or laid into the earth, destined to decay. The body grows old, our senses fail, our eyes grow weak, our ears hear less. Even taste, touch, and smell diminish. Eventually, there will come some disease and then friend death.

What if, in its entirety, this sorry picture—and what we call the "outside" world—could all be called into question? What if you knew that instead of this sad picture, you were pure spirit? What if you knew that the only real permanency is found in the mind of God? What if it is possible to know Heaven by being alive, awake, and aware right now? Heaven seems like a dream, and this world seems like reality. In truth, it is the other way around.

> *If your perfection is in Him and only in Him,*
> *how can you know it without recognizing Him?*
> *The recognition of God is the recognition of yourself.*
> *There is no separation of God and His creation.*
>
> T-8.V.2:6–8

CHAPTER 5

Perfect Happiness

Do you have any idea how many lives we must have gone
through before we even got the first idea that there is more
to life than eating, or fighting, or power in the Flock?
A thousand lives, Jon, ten thousand! And then another
hundred lives until we began to learn that
there is such a thing as perfection,
and another hundred again to get the idea that
our purpose for living is to find that perfection
and show it forth.

SULLIVAN, JONATHAN LIVINGSTON SEAGULL'S TEACHER IN
JONATHAN LIVINGSTON SEAGULL, BY RICHARD BACH

I was ordained a minister in the United Methodist Church in 1970. At the time of the ordination, you had to promise that there were certain things you would and would not do. Making promises is always problematic. Making promises puts us in a box. It ties our hands and restricts our freedom. Once you make a promise, if you break that promise, you are in trouble. To be ordained:

1. We had to affirm that we were "called" to ministry.
2. We had to say that we had accepted Jesus as our personal savior.

3. We had to say we believed in a Triune God (as opposed to a Unitarian) God.

4. We had to say that we believed that the Bible was *the* authoritative standard for all life.

5. We had to say that we would abstain from the use of alcohol.

6. Single ministers had to take a vow of celibacy.

7. We had to say that we were headed toward perfection.

Perfection Is the Goal

The late 1960s and early 1970s was a time of sexual revolution. The musical *Hair* opened on Broadway in 1971; we were experiencing the "dawning of the Age of Aquarius." I was twenty-eight, single, and recoiling from a marriage I'd entered into, in part, to have a "legitimate" sexual experience. I was studying for my doctorate while also teaching at the New School University in Greenwich Village in New York City. I had not yet met my wife Dolores. There were many beautiful women around.

At a retreat before the ordination, several of us "ordinantia" expressed our ambiguous feelings about the vows. We had each completed three years of full-time seminary studies. Most of us were already employed as ministers, so not going through with ordination would mean that we would not advance in the church. One young man was particularly unhappy about having to pledge allegiance to the Bible, which he saw as a rather mixed bag.

We were told that only the more conservative members supported the prohibition against alcohol and the insistence on celibacy for single clergy, and we should say "yes" to each of the questions even though we "might not" be observing them to the "letter of the law." In other words, we should lie! No one wanted to lie. No one wanted to be dishonest. We all wanted to be ministers. Here we were vowing that we were aiming for perfection and at the same time being asked to be lie. It was an unpleasant no-win, catch-22.

One deeply spiritual young woman, refusing to perjure herself, declined the ordination. I was proud of her. She later became a respected college professor. Most of the rest of us lied. There were two vows I had no trouble making—the first and the last. I had no doubt that I was *called* into ministry. The ministry was in my DNA. Other than teaching and writing (an integral part of any ministry), I never thought of any other profession.

The second part I agreed with fully was the last vow—that "we were headed toward perfection." Perfection was the goal.

The *Manual for Teachers* of the Course begins:

> *This is a manual for the teachers of God.*
> *They are not perfect, or they would not be here.*
> *Yet it is their mission to become perfect here,*
> *and so they teach perfection over and over,*
> *in many, many ways, until they have learned it.*
>
> M-IN.5:4–6

> *The Kingdom is*
> **perfectly united and perfectly protected,**
> *and the ego will not prevail against it.*
>
> T-4.III.1:12

Where is the Kingdom of Heaven? "It's inside you"—not in the body, but in the mind. The body is ephemeral. It will die. The Mind never sleeps and lasts forever in a place we call Eternity. We can put God temporarily out of our minds, yet, He is always with us. We can no more separate ourselves from God than He can separate Himself from us.

Does God Have Sex?

I once gave a sermon titled "Does God Have Sex?" The topic drew considerable attention. It was nothing extraordinary or dramatic. The word sex comes from the Latin *secare*, meaning "to split or divide into two"—that is, male and female, the two sexes. God does not have sex. God is One and not divided. There are religious traditions in which Heaven is divided into different levels and stages, where people walk around imprisoned in bodies like our own. It's all mythology and projection.

> *Spirit has no levels, and all conflict arises*
> *from the concept of levels.*
>
> T-3.IV.1:6

The Course refers to God as our Father. God is not a person. God does not have a body. God is neither a man nor a woman. Still, it is helpful "imagery" to speak of the function of God as Father or Mother, as that which created and loves us, our eternal, spirit Self—that which is on the inside. Jesus and the Holy Spirit are symbols of the Right Mind, or true Self, within everyone. They represent a love "not of this world." They are not bodies, nor are they people.

If the word *He* is used to describe God, don't take it literally. God is not a man. There is a wonderful Jewish saying: "*Mother* is the name for God on the hearts and lips of children." There are only two possible genders in this world. We often use the image of father for God as in the story of the Prodigal Son. The image of mother works just as well. There is no sex because there is no division. Perfect oneness has nothing to do with bodies.

> *The goal of life is to make your heartbeat match*
> *the beat of the universe, to match your nature with Nature.*
>
> AMERICAN MYTHOLOGIST AND AUTHOR
> JOSEPH CAMPBELL (1904–1987)

Perfect Happiness

True, lasting happiness is perfectly possible. This is what "enlightenment" is. We may experience elation or temporary joy or take some delight in a new idea, a new opportunity, a new car, improved health, a new love, extra money in the bank, or a good report from the doctor. But no "forms" of happiness last.

Ideas leave not their source.
This is the story of the Course.

The world is an unhappy dream. We think (within the dream) that the Truth is yet to be and yet,

Everyone already knows.
Everyone is already free.
Everyone is already perfect.
Everyone can already see.

All that is ever realized is what is already known. There is one life that we share with God. "The sleep of forgetfulness is only the unwillingness to remember Your forgiveness and Your Love" (T-16.VII.12.4).

Time is a trick, a sleight of hand, a vast illusion
in which figures come and go as if by magic.

W-158.4:1

The Unreality of Sin

When we read the word *sin* in the Course, we can substitute the word *separation.* When we read *separation,* we can use the word *sin.* Sin is the belief that it is possible to do something against God. Having done something against God, the ego believes that, in order to be happy, it is necessary to suffer or "pay a price" as a penance for sins. Sin calls for punishment. Mistakes call for correction in perception. The ego believes punishment "is" correction. There is then no hope for the poor sinners of the world. They *will be* found and they *will be* punished. Thus it is impossible to think of sin as true and not believe forgiveness is a lie (W-134.4:2).

> *If sin is real, then happiness must be illusion,*
> *for they cannot both be true.*

> W-101.2:3

God Wills You Perfect Happiness Now

The world is ever-changing. The weather changes, babies are born, people's bodies age, people die. Such is the nature of time. The changelessness of Heaven is perfect. There are no storms or wars in Heaven. Perfect happiness cannot be found in a world of change. Perfect happiness is, however, possible because there is no world apart from what we think. Lesson 138 from the Course is this: "Heaven is a decision I must make." We will each inevitably make the decision for Heaven, so why not now?

Guilt is an illusion based on the thought that I have sinned by separating myself from God. I can only be separate from God within a nightmare dream. If I'm in my bed dreaming, I awaken in a place I never left. My body is still lying there in the same bed.

> *What makes this world seem real except your own denial*
> *of the truth that lies beyond? What but your thoughts of misery*
> *and death obscure the perfect happiness*
> *and the eternal life your Father wills for you?*
> *And what could hide what cannot be concealed except illusion?*
> *What could keep from you what you already have*

except your choice to see it not, denying it is there?

W-165.1:1–4

A woman who is a guest in a hotel calls up the front desk and says, "There is a naked man walking around in the apartment directly across the street from my room. You must do something!" The manager goes up to her room to investigate. He looks out her window across the street and says, "Ma'am you can only see down to his waist. You don't know. He may only be missing his shirt." "No, no," she says, "He is completely naked." "How do you know that?" asks the manager. "Just stand on the bed," she says, "and you will see." Remember:

It's not what we look at that matters.
It's what we see!

We manifest what we make judgments about and *we* will continue to manifest everything *we* make judgments about until *we* stop judging what *we* manifest. If you don't like what you are manifesting, stop judging it. When we don't judge where we are or who we are with, we get to be happy.

Space and time are opposite sides of one illusory coin. Time is literally *temporary*. It is past or future but it is never now. The only part of time that is eternal is now. Eternity is "timelessness." Jesus, in the Gospels, says, "Before Abraham was, I am." He did not say, "Before Abraham was, I was." He said, Before Abraham was, I *am*" (John 8:58).

What time but now can truth be recognized?
The present is the only time there is. And so today,
this instant, now, we come to look upon what is
forever there; not in our sight, but in the eyes of Christ.
He looks past time, and sees eternity as represented there.

W-164.1:1-4

Perfect Happiness Now

A day of grace is given me
And now I do clearly see it.

There is a light my eyes see not
And yet my mind beholds it.

Now do I see there is no loss
When I have left illusion.

The world holds nothing that I want
And so my choice is clear.

I find it not by leaving here
But in the Mind Eternal.

There is a place of timelessness,
Where love endures forever.

Here losing is impossible.
And vengeance has no meaning.

Here God speaks clearly to his Son.
And now his Son does answer.

God's Will is perfect happiness
Why choose against myself?

God's Will is perfect happiness
For all sisters and all brothers.

God's Will is perfect happiness
For all who will declare it.

There is now nothing left to find
Perfection has been given.

I move now forward home to God.
Now is the last step certain.

CHAPTER 6

Perfect Vision

When we choose the ego's distorted perception, the ego's shadow is cast across everything. However, "the day is coming and now is," when we will experience "perfect vision," and therefore, "perfect happiness." Perfect vision enables perfect oneness. The first step is a matter of willingness.

Perfect Purity

According to mythological lore, the hero or heroine (the Self we are) is always born in perfect purity. *Immaculate* means "without spot." (Thus, a *mackerel* is a "spotted fish.") Pythagoras, Buddha, Confucius, and Jesus were all said to have "immaculate" conceptions. Let's not take this too literally. This is one place Christianity got caught by worshipping the body of Jesus. It's not just any body, it's a bleeding, sacrificial body hanging on a cross. Thus, we say in the liturgy of the mass—"This is my body broken for you. This is my blood poured out for you." Bodies are not immaculate. It is the mind that remembers God.

Heaven is the home of perfect purity,
and God created it for you.

T-33.II.13:6

Perception did not exist until the separation introduced
degrees, aspects and intervals. Spirit has no levels,
and all conflict arises from the concept of levels.
Only the Levels of the Trinity are capable of unity.
The levels created by the separation cannot but conflict.
This is because they are meaningless to each other.

T-3.IV.1:5

Though born a king, the hero frequently stumbles, falling prey to his own ego. We are all created in perfect purity. Nothing can shake God's conviction of the perfect purity of everything that He created (T-14. III.12:2). God knows that we, His children, are asleep, and He has a plan for our awakening.

For the Son of God is guiltless now,
and the brightness of his purity
shines untouched forever in God's Mind.

T-13.I.5:6

Jesus says, "Blessed are the pure in heart for they shall see God." Peace comes in the remembrance of perfect purity. We love children because it is so easy to see innocence in them. I fell in love with both my high school sweetheart and my wife because I saw the innocence within. Jesus asks us to look upon all brothers and sisters as though we were looking upon an innocent child, asking for our love. The man who just stepped in line in front of you is one of those children.

The Holy Spirit is the Translator of the laws of God
to those who do not understand them....
He translates only to preserve the original meaning
in all respects and in all languages.

Therefore, He opposes the idea that differences in form
are meaningful, emphasizing always that
"these differences do not matter."

T-7.II.4:5 & 5:2–3

The miracle is the one thing you can do that transcends order
being based not on differences but on equality.

T-14.X.2:7

Jesus remembered the Christ by not seeing differences in form.
Recognizing the truth, He could say, "I and the Father are One." There is
no difference between us except in time, and insofar as there is no time,
there are no differences.

I was created like you in the First, and I have called you to join
with me in the Second. I am in charge of the Second Coming,
and my judgment, which is used only for protection,
cannot be wrong because it never attacks.
Your ego is trying to convince you that it is real and I am not,
because if I am real, I am no more real than you are.
That knowledge, and I assure you that it is knowledge,
means that Christ has come into your mind and healed it.

T-4.IV.10:3–4 & 8–9

This is the way reality is made by partial vision,
purposefully set against the given truth.
Its enemy is wholeness.
It conceives of little things and looks upon them.
And a lack of space, a sense of unity or vision that sees

differently, become the threats which it must overcome,
conflict with and deny.

W-184.4:1–3

The ego sees a fearful, disturbing world—a place of darkness filled with sin. Lesson 12 from the Course says, "I am upset because I see a meaningless world." The lesson goes on to say, "I think I see a fearful world, a dangerous world, a hostile world, a sad world, a wicked world, a crazy world" (W-12.3:2). The ego looks upon a dark world, and in darkness we are deceived.

Do not seek vision through your eyes,
for you made your way of seeing that you
might see in darkness, and in this you are deceived.

T-13.V.9:1–3

Seeing through the ego's "eyes," we are deceived. The ego sees sin, sickness, sadness, and separation. The vision of Christ looks on all things in light and sees only oneness. The ego-mind does not, indeed cannot, see oneness. The ego sees only separation, difference, and division. Identifying with the ego, we do not see wholeness. What is seen instead are discord, difference, and division.

True light that makes true vision possible is not the light the
body's eyes behold. It is a state of mind that has become so
unified that darkness cannot be perceived at all.
And thus what is the same is seen as one, while what
is not the same remains unnoticed, for it is not there.

W-108.2:1–3

Story Time

A Sufi story tells of a young girl on her way to see her beloved. She passes by a mullah (holy man) who is saying his prayers. Intent upon seeing her beloved, she unknowingly walks right in front of him. This is something forbidden by religious law (an "order" one is supposed to obey). The mullah, his prayers having been disturbed, becomes upset. Later, upon returning, she again passes near him. This time he scolds her for her mistake, saying, "It was not right for you to cross in front of me while I was offering my prayer. I was thinking of God, the Lord of Heaven." She replies, "I'm sorry. I don't yet know of God and prayer. I was on the way to see my beloved and, thinking only of my beloved, I did not see you praying. How could you, who were thinking of God, see me?"

Nothing lasting lies in dreams
or any of the ego's schemes.

A miracle, or the shift from ego-perception to vision, is a reflection of the union of will between Father and Son. The right mind sees only brothers and sisters, because it sees only its own light. Perfect clarity of vision enables us to see Heaven, even if what the world sees looks like hell—as it does when we are in pain, in times of war, during the reign of any despot, and as it did during the Inquisition and the Holocaust. The real world, a vision of Wholeness is seen *only* by the light of Spirit.

And There Was Light, one of the best books I ever read, was written by Jacques Lusseyran (1924–1971). Lusseyran was a Frenchman who became blind at the age of eight when his glasses shattered into his eyes after he ran into the corner of a school desk. He decided to learn German as a youth, so he could listen to German radio. As part of the French underground resistance to Hitler during World War II, he was captured and sent to the Buchenwald concentration camp, where he was an inspiration to many who gravitated to him for spiritual guidance. Because he was blind and could speak German, he survived Buchenwald and came to the United States, where he taught French literature. Lusseyran died, along with his wife, in a car accident in 1971. Here is a quotation from his book:

> Inside me there was everything I had believed was outside. There was in particular, the sun, light, and all colors. There were even the shapes of objects and the distance between objects. Everything was there and movement as well. . . . Light is an element that we carry inside us and which can grow there with as much abundance, variety, and intensity as it can outside of us. . . . I could light myself . . . that is, I could create a light inside of me so alive, so large, and so near that my eyes, my physical eyes, or what remained of them, vibrated, almost to the point of hurting. . . . God is there under a form that has the good luck to be neither religious, nor intellectual, nor sentimental, but quite simply alive.

Innocence

The English mystical poet William Wordsworth (1770–1850) expressed it simply when he said, "Heaven lies about us in our infancy." We could also say, "Heaven lies about us in our innocence." Eyes of innocence can see perfection. Eyes of innocence see *without* projection and the perception of differences. When preverbal infants look at us, they just see—with no thoughts of differences or judgments.

> *Innocence is wisdom because it is unaware of evil,*
> *and evil does not exist. It is, however,*
> *perfectly aware of everything that is true.*
>
> T-3.I.7:4

My friend and co-minister, the Reverend Emily Boardman, who counsels the dying, tells the story of being with one of her friends at the time of his death. The following are her words:

"My most beloved friend had fought a long, hard fight and was finally coming to the end of it. He knew it, and it didn't seem to scare him anymore. He had faced death often, and by now it felt like he was ready to join this new leg of the journey and was bidding us a most loving good-bye. I sat next to his bed when the secretary from the office he had worked for came in. She stood at the foot of the bed with a face full of love, light, and bewilderment and said, "You are *flawless!*" I turned and looked at him and, indeed, he was. I'm not sure what that means, but together we saw it, knew it, and rested in it. When she left, Charles asked me what she had said, what word she had used. I said, *flawless.* He looked at me and said, "Oh, Em, yes, we all are." Charles died two days later.

The innocence of God is the true state of the mind of His Son.

T-3.I.8:1

The Boy in the Boat

On the Sunday after the bombing at the Boston Marathon in April 2013, I gave a sermon titled "The Boy in the Boat." I spoke to the congregation about how we were to see the boy in the boat. His brother has been killed. He is bleeding, perhaps dying; perhaps the largest posse of police officers and police dogs ever assembled is carefully hunting him down. I asked them to think of the nightmare in his mind. He has killed three people, including a nine-year-old boy; he has maimed and scarred for life dozens more. I asked them to imagine the hellish guilt—his sense of fear and loneliness—knowing how hated he is, knowing he will be found. There is no place he can go for solace. No one loves him now. At best he will spend the rest of his life in prison.

Then, I asked the congregation to think about the way God sees him, the way God sees you and me. In God's eyes, we are all His children, all equal. While the world was hating him, what the boy in the boat needed was for someone to love him.

A similar tragedy was averted in August 2013 when a gunman entered a Georgia school with an AK-47 and five hundred rounds of ammunition. A quick-thinking and openhearted school bookkeeper, named Antoinette Tuff, told him, "It's going to be all right, sweetheart. I just want you to know I love you and I'm proud of you. That's a good thing that you're giving up, and don't worry about it. We all go through something in life. You're going to be OK."

The present offers you your brothers in the light that
would unite you with them, and free you from the past.
Would you, then, hold the past against them?
For if you do, you are choosing to remain in the darkness that is
not there, and refusing to accept the light that is offered you.
For the light of perfect vision
is freely given as it is freely received,
and can be accepted only without limit.

T-13.VI.7:1–4

God does not judge His guiltless Son. Only from a higher perspective is it possible to attain to the vision of Christ and see that which God condemns not.

Beyond this darkness, and yet still within you, is the vision of
Christ, Who looks on all in light. Your "vision" comes from

fear, as His from love. And He sees for you,
as your witness to the real world.

T-13.V.9:2–5

We have all gone astray, and yet God has a plan for every child to awaken from the nightmare dreams we have created. No matter how far away any child of God may wander, we shall all one day return to perfect vision, perfect wholeness, and thus, to perfect happiness. The only way we truly can see the boy in the boat is the way God does.

What happens to perceptions if there are
no judgments and nothing but perfect equality?
Perception becomes impossible.
Truth can only be known.

T-3.V.8:1–3

The boy in the boat made a mistake. As the world sees it, it was a huge "mistake." He had to be found and arrested. There is, however, no order of difficulty in miracles: One is not bigger than another. In the mystical state, there is just seeing. There is no evaluation or condemnation. We can love anyone when we see her with eyes of innocence. What the boy in the boat needed most was for someone to love him despite the severity of his aberration.

God offers only mercy.
Your words should reflect only mercy,
because that is what you have received
and that is what you should give.

T-3.VI.6:1–2

Infancy is a time of innocence. The ego is present in a nascent form, though not fully developed. Having so recently come from home—that is, Heaven, as children, we are, by nature, innocent. Even the most "hardened" of criminals have innocence buried deep within. Innocence is being home with God, not symbolically or intellectually, but experientially—without any doubt or belief to the contrary.

No one knows how many miracles occur without our awareness. Indeed, it is only when miracles do not occur that something has gone wrong (T-9.IV.6:2). All miracles are expressions of perfection, our natural, God-given state of innocence and purity. The first step on any spiritual journey, or returning to our God-given innocence, is purification. We begin by letting go of the unessential—the distortions of reality. We're looking to remove "the blocks to the awareness of love's presence" (T-In.1:7).

> *In shining peace within you is the perfect purity*
> *in which you were created.*
>
> T-13.X.9:4

In order to see clearly, we need to see beyond the body's eyes with their distortions of reality. We need to see without prejudice and projection. We need perfect vision.

> *Or how can you say to your brother,*
> *"Brother, let me remove the speck that is in your eye,"*
> *when you yourself do not see the plank that is in your own eye?*
> *First remove the plank from your own eye,*
> **and then you will see clearly**
> *how to remove the speck that is in your brother's eye.*
>
> LUKE 6:41–43

When the ego's plan fails, God's plan automatically kicks into gear. When the Prodigal Son, having failed in his own plan, returns home, the father is overjoyed at his return. The only thing that matters is that he has returned home—to a place he never left except, perhaps, in some nightmarish dream.

> *Without going out the door, you can know the whole world.*
>
> FROM THE *TAO TE CHING*, BY CHINESE PHILOSOPHER
> LAO TZU (SIXTH-CENTURY BCE)

Kick the Bucket List

In the 2007 movie *The Bucket List,* starring Jack Nicholson and Morgan Freeman, two older men, each diagnosed with terminal cancer and knowing they will soon die, take off to see the most beautiful things in the world that their eyes can behold. They see the pyramids; then they fly to see the Taj Mahal. They go around the world, beholding beauty and magnificence. In Hong Kong, Nicholson surreptitiously hires a prostitute to befriend Freeman while he sits in a bar. But Freeman declines her offer, realizing how much he loves his wife. In the end, all they both want to do is to go home, where they know love resides:

> *Look upon all the trinkets made to hang*
> *upon the body, or to cover it or for its use.*
> *See all the useless things made for its eyes to see.*
>
> T-20.II.1:1

The seeker on the path is looking—ever seeking for deeper spiritual ways of seeing. "If we make visible what is not true, what is true becomes invisible" (T-12.VIII.3:1). Man, not knowing how to reach God within, builds beautiful cathedrals.

... a temple is not a structure at all. Its true holiness lies
at the inner altar around which the structure is built.
The emphasis on beautiful structures is a sign of the fear of
Atonement, and an unwillingness to reach the altar itself.
The real beauty of the temple cannot be seen
with the physical eye.
Spiritual sight, on the other hand, cannot see the structure
at all because it is perfect vision.
It can, however, see the altar with perfect clarity.

T-2.III.1:7–12

One sees clearly only with the heart.
Anything essential is invisible to the eyes.

FROM *THE LITTLE PRINCE*, BY
ANTOINE DE SAINT-EXUPÉRY (1900–1944)

Love, which is invisible, is seen with perfect clarity by the heart and soul. Outlooks, positions, and points of view are all ego-based. Do they matter? Does it make any difference if we are Republicans or Democrats? (I said that from the pulpit at Unity Church in Chicago. Some man in the back of the room yelled, "Yes!" And the whole room roared with laughter for a full minute.) There are no Republicans or Democrats in Heaven.

Healing is a thought by which two minds
perceive their oneness and become glad.

T-5.I.1:1

Comparison must be an ego device, for love makes none.
Specialness always makes comparisons.

T-24.II.1:1–2

The Course often speaks of *constancy*. Constant vision, it says, can be given only those who wish for constancy (T-12.VII.13:4). Constancy arises in the sight of those who look on the world and see no sin or guilt, who advocate not for punishment and payment for transgressions. To be perfect, a mind must be pure; to be pure, it must be true; to be true, it must be simple; it must be innocent; it must be immaculate. It must be constant. And if it is, it will know only perfect happiness.

CHAPTER 7

Perfect Love

Perfect love casts out fear.
If fear exists,
Then there is not perfect love.
But:
Only perfect love exists.
If there is fear,
It produces a state that does not exist.

T-1.VI.5:4–8

A miracle is a correction introduced into false thinking by me.
It acts as a catalyst, breaking up erroneous perception
and reorganizing it properly. This places you under
the Atonement principle, where perception is healed.
Until this has occurred,
knowledge of the Divine Order is impossible.

PRINCIPLE 37 FROM THE "FIFTY MIRACLE PRINCIPLES," T–I.37

Divine Order

I watched a documentary on life in India that showed an Indian woman playing with her baby. She held her baby up over her head, lowering him down to her face, and then lifted him back up and away again. The baby was laughing with delight, playing with Mommy, looking deeply into her eyes, laughing every time she pushed him away and then pulled him closer. It was a wonderful sight! Slowly, slowly, the camera panned out and down, gradually exposing the surroundings. The mother was standing barefoot on a garbage heap. Below her were dozens of people bent over, digging through the garbage. Smoke rose in heavy columns all around them, but there were such joy and happiness on the face of the mother and her baby. In one holy instant, they were out of time, out of the garbage heap—experiencing love, remembering Heaven.

The role, power, and place of the Mind is so important in our lives that it behooves us to look at the "mind" up close and carefully. Appreciating the sovereignty of the Mind and our ability to choose determines our happiness. Remember, the main question:

Who is the chooser and who wants to know?

The Course teaches us to control our thoughts, rather than being at the mercy of our lower mind. We automatically adopt right-minded (Spirit-guided) thoughts as we let go of selfish defensive, ego-based thoughts.

This is salvation's keynote:
What I see reflects a process in my mind,
which starts with my idea of what I want.
From there, the mind makes up an image of the thing
the mind desires, judges valuable, and therefore seeks to find.

W-325.1:1–2

Ultimately means "eventually," "finally," or "at last." Whenever the word *ultimate* or *ultimately* appear in the Course, you can be sure that whatever appears after it is true, as in, "In the *ultimate sense,* reincarnation is impossible. There is no past or future, and the idea of birth into a body has no meaning either once or many times"

(M-24.1:1–2). What is ultimately true is always true. *Ultimately,* no compromise is possible between everything and nothing (T-2.VII.5:10). Separation from God is *ultimately* impossible. It never happened and can only occur in a nightmare that has no reality. For this reason, everyday life is a dream.

Ultimately, Only Mind Exists

Nothing exists outside the Mind.

Mind is eternal, invisible, and formless.

Mind is everywhere, encapsulating everything.

Mind cannot be dissected, analyzed, or broken down into parts.

The Mind is nonlocal. It is not bound by space-time.

Space and time are beliefs. Belief is an ego-function.

Belief is an opinion, a point of view. It is not the truth.

"*Ultimately,* space is as meaningless as time" (T-1.VI.3:5).

Because the Mind is atemporal, it is free of limitations.

The world we see is "the outside picture of an inward condition." (T-21.In.1:5). Do I see with the eyes of the ego or the eyes of Spirit?

> "To fly as fast as thought, to anywhere that is," he said,
> "you must begin by knowing that you have already arrived."
> The trick, according to Chaing, was for Jonathan to
> **stop seeing himself as trapped inside a limited body**
> that had a forty-two-inch wingspan
> and performance that could be plotted on a chart.
> **The trick was to know that his true nature lived as perfect**
> **as an unwritten number,**
> **everywhere at once across space and time.**
>
> FROM *JONATHAN LIVINGSTON SEAGULL,*
> BY RICHARD BACH

The Mind/Body Problem

Philosophers have toiled for years over "the mind/body problem."
"Where," they ask, "does the mind end and the body begin, or where
does the body end and the mind begin?" No such problem exists and the
solution is simple: There is no Body! There is only Mind!

> *A major source of the ego's off-balanced state is its lack of*
> *discrimination between the body and the Thoughts of God.*
>
> T-4.V.2:1

The word *everybody* never appears in the Course—not once. Every
"body" cannot join on the physical level. You wouldn't want to. The word
everyone appears 255 times because the Course is about Everyone in
Oneness. The mind is "wholly" real. The body is "wholly" illusory. At the
moment, there is a "temporal connection." It is strictly time-based, and,
therefore, a fantasy, a dream. When we awaken, we realize that we were
sleeping.

The following is a description from my friend, Rod Chelberg, MD,
one of the most deeply spiritual people I know. He called the following a
"dream memory":

> It was World War I, and I was lying in a trench. I was wearing
> military combat fatigues. It was a typical trench from World War
> I, about four feet deep and muddy. There were ladders and barbed
> wire as well. I saw a bright blue sky with white clouds floating
> about. All around me was the sound of screaming men, gunfire,
> and cannon fire. The smell of battle was there, as well as the feeling
> of fear. I was shot in my lower body and could not move. As I lay
> there, another shell came in and landed a few feet above me. It did
> not explode right away. As I looked around me, I saw my friends
> running away. I turned and looked at the shell again, and
> it exploded.

In that instant, I was free. I was again a thought of consciousness surrounded by peace and quiet. My first thought was "That's
it?" Nothing hurt. The transition was instantaneous. I was
complete peace and freedom. No horrible or pleasurable experience to go through. Why was I so afraid of death when it is, in fact,
a nonevent? I cannot even say that it was amazing. It was nothing.
Blink, I was free.

I suspect that the first thing that occurs when we let go of the body
is this thought: "I'm still here!" There is no permanence in any body.
Perfection cannot be assailed. The Mind cannot be assailed. Unless
I think it can, in which case I've fallen into the little "m" ego-mind,
which is "mindlessness." Being "mindless," we have no memory that we
are a Mind. Words like *unconscious, sleep, irrationality, compulsions,
dreams, fears, obsessions, insanity, judgments, projections, ego,
unreasonableness, body,* and a host of synonyms all speak of our
dreaming. The body is mindless. It is neutral. An awakened mind is not
subject to compulsions and addictions. It knows nothing of attachments
or aversions. A body is a fantasy we ultimately awaken from, not in
death, but in no longer being ego-possessed sleepwalkers through a
world we call life.

*Miracles reawaken the awareness that
the spirit, not the body, is the altar of truth.*

PRINCIPLE 20 FROM THE "FIFTY MIRACLE PRINCIPLES," T-1.I.20

The body is the thought of separation taken seriously. It is an isolated
speck of darkness, a hidden secret room, a meaningless enclosure
carefully protected. If there is a body and a world, there is separation,
levels, and division. Then there is no Spirit. There is no God. There is no
Perfection. There is just the body and the world, and time, sickness, old
age, and death.

The Mind and the Body

The mind is not in the body. The body is in the mind.

The mind is not in the brain. The brain is a computer.

The body is "a wall of flesh around the mind, keeping it prisoner in a tiny spot of space and time" (T-20.VI.11.2).

Mind transcends space-time. Bodies are bound by space-time.

Possessed by the body, we forget the Mind. As we awaken, as our awareness is raised, the proper use of the body is realized—*to let God's Voice speak gentle words to human ears* (M-12.4.2). The mind can be possessed by illusions, but Spirit is eternally free (T-1.IV.2:8).

Spirit Is the Thought of God

In German, the word Geist *means "Mind" and "Spirit."*
In French, the word Esprit *means "Mind" and "Spirit."*
"Life is the result of the Thought of God."
"Death is the result of the thought we call the ego."

T-19.IV.C.2:15

Believing that I am a body, I don't realize that I am, in fact, a Mind (Spirit). If my little mind is "possessed" with bodily thoughts, I am no longer in control of my mind. If I am addicted to any bodily based compulsions of any kind, I am not free. I am not in control of the mind. As much as I can, as long as I can, I want to keep the body light, fluid, free, and flowing. I want to keep it from becoming a distraction. The word *obsession* comes from the Latin *obsessionem*, meaning to be "besieged," "sieged," or "blockaded." I have trouble turning to Spirit if I'm feeling besieged. Where Spirit is, freedom is. There is no greater happiness than doing God's will because it is our will.

The Holy Spirit leads you steadily along the path of freedom,
teaching you how to disregard or look beyond everything
that would hold you back.

T-8.II.4:4

As we walk the path of ever-increasing awareness, we focus less on the body and the world and progressively more on Spirit. *Ultimately,* the body is clay, dust, ashes. Minds can join. Bodies cannot. We can be "of one mind." We cannot be "of one body."

The body represents the gap between the little bit of mind
you call your own and all the rest of what is really yours.
You hate it, yet you think it is yourself, and that,
without it, would your self be lost.

T-28.VI.4:1–2

My mother Milly left her body on Christmas Day 2001, at the age of eighty-five. Mother asked that her casket not be open at her funeral, and we honored her request. On the evening before the funeral, my sister, Ann, and I and our immediate family went to the funeral home. They brought out Mother's body. I reached out and touched her. She was ice-cold. (They must keep bodies in refrigeration.) I looked at her corpse and thought, "That is not her." I looked at a picture of her on top of the coffin. She had bright eyes and a beautiful smile. "That is the way," I thought, "that I shall remember her." I never doubted that Mother loved me completely. Love knows nothing of space and time. Nor is space and time within the Mind. On the level of mind, where true love is, Mother and I have always been and will always be connected.

Mind Causes Everything

Mind is the cause. The world is an effect.

Fear, guilt, and suffering are of the ego.

Love, truth, eternity, and knowledge are all in the Spirit-Mind.

Higher and Lower Mind

Another way to speak of right-mindedness and wrong-mindedness is to speak of a *higher mind* and a *lower mind*. The lower mind is the domain of the ego. The higher mind is the realm of Spirit. Only one "mind" is real and eternal. The lower mind is a dream state in which we live out a story of who we think we are.

I do not attack your ego.
I do work with your higher mind, the home of the Holy Spirit,
whether you are asleep or awake, just as your ego does with
your lower mind, which is its home.
I am your vigilance in this, because you are too confused
to recognize your own hope. I am not mistaken.
Your mind will elect to join with mine,
and together we are invincible.

T-4.IV.11:1–5

We do not doubt the existence of the mind because we partake of mind. It is possible to think of life without a body. It is not possible to think of life without a mind. While *ultimately* there is only one Mind (God), we experience a "split mind" we call *ego*, or *me*, or *Ken*, or *Rob*, or *Doris*. This "character" chooses between the Mind of God and the ego-body.

When Adam bites into the fruit of the Tree of Knowledge of Good and Evil, guilt enters his mind, and his mind becomes divided between what is to be hidden and what can be disclosed. A divided mind is not a whole mind. Therefore, it cannot be an open mind. To be completely open, the mind must be completely whole, or undivided.

> *You cannot learn of perfect love with a split mind,*
> *because a split mind has made itself a poor learner.*
>
> T-12.V.4:3

A patient suffering from indecisiveness goes to a psychiatrist. The psychiatrist says, "Mr. Goldstein, it seems you have trouble making decisions. Would you agree?" Mr. Goldstein replies, "Well, yes and no." A divided mind is caught between yes and no, back and forth, maybe and maybe not.

> *A separated or divided mind must be confused.*
> *It is necessarily uncertain about what it is.*
> *It has to be in conflict because it is out of accord with itself.*
>
> T-3.IV.3:4–6

These two options are the only alternatives for the mind. God or the ego—it is that simple. The Course is a course in mind training and the goal of the Course is to help us "wake up" by moving from wrong-minded to right-minded thinking. It takes a lot of patience and consistent practice to get it right. Just keep trying. At some point, any serious Course student needs to do the workbook of the Course. Doing the workbook shortens time and speeds the process on the road to perfect happiness.

> *"Why is it," Jonathan puzzled,*
> *"that the hardest thing in the world*
> *is to convince a bird that he is free, and that he can prove*
> *it for himself if he'd just spend a little time practicing?"*
>
> FROM *JONATHAN LIVINGSTON SEAGULL*, BY RICHARD BACH

Only the Mind

Only the mind is real.

Only the mind is responsible for seeing.

Only the mind can be illuminated.

Only the mind can be sick. Only the mind can be healed.

Only the mind can evaluate. Only the mind can decide.

Only the mind can be shared.

Spirit Is One

The ego is legion, broken into a multitude of forms ad infinitum. Spirit is God's answer to the ego. A mind in the service of Spirit becomes invulnerable. Unified Spirit is God's One Son. This One Son is the Christ. You are the Christ, a child of God. Everyone is. It must be so.

> The Holy Spirit is in your right mind, as He was in mine.
> The Bible says, "May the mind be in you that was also in
> Christ Jesus," and uses this as a blessing. It is the blessing of miracle-mindedness.
> It asks that you may think as I thought,
> joining with me in Christ thinking.

> T-5.I.3:3–6

Atonement cancels out error (wrong-mindedness), restoring the awareness of Spirit. A miracle does not change the form (the outer world of perception); it transforms the transformer (the inner world of the mind). A miracle places the mind in the service of Spirit, instead of the ego (the bodily self). The Holy Spirit speaks for the right mind, restoring sanity. Spirit is sanity. Insanity is not the will of God. It is insane to persist in maintaining an illusion.

You may believe that you are responsible for what you do, but not for what you think.
The truth is that you are responsible for what you think,
because it is only at this level that you can exercise choice.
What you do comes from what you think.

T-2.VI.2:5–7

When the mind is identified, associated, and connected with Spirit, everything changes. Life works. Miracles occur. Doors long closed are opened. Revelation once blocked becomes clear, and we experience "in-sight." God's creations are more clearly seen. Love automatically flows freely. We need not struggle to achieve love. We are Love. When we give it away, it comes back in abundance.

See how the body's eyes rest on externals
and cannot go beyond.
Watch how they stop at nothingness,
unable to go beyond the form to meaning.
Nothing so blinding as perception of form.

T-22.III.6:6–7

Plato, Sufism, the Course, God, and Formlessness

Plato (427–347 BCE) observed some 2,500 years ago the abstract nature of Mind. Ideas are "real" and "formless" unless we give them form, as a builder gives form to the ideas of an architect. What the builder creates is "temporal." Form can be an idea, like a religious or political dogma, a creed or system of belief. Every "thing" (form) is an emanation of mind. If there were no mind, there would be no concepts. According to Sufism, physical form and that which is empirical are a camouflage for reality. We must therefore move beyond appearances to find reality. No form is eternal. Love, which has no form, is eternal.

As nothingness cannot be pictured,
so there is no symbol for totality.
Reality is ultimately known without a form.

T-27.III.5:1–2

The Course "seems" difficult because it is teaching us about formlessness. Reality can only be known in the Mind. The mind is formless. Eyes see the outside world. If the "form" looks good, that is all that matters to the ego. God is "divine abstraction." *Abstract* means "nonspecific." What is abstract is not seen with physical eyes.

Form Is Mindless

The English physicist Dr. Stephen Hawking (1942–present) has said that there is no perfection in the universe. He is right insofar as he is thinking about the "formal" universe—the one that partakes of form, the one in which stars are being born and dying. There is no eternity in form. All idols are mindless. Bodies, mountains, planets, and stars all disappear in time. Religious systems of belief also disappear in time. We are now experiencing the birth of the interspiritual, interfaith age. Old systems of belief are falling away and the truth as seen within these different "forms" is coming to the fore. The Course represents one expression of this "universal" experience.

But overcome space, and all we have left is Here.
Overcome time, and all we have left is Now.
And in the middle of Here and Now,
don't you think that we might see each other once or twice?

FROM *JONATHAN LIVINGSTON SEAGULL,* BY RICHARD BACH

As ego-bodies we live on the outside of the planet, in the world of fashion, trends, and fads. We live in films, television, magazines, and newspapers. Focusing on the body, we are left mindless, unaware of the power of the mind. Still, in all things, the mind—the programmer, the decider—determines the world we see.

Forever Everywhere

The words, God, Love, and Truth are synonyms. They are all non-dualistic and not separate from each other. There is no subject/object. Love is wholly without ego-mind illusion, or fear. The ego's experience of love is always ambivalent. Perfect Love is, therefore, beyond its understanding. Love is a miracle. It is strength, it is sharing, it is freedom, it is guiltless, it is not special, it is not learned. There never was a time when Love was not. The pre-Socratic philosopher Anaximander (610–546 BCE), held that *reality* was *apeiron*, meaning "boundless" or "unlimited" (*a* meaning "without" and *peirar* meaning "end"). God, Mind, Life, Spirit has always been everywhere without end.

> *Everything is accomplished through life,*
> *and life is of the mind and in the mind.*
> *The body neither lives nor dies,*
> *because it cannot contain you who are life.*
>
> T-6.V.A.1:3—4

God Is Life

Life is an eternal attribute of everything that God created. The love of God is in everything He created. *Being alive* means being in communion with God (T-14.IV.10:6). What already exists is not "coming someday." Experiencing Heaven is a matter of vision. The Kingdom of Heaven *is* us. How can what already is be "coming someday"? Life is Being itself. It is Essence, it is quintessence. It is what is. It cannot not be. "You cannot

not teach" (T-6.III.4:1). Life cannot not be. You cannot not be perfect. The fear of God is fear of Life, not of death (T-23.IV.1:2).

> *To the ego the goal is death, which "is" its end.*
> *But to the Holy Spirit the goal is life, which "has" no end.*
>
> T-15.I.2:8

If God is Love and God is Life, then Life is Love and Love is Life. The more in love we are, the more alive we are, and the more alive we are, the more in love we are. The more we know God, the more we know Life, the more we know perfect happiness.

Light Is Life

Light reflects Life. Light and Life are aspects of creation.
   Light, Life, and Love are all reflections of perfection.

> *God has lit your mind Himself,*
> *and keeps your mind lit by His light*
> *because His light is what your mind is.*
>
> T-7.III.5:1

Life, Mind, Spirit, Love, and Light Do Not Have Form

Mind supplies Spirit with energy. Light has energy and momentum, but no form. Darkness disappears in light. Light is unlimited. Light is understanding. Light does not oppose the will of God. In light, there is tranquility and peace.

> *Where God created life, there life must be.*
> *In any state apart from Heaven life is illusion.*

At best it seems like life; at worst, like death.
Yet both are judgments on what is not life,
equal in their inaccuracy and lack of meaning.
Life not in Heaven is impossible,
and what is not in Heaven is not anywhere.

T-23.II.19:2–6

Knowledge and Perception

The Course distinguishes between knowledge and perception. Perception is dualistic. Since perception "sees" the outside, there must be a subject and an object for perception.

+ Knowledge is of the Mind and of wholeness where there is no subject and object.
+ Knowledge is awareness, or vision of perfection, or perfect wholeness.
+ Knowledge is of the pre-separated world of God and unified creation, where there are no forms and differentiations.
+ Knowledge is timeless and conflict-free.
+ Knowledge is wholly shared and wholly one.
+ Knowledge is total.

The separated mind cannot understand perfection
and its wholeness.

T-7.VI.4:2

Life and death, light and darkness,
knowledge and perception, are irreconcilable.

T-3.VII.6:6

There is no life, truth, intelligence, nor substance in matter;
all is Mind, there is no matter.
Spirit is immortal Truth, matter is mortal error.
Spirit is the real and eternal; matter is the unreal and temporal.
Spirit is God, and man is His image and likeness; hence, man is spiritual
and not material.

—FROM *SCIENCE AND HEALTH WITH KEY TO THE*
SCRIPTURES, BY MARY BAKER EDDY (1821–1910)

How holy are our minds!
And everything we see reflects the holiness within the mind
at one with God and with itself.
How easily do errors disappear,
and death gives place to everlasting life.

W-124.2:1–2

PART III

Basic Principles in
A Course in Miracles

CHAPTER 8

Mythology, Metaphysics, and Miracles

THE COSMIC EGG

Humpty Dumpty sat on a wall,
Humpty Dumpty had a great fall.
All the king's horses and all the king's men
Couldn't put Humpty Dumpty together again.

OLD ENGLISH NURSERY RHYME

Is That All There Is?

Let's start with a little logic:

1. Only knowledge has being.
2. The ego has no knowledge.
3. Therefore the ego has no being (T-8.VIII.7:7).

In 1969, the American singer Peggy Lee had a hit song, written from the point of view of someone who is disillusioned with life, titled "Is That All There Is?" If the body and the world and time were all there is, then there would be room for despair and disillusionment. Fortunately, neither the body, the world, nor time is real (unchanging, eternal truth). There is, therefore, reason for joy.

The Ego-Body: Our Best Friend and Worst Enemy

The ego is the seemingly separated self, "born in a body, doomed to suffer and to end its life in death." The ego-body is "the 'will' that *sees* the will of God as enemy" (W-pII.12:1–2). This tiny, mad idea has become so shattered, so split, so fragmented, so . . .

> *splintered and subdivided and divided again, over and over,*
> *that it is now almost impossible to perceive it once was one,*
> *and still is what it was.* ***That one error,*** *which brought truth to illusion,*
> *infinity to time, and life to death, was all you ever made.*
>
> T-18.I.4:3–4

The ego (the "mad idea" of separation) appears as legion, broken into a multitude of forms—running in a myriad of directions, in fact, so many directions that this "Humpty Dumpty" cannot be put back together again. A body shattered in an explosion cannot be brought back to "life" again, no matter how many horses and how many men there are to put it back together. The good news is that there is no "reality" in a body.

Inflation

Cosmologists tell us that the universe began with the big bang or what they call "inflation." It's the same word we use to describe economic inflation or the inflation of a tire. With just one insane thought—in a fraction of a second—the ego, the world, and the whole of the universe *appeared* to erupt into form.

When people get mad, they often explode. We say they are "venting." Spewing vitriol in this fashion can have an adverse effect on those who are nearby. If alcohol and weapons are involved, such inflation, or ego venting, can get ugly, even deadly. The resulting fighting and argumentation, stemming from one mad idea, can take on a life of its own and, literally become "something made out of nothing."

Here is where the metaphysics of the Course concerning the ego-body gets deep and interesting. We are separate and different from each other "only" on the level of form, only on the outside. Look around. Every "body" is different, and every "body" dies.

> Only mistakes have different forms, and so they can deceive.
> You can change form "because" it is not true.
> It could not be reality "because" it can be changed.
> Reason will tell you that if form is not reality
> it must be an illusion, and is not there to see.
>
> T-22.III.7:1–4

Looking for the Inside on the Outside

God/Love/Truth/Spirit is eternal, formless, and unchanging. Form in all its variations is a projection, an illusion of separation from oneness. Form, therefore, is a hiding place from God. Form is what is going on, on the outside. Form is what we see in the world. It is what we see on television. Despite the appearance of "everything" (a multitude of forms), when this big bang, this tiny, mad idea, this bleep occurred, "Not one note in Heaven's song was missed" (T-26.V.5:4). The perfect cannot be made imperfect.

Astropixie

The word *pixie* means "little." Cosmologists tell us that there are about one trillion galaxies in our known universe, each containing about one trillion stars. This puts the number of stars at 10^{22}–10^{24}! We're now looking at a number with so many zeros after it that typing it by hand would be nearly impossible! To top it off, our galaxy is tiny compared to some others! Astropixie, the *largest* galaxy on record, is approximately one billion light-years from earth. It is six million light-years across and sixty times the size of our galaxy—somewhat like putting a marble beside a basketball. Nevertheless, it's still all on the outside in the realm of form and, thus, illusion.

A tiny mad idea made (or seems to make) the entire universe. In reality, nothing happened. Love continued to be Love. Truth continued to be Truth. God continued to be God, and Reality continued to be Reality—unaffected by form.

Emptying the mind of all its projection
is the way we remember perfection.

Here is the good news. This misperception, this tiny, mad idea of attributing Reality to nonreality, can be corrected. That correction cannot be accomplished outside the mind because there is nothing outside the mind. "All the king's horses and all the king's men" can't put "it" back together again. We can, however, attain complete open-mindedness (willingness to choose again, or see differently) and thereby remember One-mindedness. When the mind, which is formless, is reunited with the Mind that created it, we can find ourselves back home.

Consciousness, the level of perception,
was the first split introduced into the mind after the separation,
making the mind a perceiver rather than a creator.
Consciousness is correctly identified as the domain of the ego.
The ego is a wrong-minded attempt to perceive yourself
as you wish to be, rather than as you are.
Yet you can know yourself only as you are,
because that is all you can be sure of.
Everything else "is" open to question.

T-3.IV.2:1–5

As consciousness is the domain of the ego, consciousness says that what is real is "outside." Without consciousness there cannot be a subject and an object. There is no separation, no other. All there is is God, or Oneness. To see (know) Oneness is to attain perfect happiness. As it is, we see only the outside.

Sometimes I forget that this is all a dream.

ALICE, FROM *ALICE IN WONDERLAND*, BY LEWIS CARROLL

In *Alice in Wonderland,* everything is upside down and backward. To get out of this upside down, backward world, all Alice needs to do is awaken from her own dream. In a similar way, the world we see is upside down and backward. We think reality is outside the mind, but it's in the mind. Fortunately, there remains a "little spark" in everyone and a way out of the rabbit hole. We might think of the little spark within as a tiny burning ember. The Holy Spirit is often identified in mystical literature as "wind," "breath," or "air." Blow on this little ember ever so gently, and it can come back fully into flame. Once re-enlivened, we again have the experience of joy.

There are more things in heaven and earth, Horatio,
Than are dreamt of in your philosophy.

—HAMLET TO HORATIO IN *HAMLET,*
BY WILLIAM SHAKESPEARE (1564–1616)

Not seeing any way out of the mad dreaming of the world leads to what philosophers often call "existential angst." It is possible, however, to see through the cracks in this cosmic egg. With time, "everyone" comes to see that we've had it all upside down and backward. We've been looking at the outside, thinking it was the inside. No wonder we cannot find happiness in the world.

You see no neutral things
because you have no neutral thoughts.
It is always the thought that comes first,
despite the temptation to believe that it is the other way around.
This is not the way the world thinks,
but you must learn that it is the way you think.

W-17.1:2–4

The world of form and separation is the ego's world, a place of fantasy and dreaming. It is a world of war, disease, and insanity. It is a world of anger, attack, greed, and selfishness. This is not Heaven. Heaven is undivided. Heaven is always heavenly. God is only good. Love is ever-loving. This fantasy world is a world of division: good and bad, war and peace, love and fear, and sickness and health.

If this were the real world, God would be cruel.

T-13.IN.3:1

The Course Is All About . . .

Let's look at four basic principles from the Course that will help us remove blocks to an awareness of Love's presence by purifying, or ridding, the mind of its illusions.
1. *There is nothing outside you* (T-18.VI:1).
2. *The body is outside you* (T-18.VI.9:1).
3. *You are not a body* (W-91.5:2).
4. *You are mind* (Spirit) (W-158.1:2).

As long as I'm dreaming (what we call "living") that I'm in a body, in a world, in space, and in time, I would rather have a clean car than a dirty one, an orderly home than a messy one, and a healthy body than a sick one. Feeling depressed and don't know what to do? Start cleaning!

There is something about setting the outside world in order that helps to bring the mind in order. Perfect happiness has nothing to do with the outside. Jesus could thus go to the cross because he knew he was not a body. Perfect happiness comes in discovering the reality of the Self within, where there is always order, regardless of external conditions.

> *No one who comes here but must still have hope,*
> *some lingering illusion, or some dream that there is something*
> *outside of himself that will bring happiness and peace to him.*
> *If everything is in him this cannot be so.*
>
> T-29.VII.2:1–2

I could say, "The Course is all about . . ." several times, in different ways and not contradict myself. Many arrows with different names— trust, honesty, tolerance, gentleness, joy, defenselessness, generosity, patience, faithfulness, and open-mindedness—all point the way to full remembrance of our eternal home and, therefore, to true and everlasting happiness.

The Course is all about . . .

1. *The Course is all about the mind.* The mind is the deter-miner of everything seen and unseen.

2. *The Course is all about helping us remember the power of the mind.* The mind is very powerful. My mind can be ego-oriented, building an empire in the world if that is what I want to do. My mind can be turned over to God and I can learn of my place in God's Kingdom. It is all a matter of choice.

3. *The Course is all about unlearning or undoing error.* Once we understand the dynamics of the ego, we can look beyond the ego. First, however, we must understand how we got ourselves into a fearful dreamlike world. Unlearning

brings "correction" to a mind that has gotten stuck in
dreaming and illusion.

> *It is obvious, then, that inducing the mind to give up its
> miscreations is the only application of creative ability
> that is truly meaningful.*

T-2.V.1:11

4. *The Course is all about realizing that we have the power to
   choose and we can choose God.*
5. *The Course is all about cleaning house.* It is about getting
   rid of the unessential, purifying, clarifying, and thus
   moving ever deeper into the center of Being.
6. *The Course is all about looking at the ego.* We look at the
   ego not to affirm its reality. We look at it in order to understand that it is an illusion, which, in fact, does not exist.
   This is a course in becoming aware of how possessed we
   are by illusion.
7. *The Course is all about raising our awareness.* The Course
   takes us higher and deeper at the same time. Raising awareness, we can more clearly see when the ego is operative,
   when the ego has taken hold of us, and, therefore, what we
   can do to disengage unconscious, compulsive, obsessive,
   insensitive, ignorant, arrogant, angry, attack thoughts and
   acts, which make us unhappy.
8. *The Course is all about being responsible.* It's about being
   absolutely responsible for absolutely everything that comes
   our way. We can then no longer complain about what
   happens to us. We can then no longer be in denial, knowing that whatever comes our way is a lesson we have given
   ourselves.

9. *The Course is all about Self-discovery.* Self-discovery means awakening from a dream. It means remembering the truth of our identity. Self-discovery is the only way to lasting happiness. Self-discovery is enlightenment. Enlightenment is "going all the way" to God.

> *Enlightenment is but recognition, not a change at all.*
>
> W-188.1:4

Enlightenment means remembering who we already are and becoming aware of what we already know. Rebirth, then, is merely the dawning in the mind of what is already in it (T-6.I.7:2).

10. *The Course is all about waking up and recognizing what we already know.*

11. *The Course is all about not judging.* In this sense, a Course student is simply someone who becomes progressively more aware of how judgmental he is. He actively engages in the process of progressively letting go of judgments.

12. *The Course is all about giving back to God what belongs to God.* We cannot steal from God and miscreate a world of illusion, but we can think that we can.

> *It is given you to know that God's function is yours, and happiness cannot be found apart from Your joint Will.*
>
> T-11.V.12:4

13. *The Course is all about liberation,* finding freedom from the tyranny of the ego.

The Basic Metaphysics of Miracles

1. Projection makes perception.

The world is what we make it.

It is our construct—totally.

We make up every aspect of the world.

That is why (hold on to your hat!) there is no world!

Another way to say this is: There is no outside.

This world looks nothing like our real home—Heaven.

There is no world because the thought system that gave rise to the world does not exist.

> *It is hard to understand what*
> *"The Kingdom of Heaven is within you" really means.*
> *This is because it is not understandable to the ego,*
> *which interprets it as if something outside is inside,*
> *and this does not mean anything.*
> *The word "within" is unnecessary.*
> *The Kingdom of Heaven is you.*
>
> T-4.III.1:1–4

2. Time is relative.

This is Einstein's big discovery.

Time can speed up. It can slow down.

It can stop. In which case—

(Have you still got your hat on?) There is no time!

Time cannot intrude upon eternity.

Eternity is not in space and time.

Eternity is "timelessness."

Eternity, by definition, is where Heaven is.

Heaven is, by definition, where eternity is.

Space and time appear on the outside.

When correction is completed, time *is* eternity.

> *It is a joke to think that time can come to*
> *circumvent eternity, which means there is no time.*
>
> T-27.VIII.6:5

3. We are not bodies.

> *We mistake our bodies for our "Selves."*
> *It is an easy mistake. After all, the body looks pretty obvious.*
> *At no single instant does the body exist at all.*
>
> T-18.VIII.3:1

> *. . . it is almost impossible to deny its [the body's]*
> *existence in this world.*
> *Those who do so are engaging in a particularly*
> *unworthy form of denial.*
>
> T-2.IV.3:10–11

Bodies are temporal.
In just a few years, neither my body nor your body will exist at all.
It does not matter, and it doesn't matter now!
(You don't need a hat if you don't have a head to put it on.)
Life does not begin with the birth of a body.
Life does not end with the death of a body.

> *Physical birth is not a beginning; it is a continuing.*
>
> T-5.IV.2:4

> *Learning is living here, as creating is being in Heaven.*
>
> T-14.III.3:2

Once we complete the work, the tool is no longer needed.

4. There is no duality.

There are no opposites.

Judgment implies duality—that there is something to judge against.

There is no "other."

Again, there is no *outside*.

There is only Oneness.

We are all already, and have always been, one with God.

We remember Oneness by not projecting illusions that negate it.

5. I'm nobody.

Not only are we not bodies, neither do any of us exist in an individualistic (egocentric) way.

We cannot and do not exist apart from God.

I am not my resume. Resumes are about the past.

6. The script is written.

There are no accidents!

This is not fatalism and we're not talking about predestination.

The older we are, the more we can look backward through the spectrum and see that things happened exactly as they were supposed to, given our level of awareness, maturity, and our ability to make decisions. Every decision I make in every single moment determines how the script is written. As Albert Einstein said, "God does not play dice with the universe."

7. All decision making must be turned over to God.

The sooner we do so, the happier we will be.

CHAPTER 9

Let's Play Make-Believe

GETTING TRAPPED BEHIND THE MASK

It is certain that you will never find satisfaction in fantasy,
so that your only hope is to change your mind about reality.

T-9.IV.10:2

Making and Creating

Since the separation and our choice of the ego's thought system over
Oneness, the words *create* and *make* have become confused. We have
not created ourselves. Spirit creates. The ego makes, as in "Do you
want to make something of it?" Thirty-five times the Course says, "God
created you." In fact, "God created you perfect." We did not "create"
ourselves, and we certainly did not "create" God. Rather, we made up
both an image of God and an image of ourselves.

God created man in his image,
and then man returned the favor.

ANONYMOUS

Perception's Fundamental Law

The mythic dream-image we find in the story of Adam and Eve is one of an angry father who casts His children out of Heaven. Projection makes perception and perception's fundamental law is:

> *I see what I believe is there,*
> *and I believe it is there because I want it there.*

> T-25.III.1:3

I was washing my hands in a men's room and overheard what seemed to be a conversation coming from one of the stalls. A moment later, a young man came out. He continued to carry on a one-sided conversation, speaking aloud to someone who was not there. I looked to see if he was wearing a Bluetooth microphone for his cell phone. He was not. He looked back at me as though my looking at him were an affront of some kind, and I decided it was time to leave the men's room.

We regard someone who carries on a conversation with someone who is not there as delusional or insane. The word *insane* comes from the Latin *in,* meaning "not" and *sanus,* meaning "healthy," "whole," or "well." To be *insane* is to be trapped within one's own mind. The ego is insane because it is not whole. The more we experience being trapped inside our minds and our ourselves, the more insane we are. Lesson 52 from the Workbook, which is a review of Lesson 10, concludes by asking us to say to ourselves,

> *Would I not rather join the thinking of the universe*
> *than to obscure all that is really mine*
> *with my pitiful and meaningless "private" thoughts?*

> W-52.5:7

The Course repeatedly asks us not to condone insane thinking. The more "make-up" we use (symbolically, not literally—there is no "sin" in putting on makeup), the more distorted our frame of reference becomes, the greater our feelings of isolation and insanity. The more we make up a "story" that is not true, the more artificial our world becomes and the deeper our unhappiness. The fellow in the men's room was living in a world inside his own mind, a world of his own making. The Course opens us up to the "Thinking of the Universe," and an awareness of One-mindedness. First, we have to get to right-mindedness, and we do that by giving up the insane ego.

> A sense of separation from God is the only lack you
> really need correct. This sense of separation
> would never have arisen if you had not
> distorted your perception of truth,
> and had thus perceived yourself as lacking.
>
> T-1.VI.2:1–2

The Dream (Nightmare) of Self-made Men and Women

The more we make up a separate "self," the more isolated we feel and the more desperate we become. The more disconnected we are from our brothers and sisters, the greater our loneliness and desperation.

> All loneliness is homesickness for Heaven.

Everyone makes up a self and then dreams the dream of that self. This making up of a self is not reality. It is dreaming. In Kabbalah, this unreal self-image is called a "shell." Swiss psychotherapist Dr. Carl Gustav Jung described this false self as one's "persona," a mask designed to make an impression on others while also concealing our true feelings, much as a hypocrite acts one way while thinking another. The word *hypocrisy* comes from the Greek *hypocrisies,* meaning "playacting or pretense."

From 1982 to 1990, I taught philosophy, religion, and psychology courses for Mercy College inside Sing-Sing Prison in Ossining, New York. Many of the inmates there invented a "persona" (a fantasy world of their own), in the midst of others who were doing much the same thing. They thus moved ever deeper into separation, solitude, and aloneness, even while surrounded by hundreds of other people.

Some of the inmates adopted tough-sounding nicknames. I met "Big Lynn," "Butch," "Cowboy," "Doc," "Tiger," and "King." They pumped iron, developed big muscles, wore distinctive tattoos and bandannas, grew beards, and wore sleeveless shirts. The only things that the inmates were not permitted to use to enhance their "personas" were items that might become a weapon, like metal body piercings, rings, and jewelry.

Deeper and more isolating, however, was the frequent adoption of a cool, seemingly noncaring attitude and an air of toughness. Behind each mask, there remained a frightened, forlorn, unhappy man. A heavy security wall surrounded the exterior of the prison, while inside, many of the men were building dense, nearly impenetrable walls around themselves.

There is nothing deadlier than the religionized ego.

AMERICAN PSYCHIATRIST
DR. DAVID R. HAWKINS (1927–2012)

Similar personas can just as easily be developed in someone leading a "good life"—as the chairman of the board of trustees, as an army officer, a police officer, a doctor, a psychologist, a professor, or a "royal master" of the local Masonic lodge. I attended a conference where a martial arts expert insisted on being called "Master." There are no masters, captains, lieutenants, reverends, or doctors in Heaven.

Beware of all enterprises that require new clothes.

—AMERICAN TRANSCENDENTALIST
HENRY DAVID THOREAU (1817–1862)

A fellow dies and finds himself standing in front of St. Peter. While he is being interviewed by St. Peter, the fellow sees a little man running around the Pearly Gates, wearing a white doctor's smock with a stethoscope around his neck. The man who just died asks St. Peter, "Who is that little man running around here? Is he a doctor?" "Oh no," says St. Peter, "That's God. He just likes to pretend that He's a doctor."

Do not be afraid to look within.
The ego tells you all is black with guilt within you,
and bids you not to look.
Instead, it bids you look upon your brothers, and see the guilt
in them. Yet this you cannot do without remaining blind.
For those who see their brothers in the dark,
and guilty in the dark in which they shroud them,
are too afraid to look upon the light within.

T-13.IX.8:1–5

In the film *Star Wars*, Darth Vader is half-robot, half-man—a towering, malignant figure with no visible eyes. His machinelike voice issues from a frozen, menacing mask, devoid of love. Darth Vader is symbolic of someone who has lost his identity in a fantasy world. If you wear a mask for too long, you run the risk of forgetting who you are. Fantasies, like dreams, are projections. They are distortions of reality. They are attempts to control reality based on false needs. Reality is then lost through usurpation. Fantasies are deficient and lacking in gratification. There is no lasting happiness in a fantasy. Fantasies are private, fleeting, and temporal. Fortunately, fantasies become unnecessary as the wholly satisfying, fulfilling, and perfect nature of reality becomes apparent.

We are afraid that the annihilation, or loss, of our ego's thought system will mean the loss of our individual self. Nothing could be further from the truth! Those who have made the greatest contributions to humanity are those who have been most willing to turn total direction over to God. Englishman William Booth (1829–1912), the founder of the Salvation Army, one of the most successful humanitarian organizations of all time, said, "I told God He could have all there was of William Booth."

I follow in the way appointed me.
I have a special place to fill; a role for me alone.
Salvation waits until I take this part as what I choose to do.
Until I make this choice,
I am the slave of time and human destiny.

W-317.1:1–3

Think of some individuals who have been most willing to turn their will over to God: Buddha, Jesus, Saint Francis of Assisi, Meister Eckhart, Ramakrishna, Helen Keller, Gandhi, Albert Schweitzer, Martin Luther King Jr., Mother Teresa, Desmond Tutu, and the Dalai Lama. Those who have been the most selfless—who gave the most and who loved the most—lost nothing. In fact, they gained the respect of the whole world.

There are no divisions in Heaven, no ranks, no levels, no titles. The more we project (make up) the world, the more we believe the dream of separation and division is real. So "the thoughts we think we think, are not our real thoughts" (W-15.1.1). Our real thoughts are those we share with the Thinking of the Universe.

You believe you can harbor thoughts you would not share,
and that salvation lies in keeping thoughts to yourself alone.
For in private thoughts, known only to yourself,
you think you find a way to keep what you would have alone,
and share what "you" would share.
And then you wonder why it is that
you are not in full communication with those around you,
and with God Who surrounds all of you together.

T-15.IV.7:3—5

When the Mask Freezes Over

George Reeves (1914–1959), who played Superman during the 1950s, was a good actor, and he played many roles. However, once he became Superman, he was so typecast that he found he couldn't get out of what he called his "damn monkey suit." After the Superman series ended, Reeves was offered a role as a romantic character in the movie *From Here to Eternity*. When the audience (children in particular) saw him on the screen, they yelled out, "Hey, look—that's Superman!" The movie was recut and his part taken out.

Subsequently, Reeves could not land parts in other movies. To earn a living, he was forced to make appearances at children's events dressed in his "monkey suit." With his arms folded across his chest, smiling broadly, he would tell children they should be good and brave boys and girls. On June 16, 1959, after a decade of playing Superman, George Reeves was found dead of a self-inflicted gunshot wound. Three years later, Marilyn Monroe (1926–1962) would be found dead of a drug overdose. Two months before she died, she told an interviewer from *Look* magazine, "I am not a sex goddess. A sex goddess is a thing, and I am not a thing. I am a person. I'm just Norma Jean."

If we lose control of what is happening to us
our lives become controlled by fate.

FROM *THE ALCHEMIST*, BY BRAZILIAN
AUTHOR PAULO COELHO (1947–PRESENT)

A wonderful example of a famous person who refused to get trapped behind a mask is German-born physicist Albert Einstein. Einstein saw the game that society played, and he refused to play it. He was too smart for that. We're probably all familiar with the picture of Einstein sticking his tongue out at photographers. Einstein was so well-known that he would be stopped on the street by people wanting him to explain "that theory." In response, he would apologize. "Pardon me, sorry! Always, I am mistaken for Professor Einstein." Einstein was just Einstein, a great mystic who said that, more than anything, he wanted to know the "mind of God."

If the mask freezes over, if we get caught in the "dreaming of the world," we may not see a way out. Our Self seems to be asleep, while the mind that weaves our illusions appears to be awake. Caught in the dreaming of the world, Reality remains elusively beyond our reach.

Psychotherapy is necessary so that an individual
can begin to question their reality.

P.IN.1:5

Therapy works as a patient begins to let go of the need to hold on to his insane stories. Enlightenment comes to every mind that lets go of the ego's story.

You will awaken to your own call,
for the Call to awake is within you.

T-11.VI.9:1

CHAPTER 10

Who Pulls the Puppet's Strings?

THE EGO, THE BODY, AND THE
DREAMING OF THE WORLD

The dreaming of the world takes many forms, because
the body seeks in many ways to prove it is autonomous and real.

T-27.VIII.2:1–3

The first thing every morning, we get up and take care of some
bodily needs. We look at ourselves in the mirror and say something
like, "Oh my God, what can I do to straighten this mess out so other
bodies can look at it?" I once had a good friend I loved dearly. We were
buddies since the '60s. He was a sweet soul, a disabled Vietnam veteran.
Each morning after his obligatory trip to the bathroom, he would go to
the kitchen, open the refrigerator door, take out a can of beer, flip open
the tab on top, sit down at his kitchen table, light a cigarette, and stare at
the floor.

An "imprisoned" mind is not free because
it is possessed, or held back, by itself.

T-3.II.4:3

Question: Who opened that refrigerator door? Who popped the top on the can of beer? Who lit the cigarette? Who issues the directions that any body follows? Who pulls the puppet's strings? Who speaks through any mannequin's mouth?

The body thinks no thoughts.
It has no power to learn, to pardon, nor enslave.
It gives no orders that the mind need serve,
nor sets conditions that it must obey.

T-31.III.4:2–4

The body is the central figure in the dreaming of the world.
There is no dream without it, nor does it exist without the dream
in which it acts as if it were a person to be seen and be believed.

T-27.VIII.1:1–2

It's Always Something

The ego-mind keeps us asleep by keeping our attention rooted in the body. The average person spends one-quarter to one-third of her lifetime sleeping. Psychologists tell us that we have an average of six dream cycles per night, lasting from a few minutes to a half hour or more. We may have several different dreams within each dream cycle, one dream scenario morphing into another. The average person spends six years of his life in a myriad of often distressing nighttime dreams.

Our dreams are filled with a variety of problems and much frustration. Something or someone may be blocking our way, foiling our endeavors; luggage might be lost; water might be rising all around us and we desperately need to get to higher ground. There is almost always some "unfinished" business addressed in a dream. We awaken from our nightmare dreams to a different (ongoing) dream and a new set of problems. One morning, I woke up thinking that I had forgotten to show up to give a lecture. I felt as though I'd let people down. I realized as I awakened that I hadn't missed anything! I had not let anyone down. It was just a dream. Our night dreams and our day dreams have different forms—that is all (T-18.II.5:13).

Suffering of any kind is nothing but a dream.

W-284.1:4

Each morning on our farm in Missouri, we awoke to a long list of required chores. We had to spend more than an hour milking the cow, and feeding and watering the pigs, horses, and chickens—all before we got ready for school. We each awaken to a list of daily "chores": We have to take care of the kids, fix breakfast, drive to work, pay bills, get the car fixed, go to the doctor, deal with unpleasant people, confront the boss— the list goes on and on.

In our waking and sleeping dreams, our many problems become the mechanism by which the ego keeps us from becoming *mindful.* The dream of the world, often a mindless, trancelike reverie, is a diversion that keeps us dreaming. In the soap opera of our everyday lives, we wander around in a monotonous fantasy.

The Illusionary Autonomy of the Body

The ego calls on us to carry out habits or tasks that we think we mustn't stop performing because the ego-body tells us we have to do them. In *The Little Prince* by Antoine de Saint-Exupéry, the little Prince journeys to a planet where he meets a drunk. When he asks the drunk why he drinks, the drunk says, "Because I am ashamed." When the prince asks why he is ashamed, the drunk replies, "Because I drink!" This downward spiral of reasoning dominates much of ego-thinking. The illusion of the autonomy of the body teaches us that the body can act like the mind (T-15.VII.12:1). We think that the body is sufficient unto itself. We think our body is who we are and yet the body is completely dependent on the mind. It is always the mind that decides whether the body is to be placed in the hands of the ego, or in the hands of Spirit.

> *What you do comes from what you think.*
> *You cannot separate yourself from the truth*
> *by "giving" autonomy to behavior.*
>
> T-2.VI.2:7–8

The body is a puppet, a marionette. It is sometimes a dummy, sometimes G.I. Joe, sometimes a prisoner, sometimes a doll. The body is a tool, a computer, and a vehicle in which we move around. *Ultimately* (which means now), it is no thing at all. Thus, we say, *ashes to ashes— dust to dust.* The Course calls the body *a little mound of clay.* In *The Razor's Edge* by W. Somerset Maugham (1874–1966), Larry Darrell, the hero, describes his experience as a pilot during World War I.

> I remember after a battle seeing a pile of dead French soldiers heaped upon one another. They looked like the marionettes in a bankrupt puppet show that had been cast pell-mell into a dusty corner because they were of no use anymore. I thought then . . . the dead look so awfully dead.

The Universe's University

The body is a learning device for the mind. It is a tool with which we develop our abilities. Life is our curriculum. Everyone we meet is our teacher and the world is our classroom—a university without walls.

The purpose of the body is to facilitate learning (T-2.IV.3:1–3). The only natural use of the body is as an instrument in facilitating learning.

> As a learning device it [the body] merely follows the learner,
> but if it is falsely endowed with self-initiative, it becomes a
> serious obstruction to the very learning it should facilitate.
> **Only the mind is capable of illumination.**
> **Spirit is already illuminated and the body in itself is too dense.**
> The mind, however, can bring its illumination to the body
> by recognizing that it is not the learner,
> and is therefore unamendable to learning.
> The body is, however, easily brought into alignment with
> a mind that has learned to look beyond it toward the light.

T-2.V.6:2–6

Spirit is that part of us which is already illumined.

Mind is that which seeks to be illumined.

Body is who we think we are.

It's up to our mind to change our perspective and to move from its false, bodily orientation to its true, spiritual orientation.

Look around. Everything we do is done for the sake of the body. Pick up a magazine. Ads for clothing, jewelry, cosmetics, food, drinks— and more and more drugs—abound. Standing on line at the checkout counter at the grocery store, I find myself face-to-face with a copy of *The National Enquirer.* On the cover are pictures of a variety of "celebrity" bottoms, taken at various beaches with the question "Whose cellulite is this?" under the photos. Enquiring minds want to know.

Some of us hate our bodies, and try to hurt and humiliate it. Some of our greatest mystics misperceived their bodies, thinking of them as they would an enemy. Saint Francis of Assisi (1181–1226, Italy), who lovingly called his body "brother ass," sprinkled ashes on his food to dull the pleasant taste. Heinrich Seuse (1295–1366, Germany), a famous Dominican mystic, endured fasting, sleep deprivation, extreme cold, iron chains, self-flagellation, and a nail-studded coat. He rubbed salt and vinegar into his wounds. Eventually, Seuse was healed of this obsession, after he heard the Holy Spirit tell him that God wanted him to stop hurting his body. There are no perfect bodies, there are only perfect minds.

The body is neither bad nor good. It is not an enemy, an opponent, or an adversary. It is neither a pleasure palace, nor something to be worshipped. Dolores and I enjoy going to movies, so we usually watch the Oscars. On Oscar night 2011, I was visiting with friends and I missed the show. The next morning, I turned on *Good Morning America* to see who won, but the show was only about who wore what and how they looked on the red carpet.

Thinking that we are the tool—the computer, the vehicle, the communication device—is a limit in perception, and therefore, a misperception. The body can never be "who" we are. Just like our cars, our bodies obviously last longer, and we get a lot more mileage out of them, if we respect and care for them. The "time" we spend as bodies is a dream! We remember our Oneness not as a body, not as a vehicle, not as a tool, but as Spirit—a perfect thought in the mind of God.

Who pulls the puppet's strings? Who makes the body boogie? Who opens that can of beer? Who thrusts the hand into that bag of potato chips? Who opens the book we call *A Course in Miracles* and studies the daily lesson? The body can do nothing except what the mind tells it to do. All decision making must be turned over to Spirit; otherwise, we may let some clever puppeteer (like Stromboli in the story of *Pinocchio*) run the show.

I read a study done on diets to learn which diet was the best. The conclusion: Many diets work just fine, if you do what they ask you to do. First, there must be a mind that makes the decision to follow the diet. Although there was a science to each of the different diets (avoid sugars and fats, etc.), they all came down to four simple little words, not one of them more than four letters long: Don't eat too much!

> *Child of God, you were created to create the good,*
> *the beautiful and the holy. Do not forget this.*
> *The Love of God, for a little while, must still be expressed*
> *through one body to another, because vision is still so dim.*
> *You can use your body best to help you enlarge your perception*
> *so you can achieve real vision,*
> *of which the physical eye is incapable.*
> *Learning to do this is the body's only true usefulness.*

> T-1.VII.2:1–5

In the dream, the body looks very real and denying the "seeming" reality of the body is an unworthy form of denial (T-2.IV.3:8). The world is seductive and it is easy to think that the learning device is Reality. But it is just a learning device.

> *The ego teaches that the body's pleasure is happiness.*

> T-19.IV.B.13:7

Don't Give Power to Pleasure

Pain and pleasure are proof of separation and the seeming reality of the body. *Don't give power to pleasure* doesn't mean not to enjoy the body. There is nothing wrong with pleasure. Who doesn't enjoy a good meal, making love, taking a nice nap, or basking in a demulcent massage? All such experiences are "temporal." Saint Francis of Assisi missed out on some good food by covering his meals with ashes. *Don't give power to pleasure* simply means don't let the seeking of pleasure replace fulfilling

God's Plan for Salvation. Indulgence can lead to a wide variety of addictions. Comfort foods can easily become "*dis*comfort" foods. When it comes to eating, a brief moment of pleasure is often followed by a longer period of guilt and depression.

It is possible to misinterpret the Course, saying that since it teaches us that life, as we perceive it, is a dream, we might as well go ahead and enjoy it all we want—eating and drinking as much as we can. This process simply affirms the reality of the body and facilitates our getting caught in bodily based addictions, compulsions, and obsessions that lead away from joy, peace, and happiness. When Dolores and I go out to dinner, we order one salad and one entrée. We divide them in half and it is always more than enough for both of us. There are very few overweight folks in Japan. Every meal we ate in Japan was small and each a work of art. Dolores spent more time taking pictures of our meals than she did photographing Buddhist temples.

Power, fame, money, physical pleasure;
who is the "hero" to whom all these things belong?
Could they mean anything except to a body?
Yet a body cannot evaluate. By seeking after such things
the mind associates itself with the body,
obscuring its Identity and losing sight of what it really is.

M-13.2:6–9

The confusion of miracle impulses with physical impulses
is a major perceptual distortion.
Physical impulses are misdirected miracle impulses.
All real pleasure comes from doing God's Will.
This is because "not" doing it is a denial of Self.
Denial of Self results in illusions,

> *while correction of the error brings release from it.*
> *Do not deceive yourself into believing that you can relate*
> *in peace to God or to your brothers with anything external.*
>
> T-1.VII.1:2–7

What has brought you happiness? Did this joy come to the mind or the body? Only the healed mind experiences lasting happiness, true joy, and lasting peace.

> *Do not allow the body to be a mirror of a split mind.*
> *Do not let it be an image of your own perception of littleness.*
> *Do not let it reflect your decision to attack.*
>
> T-8.VIII.9:5–6

Projection makes perception and distorted perceptions produce a dense cover over miracle impulses (T-1.VII.1:1). The miracle impulse is to love. What is true in the moonlight is not, however, always true in the sunlight. Confusing love with lust often results in guilt. Nothing temporal lasts. Only perfect love lasts.

> *Appetites are "getting" mechanisms, representing the ego's*
> *need to confirm itself. This is as true of body appetites*
> *as it is of the so-called "higher ego needs."*
> *Body appetites are not physical in origin.*
> *The ego regards the body as its home,*
> *and tries to satisfy itself through the body.*
> *But the idea that this is possible is a decision of the mind,*
> *which has become completely confused*
> *about what is really possible.*
>
> T-4.II.7:5–9

Appetites are of the mind, not the body. If the mind can heal the body, but the body cannot heal the mind, then the mind must be a stronger thing than the body. Every miracle demonstrates this (T-6.V.A.2:6–7). While the excitement of endorphins functioning as neurotransmitters produces feelings of well-being and "feeds" addictions, the origin of addictions can always be traced to a decision in the mind to engage in some form of "sleeping." Sleep is one of those "appetites," and we can be "drugged" by sleep (T-8. IX.4:6).

The Body Does Not Have a Mind

Do not accept the ego's confusion of mind and body (T-7.V.3:3). We may think the body is saying to us, "I need a beer" or "I need sex." Eat, and the body may be temporally satiated. But after a little while, we will want to eat again. If we "overdo" eating, drinking, or sex, we run the risk of becoming addicted. Then it seems as though the ego-body has won, and awareness of Self is put into abeyance—not lost, but suspended. Then we have lost sight of the straight way and the narrow gate. Time becomes an unhappy dream until the right use of will returns and sanity (Love) reenters awareness. Not letting the body rule means not letting the ego rule.

When the body ceases to attract you,
and when you place no value on it as a means of getting
anything, then there will be no interference in communication
and your thoughts will be as free as God's.
As you let the Holy Spirit teach you how to use the body only
for purposes of communication, and renounce its use for
separation and attack which the ego sees in it, you will learn

you have no need of a body at all.

T-15.IX.7:1–2

Pain demonstrates the body must be real.
It is a loud, obscuring voice
whose shrieks would silence what the Holy Spirit says,
and keep His words from your awareness.

T-27.VI.1:1–2

Don't Give Power to Pain

Pain is a great and annoying distraction that takes our peace away. From the traditional Christian perspective, Jesus suffered, bled, and died for our sins. Only a mind can be sick and suffer. From the perspective of the Course, Jesus knew he was not a body. He recognized the truth of who he was as Spirit and did not get caught in fear. God cannot suffer.

Pain and pleasure both confirm the body. Yet, pain and pleasure are equally unreal (T-27.VI.1:7). Instead of saying, "Jesus, take this pain away" (and assigning the responsibility for your peace to someone else), ask instead, "Help me look at this differently." As we turn progressively inward toward Self, we find temptations falling away, revealing a much more joyous path. As the world loses its attraction for us, we find that God's love comes more clearly into focus. The more the mind turns toward God, the more inspired we become, the more we let our Inner Teacher guide our path, the less we know of selfishness—the more we give in to Spirit—the more we know the body is not real.

In the holy instant there are no bodies,
and you experience only the attraction of God.
Accepting it as undivided you join Him wholly, in an instant,
for you would place no limits on your union with Him.

*The reality of this relationship becomes the only truth
that you could ever want. All truth "is" here.*

T-15.IX.7:3–6

Bye and bye only the body can ever die.

I watched an acquaintance of some fifteen or twenty years shuffling slowly down a grocery store aisle. She did not know I saw her. How old and tired she looked! Her cheeks were dark and sunken in; her head bent low as she looked from one side to the other on the grocery shelves. She had lost the sparkle that once filled her eyes. Every "body" wears out; nothing physical lasts. Spirit knows nothing of death. Spirit transcends what is perishable and changeable. Spirit is everlasting. Spirit is formless. Spirit never wears out.

The body is not evil. It's not bad. It is nothing. The only proper purpose of the body, as we advance as teachers of God, is to let God's voice speak through it, conveying to human ears a message that transcends a limited world. Whose will we obey is our decision to make. The body can act erroneously only when it responds to a misthought. Given to the Holy Spirit, the body can be a useful learning tool, a vehicle, and a computer. Or it can robotically follow the ego's dictates down a path of miscreation and self-destruction. The mind is capable of illumination; the body is not. The body can, however, be brought in alignment with a mind that has learned how to look beyond differences.

*The body no more dies than it can feel.
It does nothing.
Of itself it is neither corruptible nor incorruptible.
It "is" nothing.*

T-19.IV.C.5:2–5

When peace comes at last to those who wrestle with temptation
and fight against the giving in to sin; when the light comes at
last into the mind given to contemplation; or when the goal is
finally achieved by anyone, it always comes with just one happy realization;
"I need do nothing."

T-18.VII.5:7

We attain happiness with one simple, profound revelation:
I am not a body. I am free. I am still as God created me.

W-201

Who transcends the body has transcended limitation.

M-23.3:10

PART IV

THE LAWS OF HAPPINESS

CHAPTER 11

The Fundamental Laws of Happiness

If you hold your hands over your eyes, you will not see
because you are interfering with the laws of seeing.
If you deny love, you will not know it
because your cooperation is the law of its being.
You cannot change laws you did not make,
and the laws of happiness were created for you, not by you.

T-9.I.11:7–9

Are there laws of happiness?
Are there principles we can live by that would make us happy?
Are these laws sure?
Would we be happier if we followed these laws?

Rules, Laws, and Fundamental Principles

A law is a rule, a procedure, a fundamental principle, a description of a process by which things work. The laws of physics describe how things work in the physical world. The laws of biology, such as the principle of capillary attraction, describe how things work in the biological world. The laws of chemistry explain how things work within the chemical world. Liquids, for example, freeze and evaporate according to specific laws. Water freezes at 32 degrees Fahrenheit or 0 degrees Celsius (centigrade). A "degree" is something specific. When something freezes, boils, or evaporates, it is calculated by a human-made gauge and reported in human-made increments. All measuring devices are "made up."

> *. . . laws are set up to protect the continuity*
> *of the system in which the lawmaker believes.*

T-4.I.5:4

> *Fidelity to premises is a law of mind,*
> *and everything God created is faithful to His laws.*
> *Fidelity to other laws is also possible, however,*
> *not because the laws are true, but because you made them.*

T-6.IV.11:3–4

Human-Made Laws

For good or for ill, the laws of a state or nation describe how things *should* work within that society. Human-made laws are far from perfect, though over time they may be refined and improved as the society's awareness rises. For example, the Thirteenth Amendment to the U.S. Constitution outlaws slavery. While the amendment was adopted in 1865, it wasn't until 1964—one hundred years later—that the Civil Rights Act outlawed discrimination. Women were not given the right to vote until 1919, less than one hundred years ago. Growth occurs slowly in our world, but God's laws (the laws of happiness) have always been perfect and nondiscriminatory.

> ***Miracles are thoughts.***
> *Thoughts can represent the lower or bodily level of experience,*
> ***or the higher or spiritual level of experience.***

One makes the physical, and the other creates the spiritual.

PRINCIPLE 12 FROM THE
"FIFTY MIRACLE PRINCIPLES," T-1.I.12:1–3

There are higher and lower forms of mind and, therefore, of communication. A miracle represents a higher-order cause and effect that reverses physical laws. Principle 17 from the "Fifty Miracle Principles" states:

Miracles are a kind of exchange.
Like all expressions of love,
which are always miraculous in the true sense,
the exchange reverses tho physical laws.
They bring more love both to the giver and the receiver.

T-1.I.9:1–3

Higher-Order Laws (Miracles)

Higher-order laws transcend human-made and physical laws. Human-made laws can be faulty. According to physical laws, it takes time for healing to occur. Psychologically, as well, when our hearts break (when a romance fails or a loved one dies), it takes time to heal. A miracle is not bound by time. A miracle is a release from fear and that can happen in an instant. Doctors often describe unexpected or unexplainable cures as "miracles." Higher-order laws are not dependent upon the laws of time.

Miracles transcend the body.
They are sudden shifts into invisibility,
away from the bodily level. That is why they heal.

T-1.I.17:1–3

. . . miracles violate every law of reality as this world judges it.
Every law of time and space, of magnitude and mass is
transcended, for what the Holy Spirit enables you to do
is clearly beyond all of them.

T-12.VII.3.2–3

Spiritual healing need not take time
but it does require a change of mind.

I once counseled an unhappy young woman who was having trouble forgiving a young man who had jilted her. In an attempt to comfort her, I reassured her that someday she would forgive him. I added that, if she wanted to, she could even forgive him now. Almost instantly, her face relaxed. She became pensive and calm. She realized that, indeed someday she would forgive him. So why not now? It is rare that you see a miracle happen so quickly! She left my office as a much happier young woman, saying that she did not need any more counseling. They never dated again. They each eventually married different people and they became lifelong friends.

The miracle is a learning device that lessens the need for time.
It establishes an out-of-pattern time interval
not under the usual laws of time.
In this sense it is timeless.

T-1.I.47:1–3

It must be clear that it is easier to have a happy day
if you prevent unhappiness from entering at all.
But this takes practice in the rules that will
protect you from the ravages of fear.
When this has been achieved, the sorry dream of

judgment has forever been undone. But meanwhile,
you have need for practicing the rules for its undoing.

T-30.I.13:1–4

Death of the body, for example, might be the miracle needed to free a soul from a trap called "pain." The Holy Spirit is perfectly aware of how to teach us to remember what we are, and He steps in whenever we are "willing" to do our part by bringing our mind back to God.

The higher mind thinks according to the laws spirit obeys,
and therefore honors only the laws of God.

T-5.I.1:6

We develop our higher mind by honoring the laws of God. This leads to our greatest happiness. Ultimately, the only laws we can obey in order to be happy are the laws of God.

The Most Fundamental Law There Is

I push a ball across a billiard table, it hits another ball, which rolls away from that one. This is an example of the "law" of action and reaction, or cause and effect. If there is an effect, there must be a cause. The law of karma, as described in Eastern spirituality, says that what you and I do at one moment affects what comes back at another time. All our words and deeds have consequences. Even the smallest thing, like a loving thought or an unloving, jealous thought, has its effect. Each separate deed, along with every other deed, determines our destiny. Jesus repeats this law when He says, "As you sow, so you reap." Time and again we observe, "What goes around comes around." Or, as John Lennon (1940–1980) said, "Time wounds all heels." It is, thus, that we hurt ourselves when we attack a brother or sister who is my own self.

> *If you attack error in another, you will hurt yourself.*

T-3.III.7:1

> *When you attack, you are denying yourself.*
> *You are specifically teaching yourself*
> *that you are not what you are.*

T-10.II.4:1

Ultimately, we cannot hurt the Self that is the Son of God, united in Spirit with God and each other. Cause and effect are mutually dependent. The existence of one determines the existence of the other. Belief in an effect establishes cause. Without effect, cause cannot be.

A cause produces a result, a consequence.

A cause is something that is responsible for a result.

An effect is something that is brought about by a cause.

If we remove our belief in the effect, the cause ceases to be. Thus, the Course says:

> *You may believe that you are responsible for what you do,*
> *but not for what you think. The truth is that*
> ***you are responsible for what you think,***
> *because it is only at this level that you can exercise choice.*

T-2.VI.2:5—6

God Is the Only Cause

God is the One Mind in which we are united. God, being Love, knows only love. God neither causes nor believes in guilt. The mind of God knows nothing of punishment, anger, fear, hatred, and war.

Only by changing the cause—our thoughts and beliefs—do we get the effect we desire.

We cannot be happy if we do not assume responsibility for our thoughts.

We cannot be happy if we are caught in denial and repression.

We cannot be happy when we are being projective and judgmental.

> *Psychotherapy, then, must restore to his*
> *awareness the ability to make his own decisions.*
> ***He must become willing to reverse his thinking,***
> *and to understand that what he thought projected*
> *its effects on him were made by his projections on the world.*
>
> P-1.4:1–2

Higher- and Lower-Order Laws

The laws of God (the laws of happiness) are creative, unifying, and progressive. The laws of God are reparative. They work for the good of all and move us closer to One-mindedness. Higher-order laws are "miraculous." Higher laws multiply or add to our lives, resulting in abundance. Higher laws—such as those related to generosity, patience, and tolerance—heal, make whole, and facilitate the common good.

> *Your insane laws were made to guarantee that you would*
> *make mistakes, and give them power over you*
> *by accepting their results as your just due.*
>
> T-20.IV.3:1

Laws of chaos, or lower-order laws of the ego, are regressive. Laws of chaos, governing illusion, are outside of reason's sphere. They separate and divide, and, like a bad disease, they destroy. "An eye for an eye and a tooth for a tooth" is an insane law. Following this principle, everybody winds up sightless and toothless! Laws of the ego diminish us all. They lead to loss, scarcity, and fear.

> *What you project or extend is real for you.*
> **This is an immutable law of the mind**
> *in this world as well as in the Kingdom.*
>
> T-7.II.2:4–5

The Fundamental Law of Perception

To judge is to project. To love is to extend. Loving is *much* more fun than judging! The fundamental law of perception says, *We see what we believe, and we believe it is there because we want it there* (T-25.III.1:3). Ultimately (which means now and always), God is the only cause and all that extends from God is love. Love is eternal. Projections of the ego are ephemeral, fleeting, and part of a dream that ends when we awaken.

> *Perception is a result and not a cause.*
> *And that is why order of difficulty in miracles is meaningless.*
> *Everything looked upon with vision is healed and holy.*
> *Nothing perceived without it means anything.*
> *And where there is no meaning, there is chaos.*
>
> T-21.IN.1:8–12

If projection makes perception and perception is a result not a cause, then my projection is the cause of what I see. If I lie in bed at night and project a dream, I am the projector of what is perceived within my dream. No one else is responsible for my dream. That would be impossible. This fact of projection is as true in the daytime as it is at night. Thus, the Course says, *all of our time is spent sleeping* (T-18. II.5:12).

The Fundamental Law of Vision: Extending Love

The Pharisees repeatedly tried to "trip up" Jesus, to get him to say something they could find fault with.

> But when the Pharisees had heard that he had put
> the Sadducees to silence, they were gathered together.
> Then one of them, which was a lawyer,
> asked him a question, tempting him, and saying,
> "Master, which is the greatest commandment in the law?"
> Jesus said unto him, "You shalt love the Lord your God with all
> your heart, and with all your soul, and with all your mind.
> This is the first and the greatest commandment.
> And the second is like unto it,
> You shalt love your neighbor as yourself.
> On these two commandments hang
> all the law and the prophets."
>
> MATTHEW 22:35–40

> This is perception's form, adapted to this world,
> of God's more basic law; that love creates itself,
> and nothing but itself.
>
> T-25.III.1:6

If what we do comes from Love, it will be true and in accordance with the will of God. Thus, what we do will lead to greater happiness.

You cannot change laws you did not make, and the
laws of happiness were created for you, not by you.

T-9.I.11:9

As the laws of happiness were created *for* us but not *by* us, they must have been created by a higher authority. Higher laws transcend social, institutional, and even physical laws, like those of space and time. Another example of a lower-order law is the ego's belief that it is possible to derive pleasure through "revenge." Revenge always leads only to guilt—the product of separation and anger. Revenge never leads to happiness.

The higher mind thinks according to the laws Spirit
obeys and therefore honors only the laws of God.

T-5.I.1:6

Having free will means we can "decide" to follow or go against God's laws, which means we can choose to pursue or go against our own best interest. As long as we live according to the laws of the ego, the Holy Spirit cannot help us. All is not lost, however. Being a dream, the ego disappears as we awaken and we awaken as we progressively choose to follow GPS. The sooner we respond, the happier we can be now. God's will for us is perfect happiness now.

Miracles make minds one in God.
They depend on cooperation because the Sonship
is the sum of all that God created.
Miracles therefore reflect the laws of eternity, not of time.

T-1.I.19

The Laws of Eternity

The laws of eternity are not bound by the laws of time and space. Miracles are perfectly natural. They appear "miraculous" because they are not dependent on physical laws. A healing, for example, does not have to happen over time. The healing of a mind can happen the instant truth dawns on it. Laws of eternity are reflections of higher laws. Following higher-order laws leads to our greatest happiness.

I inspire all miracles, which are really intercessions.
They intercede for your holiness
and make your perceptions holy.
By placing you beyond the physical laws they raise you into
the sphere of celestial order. In this order you are perfect.

T-1.I.32:1–4

A "teacher of God" is anyone who chooses to be one. The qualification to be a teacher of God is simply knowing that somehow, somewhere, we have already made a deliberate choice not to see our own interests as apart from someone else's (M-1.1:1–2). This choice arises from a vision of wholeness that consists in knowing only oneness. In other words, the teacher of God chooses (metaphysically) not to "see" duality.

The Course describes ten characteristics of a teacher of God. These ten characteristics are various attributes, traits, principles, or laws that describe the processes by which life works. According to the laws of happiness, as we live in harmony with the principles of trust, honesty, tolerance, gentleness, joy, defenselessness, generosity, patience, faithfulness, and open-mindedness, so are we at peace. So are we happy.

There is an order to these basic characteristics of a teacher of God, and a reason why one follows after the other. As we consider each characteristic, we'll see how they connect. Ultimately, each of these principles is the same, which will become increasingly evident as we look at them.

There Are Basic Laws Related to Trust

Trust is the first and the most basic principle. All the other characteristics of God's teachers rest on trust. Do I rely on the ego and its laws, which causes only misery and pain, or do I choose to embrace a higher-order law and trust that following God's laws will bring me perfect happiness? Trust is broken into six stages of development. We'll examine each stage in the next chapter.

There Are Basic Laws Related to Honesty

Honesty is crucial to happiness. Dishonesty leads to guilt. Guilt is the symbol of our denial of and attack on God. We spend a tremendous amount of energy denying God's truth. "The ego never looks on what it does with perfect honesty" (T-11.In.2:6). When we are dishonest, we lose our way. Hiding means being unhappy. Hiding is a trap engineered by the ego.

There Are Basic Laws Related to Tolerance

Intolerance is so pervasive and insidious, we don't realize how much of our time it consumes, how much of thought and conversation is given to fault finding and judgment. Fault finding is a way of not taking responsibility. When we don't take responsibility, we perceive ourselves as victims. We do not realize how unhappy intolerance makes us.

Judgment always involves rejection, which is a manifestation of separation. It takes a great deal of awareness to stop judging. Once we are successful in suspending judgment, we experience a tremendous release, and a deep sense of peace. Nothing is more conducive to peace of mind than not having an opinion. Jesus says, "As we judge so are we judged" (Matthew 7:12). Here's the old law of cause and effect. No one has the right to judge how far others are along their path home.

The ego speaks in judgment, and the Holy Spirit reverses
its decision, much as a higher court has the power
to reverse a lower court's decisions in this world.

T-5.VI.4:1

There Are Basic Laws Related to Gentleness

God's teachers are incapable of harm and are wholly gentle (M-4.IV.1:1).
When we are kind, kindness comes back our way. We offer kindness to
ourselves each time we hear God's voice and choose to learn the easy
lessons He teaches.

There Are Basic Laws Related to Joy

Joy is an inevitable result of gentleness and the experience of freedom
from fear. Joy is a consequence of following the laws of God. We can be
joyful only as long as we are also trusting, honest, tolerant, and gentle.

There Are Basic Laws Related to Defenselessness

Workbook Lesson 153 says, "In my defenselessness my safety lies."
Rather than bringing into play the ego's principles of retribution,
retaliation, reprisal, and revenge, defenselessness is deferential and
disarming. It is peacemaking. Defenselessness, not defensiveness,
brings us joy. Defensiveness rests on fear. When we defend the ego, we
back ourselves into further aloneness, isolation, and despair—all very
unhappy states.

There Are Basic Laws Related to Generosity

Here the law of cause and effect is clearly seen: As we give, so do we receive. "To spirit, getting is meaningless and giving is all" (T-5.I.1:7). Generosity is a blessing we give ourselves. While this kind of thinking is alien to the ego's lower mind, it is comprehensible in connection with the way ideas are shared by the higher mind. When we give our ideas away, if they are accepted, they are strengthened in both the giver and the receiver. Therefore, whatever love we give away, remains forever ours.

There Are Basic Laws Related to Patience

Practicing patience, we become patient. When we're waiting in line at the bank or at the grocery store, we can choose to wait patiently (happily) or impatiently (unhappily). When we practice patience, we also practice tolerance, open-mindedness, and defenselessness.

There Are Basic Laws Related to Faithfulness

Faithfulness is the teacher of God's trust that the Word of God will set all things right. Faithfulness, like honesty, also means consistency. Faithfulness in practicing these principles brings rewards. Hanging in there, remaining true, remaining constant and steadfast gets us home again.

There Are Basic Laws Related to Open-mindedness

Open-mindedness—complete and total open-mindedness—is perhaps the last of the attributes the teacher of God develops. Open-mindedness comes with freedom from judgment. Just as judgment closes the mind, so open-mindedness releases us to the full experience of God.

As a teacher of God, we choose to trust rather than to be distrustful, to be honest instead of dishonest, to practice tolerance instead of intolerance. When it comes to gentleness, we're talking about giving up all thoughts of harm, leaving us to act only in a gentle manner toward each other. Practicing each of the characteristics means choosing to give up the negative (ego) for the positive (Spirit).

CHAPTER 12

Stages in the Development of Trust

ON TRUST AND HAPPINESS

Give me but a little trust in the name of the complete trust I
have in you, and we will easily accomplish the goal of
perfection together.

T-12.II.8:5

The children of God are entitled to the perfect comfort
that comes from perfect trust.

T-2.III.5:1

The Unveiling of the Ego

My primary text during the years that I taught university courses on
mysticism was a delightful book, simply titled *Mysticism,* by English author
Evelyn Underhill (1875–1941). I would love to have known Evelyn. She was
herself a mystic and, I'll bet, a bit like Helen Schucman. A woman of great
intellect, she was a visionary, and like Helen, a metaphysical poet. Evelyn spent
her whole life studying different mystics, whom she saw as spiritual pioneers.

Instead of setting about saying there is a mind and I want to kill it, you begin to seek its source and then you find it does not exist at all.

ENGLISH AUTHOR AND MYSTIC EVELYN UNDERHILL

Evelyn's book on mysticism was published in 1911. Any book that is still being reprinted and sold more than one hundred years after it was first published is certainly a classic. Though she did not hold a doctoral degree, she was the first woman theologian to lecture in English universities and the first woman to lead spiritual retreats for the Church of England. She counted as her best friends the Indian poet Rabindranath Tagore (1861–1941), the first Asian to win the Nobel Prize for literature (1913), and the French Philosopher Henri Bergson (1859–1941), winner of the Nobel Prize for literature in 1927. Interestingly, each of these three died in early 1941. Upon her death, the *Times of London* said that in the field of theology, she was "unmatched by any professional theologian of her day." (See www.evelynunderhill.org.)

After many years of reading a vast collection of mystical documents from both the Western and Eastern traditions, Evelyn identified five stages in spiritual development that she felt most mystics went through. In similar manner, the Course describes six stages in the development of trust. The first two stages described in both the Course and Evelyn's book are striking similar. Evelyn's second stage, which she calls *purgation,* is similar to the second and third stages of the Course, which are called *sorting out* and *relinquishing.* The last two stages described by Evelyn and the Course are again amazingly similar—especially the next to the last stage—an unsettling period that is defined by Evelyn as the "final dark night of the soul."

The Course describes ten characteristics of a teacher of God. Everyone already possesses each of these characteristics, but the characteristics are unrecognized, undeveloped, or unappreciated. At the end of *The Wizard of Oz,* the wizard explains to Dorothy and her companions—the Scarecrow, Tin Man, and Cowardly Lion—that they already possess what they have been seeking all along. Oz simply bestows upon each of them tokens of esteem in recognition of these qualities. In this same way, the list of the attributes of God's teachers does not include those things that are our natural inheritance, such as love, sinlessness, perfection, knowledge, and eternal truth. These are not traits we need to develop. They are there already in everyone.

Our task is one of *uncovering* what is already there. We are now, and always have been perfect. We are now, and always have been filled with love. It's not a matter of developing these qualities. These qualities are a given. As we develop and deepen the attributes of the teacher of God, including trust, honesty, tolerance, and the like, we progressively come to remember these eternal truths. Glinda, the good witch in *The Wizard of Oz*, tells Dorothy that she, too, always had the power to return home. In fact, Glinda says, all Dorothy has to do is close her eyes, tap her heels together three times, and repeat "There's no place like home." Dorothy does so and awakens back at home, surrounded by family and friends.

> *Heaven is your home,*
> *and being in God it must also be in you.*
>
> T-12.VI.7:7

The Law of Trust

The first characteristic a teacher of God develops is trust. God really is in charge—always has been and always will be. Lesson 47 from the Workbook states, "God is the strength in which I trust." This is the first principle by which we must rule our lives. If there is no God, then, indeed, we have reason for despair. Then, indeed, all is chaos, all is lost. Lesson 200 from the Workbook says, "There is no peace except the peace of God." If we trust in our own strength, we have every reason to be apprehensive and unhappy. Thankfully, we need not trust in our own strength because we have God's voice, the Holy Spirit, as our guide.

In God We Trust is inscribed on American currency. If we really believed that motto, we would have no worries or concerns. As Jesus says so beautifully in the Sermon on the Mount, "Consider the lilies of the field. . . . They toil not, neither do they spin and yet, even Solomon in all of his glory was not arrayed like one of these." Trust does not mean that we trust our brother's unstable ego; that is foolishness and can lead to betrayal and loss. We do trust, however, that somewhere within every brother and sister there is a light that knows the truth.

The following steps and stages in the development of trust are not clearly defined by Underhill or the Course; there are obvious overlaps and it would be a mistake to take the steps too literally. Furthermore, we may experience the first five of these steps over and over again in different ways. Each time we go through a major test, such as the loss of a loved one, a serious health or financial challenge, and the like, we may find ourselves going through these stages all over again. As we get better at following God's law, we find ourselves progressively awakening into greater awareness and greater happiness until we reach the last and final state of perfect love and perfect happiness. The sixth and final stage is enlightenment or perfection. It is Heaven. It is home. Once reached, it is ours forever.

Corrective learning always begins with the awakening of spirit,
and the turning away from the belief in physical sight.

T-2.V.7:1

The ego, by nature, is not trusting. If we place trust in God, we will see through the eyes of Spirit. To do this, we must ask the Holy Spirit for help and trust His guidance. The deeper and more completely we place our trust in God, the more clearly inspiration will come our way.

When this power has once been experienced,
it is impossible to trust one's own petty strength again.

M-4.I.2:1

Stage 1: A Period of Undoing, Leading to Awakening and Awareness

In the first stage, we are often dealing with the external changes we see in our world: A relationship ends, a business fails, an accident occurs, a move is necessary. The Course refers to this stage as a "period of undoing." This "undoing," according to Underhill, leads to an awakening to an awareness of the Divine. The awakening often occurs due to some kind of "crash and burn" experience that makes it necessary to see things in a new way. This stage need not be painful (since nothing of real value is being lost), but it is often experienced as painful. Awakening occurs as we progressively relinquish our projective judgments and accept responsibility for what "seems" to be happening to us.

The first step toward freedom
involves a sorting out of the false from the true.

T-2.VIII.4:1

After crashing and burning, after disillusionment or, perhaps, as a result of meditation, we experience a new awareness, often followed by a deeper seeking. We are still in the world, but no longer so strongly attached to it. Now we turn more to the Kingdom of God within. "Something" questions the nature of our reality as defined by the collusion of illusion and the society of which we are a part. A change in direction, an alchemical churning, turning, cooking begins working within us. We begin to experience a reversal in thinking. While the ego continues to function on the outside, Spirit works more deeply inside.

According to mythic traditions, we find freedom from the devil by calling the devil by name. Likewise, we find freedom from the ego by seeing it for the nothing that it is, and thus, not giving it power over us. We begin the process of setting aside our useless and inhibiting behaviors. At this point, an alcoholic or addict might ask for help, join a program like AA, and begin the recovery process.

Corrective learning always begins with the awakening of spirit, and the turning away from the belief in physical sight.

T-2.V.7:1

We don't see many folks under the age of forty studying the Course. They are often busy finding mates, establishing careers, having children, buying homes, and paying bills. Once many of the externals have been attained, or after marriages or businesses fail, or when children are more a pain than a pleasure, these same folks may experience a "midlife crisis," when it may seem that things are being taken away. In truth, their lack of "real" value is being recognized.

I once met a man, a custodian in a large church, who told me that many years earlier he had been a monk. Tired of the autocratic and demanding ways of the abbot of the monastery, one day he put his working clothes on, he went to the front door, walked out, stood for a moment on the front steps, and then, without looking back, just kept walking. He knew, he said, there had to be a better way. He went into the monastery to get away from the world and in the monastery, he said, they had created another dream world just as ego-based as the world outside. Later he found the Course.

Miracles are everyone's right but purification is necessary first.

T-I.1:7

Stage 2: Purification, Purgation, Sorting Out

Underhill calls this second stage "purification." Spanish mystic Saint Teresa of Ávila calls it "purgation." The Course calls it "a period of sorting out." According to Underhill, no one can skip this stage. This is a time of cleaning, clearing, and letting go of fears, unessential anxieties, and false concepts. Changes may occur in relationships, with parents, children, careers, health issues, money issues, and more. And it's all okay. Trust is important now, as our vision is progressively being perfected.

> *Your task is not to seek for love, but merely to seek and find*
> *all of the barriers within yourself that you have built against it.*
> *It is not necessary to seek for what is true,*
> *but it "is" necessary to seek for what is false.*

T-16.IV.6:1–2

Just as a snake sheds its skin, there is a shedding of the old and a making way for the new. Teachers of God are learning how to dispose of every self-seeking motive, every addiction, compulsion, obsession, lie, embellishment, exaggeration, every unforgiving or angry thought, and complaint as soon as it is recognized for what it is. We find the truth by discarding everything that is not true.

After a few weeks of being sober, folks who join Alcoholics Anonymous often report a clarity or awareness they didn't even know existed. This clarity, awareness, and sense of self-confidence were available all along. It had, however, been blocked. To become unblocked, they first had to let go of something that seemed valuable (like alcohol) in order to find what is really valuable.

Only the hand that erases can write the true thing.

GERMAN MYSTIC MEISTER ECKHART (1260–1326)

Erase the mind. And the way to erase it is not by fighting:
The way to erase it is just to become aware.

INDIAN TEACHER OSHO

Catharsis and Regurgitation

Purgation may include a catharsis, a confession, "getting it off one's chest." Those who join AA are asked to admit to God, themselves, and at least one other person that their life has become unmanageable and they have been mistaken in their perceptions. This helps, but it does not keep us from falling back into old patterns. Consistent practices are necessary to maintain focus. This is why it is important to go through the lessons in the Workbook. It takes a lot of work to retrain the mind. We literally have to begin thinking in a whole new way. Increasing willingness "one day at a time" is required.

If you allow yourself to have in your mind
only what God put there,
you are acknowledging your mind as God created it.

T-6.V.C.5:4

A marriage therapist friend tells me she often wishes she could say to some of those she counsels, "Stop it!" "Get off it!" "Grow up!" "Be responsible!" Or "Stop whining!" Of course, she doesn't do that. Teachers of God never frighten or threaten their students. Instead, they gently lead them down a more peaceful and loving path. Still, "Getting off it"— that is, stopping the insanity—is precisely what is called for in order to gain our spiritual focus.

If you don't wash out the stone and sand, how can
you pick out the gold? Seek the path of

Heaven with firm determination.
And you will see the original thing!

CHINESE TAOIST LIU I-MING

During this second stage, we realize that all things, events, encounters, and circumstances are helpful in the spiritual journey process (M-4.I.A.4:5).

Stage 3: A Period of Relinquishment

If the stage of relinquishment is interpreted as giving up the desirable, it will engender enormous conflict. We don't want to let go of our ego (our individuality), even though that's the way to be happy. Remember, nothing real can be threatened and nothing "truly valuable" can be lost.

The soul is not empty, so long as the desire for
sensible things remains. But the absence of this desire
for things produces emptiness and liberty of soul;
even when there is an abundance of possessions.

SPANISH MYSTIC SAINT JOHN
OF THE CROSS (1541–1591)

Self-discipline deepens as we progressively realize what is truly valuable (love) and as we let go of that which is not valuable (every self-seeking motive that is not grounded in love). The point is not about giving up "things"; it's about realizing the value we place on our "desire" for things. It may seem as though we are being asked to sacrifice our best interests on behalf of truth. Truth, however, is the very thing that will lead us home. When we let the unessential go, happiness is the result.

Strangely, where we expected to find a loss, in lightheartedness. Once the bankruptcy is over, the deal, the house is sold, or the job is lost, some perspe comes our way. When English author Aldous Huxley felt after watching his house burn to the ground in the 1961, he replied, "It is a marvelous, clean feeling."

Stage 4: A Period of Settling Down: Illumination in Reasonable Peace

Underhill calls the fourth stage "illumination." Stages 1 through the Course are phases of cleaning, undoing, releasing, sorting out, letting go, leading to our realization that the only thing we had to gi up is what hurt us.

The fourth stage, seen by some as the final stage, is a quiet time, a period of reprieve, a period of "reasonable" peace. Freed of what held us back, we can now make better choices. We begin to employ many of the characteristics we'll read about in the coming pages; we're more honest, patient, generous, and open-minded, and less judgmental. We find ourselves becoming increasingly attentive to the guidance of the Holy Spirit. We give up thinking that perfection can be found in the external world and look for it inside instead. We relax a while, forgive all things that we think others have done to us, and overlook what is not there. We realize that, regardless of what is said or done, no one has the power to take the peace of God away from us.

The Course asks us to watch our minds, to watch our thoughts, and to identify with the part that is watching, not the part that is wallowing. By watching our thoughts, we disengage from dreaming, and step gently in the direction of illumination.

osmic Dancer and the Mastery of Two Worlds

Course speaks of the "Bridge to the Real World" as a symbol for this
from perception to knowledge. According to Islam, Jesus (or Isa)
, "The world is a bridge. Cross the bridge but do not build upon it."
one-time teacher, Joe Campbell (1904–1987), called this stage, the
Mastery of Two Worlds." We are in the world but are unaffected by its
olitics, its opinions, its values, and its points of view. We are achieving
n increasing equilibrium between the inner and the outer worlds.

We live in the world knowing that our real home is Heaven. Friedrich
Nietzsche spoke of this stage as that of the "Cosmic Dancer" who does
not rest in a single spot, but lightly turns from one position to another.
We stand outside Heaven's door, but not yet at the top of the ladder. As
the spiral comes around again, we move ever closer to the center. We go
on from here—not alone—but more aware of the mighty companions,
the loving thoughts we hold of everyone.

Stage 5: The Dark Night of the Soul: A Period of Unsettling

The sharp edge of a razor is difficult to pass over;
Thus the wise say the path to Salvation is hard.

KATHA-UPANISHAD

The ego is capable of suspiciousness at best
and viciousness at worst.

T-9.VII.3:7

The Big Let Go(d)

As we come closer to the center, the ego becomes more desperate,
realizing that if we give our mind fully back to God, the ego is a goner.

At this point, the fear of death (not of the body but of the ego) becomes very real. The Spanish mystic Saint John of the Cross (1541–1591) made popular the phrase *dark night of the soul* to describe this stage. In his poem of the same name, he describes the hardships the soul meets in its final journey and literal detachment from "all things," including the body.

Evelyn Underhill also calls this stage the "dark night." In the "dark night," we face the end of ourselves as distinct individuals. Unbeknownst to the ego, this is actually our greatest joy, perfect happiness, and liberation. To attain perfect happiness, everything must be given over to God, without reservation. The outlook is bleak for the ego: it is unmasked for the nothing that it is—a passing dream, no more valid than any of the other trillion dreams that temporarily consume the mind of any mortal.

Buddha meditated alone for seven years. Jesus wandered alone in the desert for forty days. Muhammad sat for days on end, alone in a cave. Having finally emptied their minds of any form of self-seeking and being completely open, God spoke to them and many more, who, having awakened, remained silent. Saint John of the Cross, Saint Teresa of Ávila, and a myriad more found trust deepening through long periods of illness and psychological distress.

> *People will do anything, no matter how absurd, to avoid facing*
> *their own soul. One does not become enlightened by imagining*
> *figures of light, but by making the darkness conscious.*
>
> SWISS PSYCHOTHERAPIST
> CARL GUSTAV JUNG

The last of the characteristics a teacher of God develops is total open-mindedness, in which all judgment is set aside. We cannot go back and going forward seems fearful—it means moving fully into the heart of God, yet we go forward knowing that "The world I see holds nothing that I want" (W-128).

The closer you come to the foundation of the ego's thought
system, the darker and more obscure becomes the way.
Yet even the little spark in your mind is enough to lighten it.
Bring this light fearlessly with you, and bravely hold it up
to the foundation of the ego's thought system.

T-11.IN.3:5–7

It's no fun descending into the murky depths of the psyche and taking a good look around. Most folks avoid it. This can be a time marked by feelings of helplessness, stagnation of will, and a sense of the withdrawal of God's presence. Some folks are surprised to hear that Mother Teresa (1910–1997), in correspondence with her spiritual directors, described in deeply moving words her struggles with faith, her doubts, and her sense of abandonment by God. In one publicly released letter to her spiritual confidant, the Reverend Michael van der Peet, she wrote, "The silence and the emptiness are so great that I look and do not see, listen and do not hear—the tongue moves in prayer but does not speak. I want you to pray for me—that I let Him have a free hand."

One thing that comes out of myths is that at the
bottom of the abyss comes the voice of salvation.
The black moment is the moment when the real
message of transformation is going to come.
At the darkest moment comes the light.

—AMERICAN MYTHOLOGIST JOE CAMPBELL

Should we be surprised to hear that the darkest night comes just before the dawn, and it comes with a final exam—perhaps the prospect of bodily death? Yet, by trusting more deeply, we see that what we let go is nothing, right up to the big "let go" of our illusory body, our persona, and the dream figure of ourselves. The body ages and our energy and motion become restricted. We may experience the loss of our home and the death of a mate while moving more deeply into the realization that our treasure is not found in anything external.

The fifth stage culminates in a final giving up of all sense of self and a surrendering to divine will. Jesus cries out, "My God, My God why have you forsaken me?" And then in total submission, "Unto your hands I commend my Spirit." As we become unidentified with the self we created, we let go of the whole illusory dream, remembering that our self is nothing and our Self is all (W-358.1:7).

Coming round again, and rising ever higher, stages 1–5 may be repeated many times in different ways at different ages. Progress, however, is ever inward and upward, and thus, more clearly focused on home. With each round comes a more refined and deeper purification and greater awareness.

To know yourself you must go beyond yourself.

INDIAN ADVAITA VEDANTIST
SRI NISARGADATTA MAHARAJ (1897–1981)

Stage 6: A Period of Achievement

Evelyn Underhill calls stage 6 "Union with God."

Perfect happiness, or Heaven, the Course tells us, is completion.

Judy Whitson tells the story of Bill Thetford on the day before he died. Bill came to Judy's home in Tiburon, California, to celebrate the Fourth of July 1988, with a group of friends. Judy noted a certain joy radiating from him. He started dancing around her living room. "Bill," Judy said, was "tripping the light fantastic." "I feel so flexible, I'm feeling so free!" he exclaimed. "All my relationships feel so completely healed and whole!" That evening at dinner, Bill told his friend Catherine, "There's no baggage. I'm cleaned out—in and out. I'm complete with everyone." The next morning, on his way out for a walk, his doctor said, "His heart blew out." Bill died instantly.

> *The song of our rejoicing is the call to all the world that*
> *freedom is returned, that time is almost over, and*
> *God's Son has but an instant more to wait until his Father*
> *is remembered, dreams are done, eternity has shined*
> *away the world, and only Heaven now exists at all.*
>
> W-PII.2.5.2

The world ends with the cessation of separation. Complete forgiveness is the final goal of the curriculum. God begins where learning ends. Returned fully to God, the mind no longer wanders, there are no more unnecessary detours, and no more decision making. Illusions are forever set aside. Following only God's plan, we are directed toward creation within the Kingdom. Peace of mind and our awareness of Heaven are complete; nothing could be more desirable. We relinquish the ego in favor of the truth. Truth steps forward in light and we are reborn in a luminescence the ego cannot imagine.

> *When he is wrong he finds correction.*
> *When he wanders off, he is led back to his appointed task.*
>
> W-131.4:5–6

Realignment with the mind of God is unilateral, unequivocal, and inevitable. To be in the Kingdom, it is necessary to focus our full attention on it. The more clearly our GPS is focused on home, the more clearly we see the "straight way and the narrow gate." The more destiny guides the process, the greater our blessing and happiness. The spiritual journey does not consist of arriving at a new destination where we gain something we did not already have. It's not about form. It's not about fame. Enlightenment is but a recognition, not a change at all (W-188.1:4). It consists in the dissipation of ignorance concerning our "selves" and the remembrance of Oneness and eternity.

> *"To fly as fast as thought, to anywhere that is," he said,*
> *"you must begin by knowing that you have already arrived."*
>
> FROM *JONATHAN LIVINGSTON SEAGULL*, BY RICHARD BACH

We come around again in time, like a circle. The circle becomes a spiral and we ascend through many levels until, at last, we reach the stage in which there are no more questions, levels, seeking, or speaking. Now there is only Knowing and Being. Though we all know it in our hearts, this is a state our poor human minds can barely grasp and words cannot adequately describe.

> *When experience will come to end your doubting has been set.*
> *For we but see the journey from the point at which it ended,*
> *looking back on it, imagining we make it once again;*
> *reviewing mentally what has gone by.*
>
> W-158.4:4–5

CHAPTER 13

Life without Lies

Honesty and Happiness

Pilate, therefore, said to him, "Are you a king?"
Then Jesus answered, "It is you who say it.
Yes, I am a king. I was born for this.
I came into the world for this; to bear witness to the truth.
And all who are on the side of truth listen to my voice."
"Truth?" said Pilate, "What is that?"

JOHN 18:37–38

Let's Review Briefly

We (the ego) decided to leave our Father (God) and run away from home, to strike out on our own, to create our own world. In doing so we "fell" into a dream. Adam biting into the fruit of the Tree of Knowledge of Good and Evil (duality) put us (everyone) in a dreamlike state. The memory of home is still within us, but it is now buried.

The ego, then, is nothing more than a delusional system in
which you made your own father. Make no mistake about this.
It sounds insane when it is stated with perfect honesty,

but the ego never looks on what it does with perfect honesty.

T-11.IN.2:4–6

In creating our own world, we put the awareness of God out of our mind. Like most adolescents, we want to do things the way we want to do them. The whole of the ego's thought system rests on the idea that it is possible to be separated from God. This is a form of self-deception. We are self-deceived when we choose the ego. It is not possible to be separated from God. An illusory dream is not reality. Somewhere deep inside, even in the darkest mind, the awareness of God remains.

The glass in which the ego seeks to see its face is dark indeed.
How can it maintain the trick of its existence
except with mirrors?
But where you look to find yourself is up to you.

T-4.IV.1:6–8

Denial and Repression

After Adam ate of the fruit of the Tree of Knowledge of Good and Evil, he ran and hid in the bushes. God finds Adam and asks why he is hiding. Adam says he is hiding because he is naked (that is, afraid and feeling guilty). Where once there was unity, now there is duality. Where once there was only Oneness, we now have both good and evil. Adam must now conceal his nakedness—his shame and guilt. Adam is us, and we are all, like Adam, still hiding.

One of Sigmund Freud's most significant contributions to the study of psychoanalysis was unearthing the ego's use of denial and repression. Afraid of our ego's possible annihilation, we choose not to look within. By not looking, we keep ourselves isolated and unhappily trapped in our own little private world. We hide in our body, in our stories, in time, in dreams. God, knowing we are His sleeping children, has placed within us a little spark, a memory of His eternal love, assuring us that one day we will awaken.

Every deceiver knows—deep inside
Deception cannot—forever hide.

The search for truth is but the honest searching
out of everything that interferes with truth.

T-14.VII.2:1–1

Acknowledging the Truth

All the other traits of God's teachers rest on trust. Those who trust can afford to be honest because they see the value in honesty. The first step in the development of trust is sorting out the false from the true. Our task is not to look for the truth. Truth is a given. Truth is seen the instant the false is set aside.

The extension of truth,
which "is" the law of the Kingdom,
rests only on the knowledge of what truth is.
This is your inheritance and requires no learning at all,
but when you disinherited yourself
you became a learner of necessity.

T-7.VI.2:6–7

Learners of Necessity and Knowers of Truth

Having disowned Self and having adopted the thinking of the ego, we become learners of necessity, rather than knowers of truth. No one can hide forever from the truth. On seven different occasions, the Course says that the truth is simple. It looks complicated because we are complicated.

Let's review two basic principles:

1. **The body does not exist, except as a learning device for the mind.** The body is a dream figure. Be glad! For many folks, the body seems like a prison—a place of confinement and pain. Once its usefulness is over and we awaken from the dream, the body will no longer be needed. Thank God! What makes this process of awakening look so complex is that we have mistaken the tool (the learning device) for the thing itself. We think the body is our home while our home remains in Heaven. This does not mean we should do away with the learning device. We are here to learn a lesson and it's best to get on with it.

2. **Time is a learning device.** Like the body, time will disappear when it is no longer useful. As long as there is need for the atonement, there is need for time. The miracle (a shift of perception from lies, or error, to the acceptance of truth) lessens the need for time.

Life without Lies

In a scene in the first *Superman* movie (1978) with Christopher Reeve and Margot Kidder, Superman is flying, carrying Lois Lane in his arms. They land on Lois's balcony. She gazes into Superman's eyes—a romantic moment with the promise of a kiss—and she says, "Superman, what do you believe in?" Superman, looking back into her eyes, says, "I believe in truth, justice, and the American way." Lois replies, "You've got to be kidding!" Unblinking, Superman responds, "Lois, I never lie."

But Superman's statement—that he never lies—*is* a lie. Clark Kent, Superman's alter ego, must hide his true identity, and Clark lies frequently, claiming that he has no knowledge of Superman. One of the most obvious contradictions in life is that while we profess a reverence for honesty, we frequently disregard the practice. Honesty means consistency: What we say reflects what we think. Honesty means that nothing we say contradicts anything we do. The ego, however, is inconsistent. By nature, the ego is dishonest; it conflicts with and hides our true identity as Spirit. This hiding causes loneliness and, along with it, unhappiness.

> *Such are the truly honest.*
> *At no level are they in conflict with themselves.*
> *Therefore it is impossible for them to be in conflict*
> *with anyone or anything.*
>
> M-4.II.1:7–8

A minister noticed a group of boys standing around a small stray dog and asked, "What are you boys doing?"

"Telling lies," said one.

"The one who tells the biggest lie gets the dog," said another.

"Why, when I was your age," the minister said, "I never told a lie."

The boys looked at one another. Disheartened, one of them said, "I guess you win the dog."

The Emotion of Secrecy

Time magazine once ran a cover story with a lead article titled "Lying: Everybody Is Doing It." One of the great temptations of the ego is to bolster its power with deception. The ego is tireless in its commitment to beating everyone else to the top of the heap.

> *Here is the one emotion that you made,*
> *whatever it may seem to be.*

This is the emotion of secrecy,
of private thoughts and of the body.
This is the one emotion that opposes love,
and always leads to sight of differences and loss of sameness.
Here is the one emotion that keeps you blind,
dependent on the self you think you made
to lead you through the world it made for you.

T-22.I.4:7–10

The emotion of secrecy protects our inner, private self and keeps us from correcting our fears and illusions. It also keeps us from knowing each other. It keeps us from union, from joining, from true intimacy, and from love.

In his book *Radical Honesty: How to Transform Your Life by Telling the Truth,* Dr. Brad Blanton (1940–present) tells about a survey in which respondents were guaranteed complete anonymity. One of the questions asked was about the frequency with which respondents perceived themselves as being dishonest or lying. Ninety-three percent of the respondents said they lied regularly and habitually. Dr. Blanton suggested that the remaining 7 percent, who said they never lied, were perhaps the biggest liars of all. Dr. Blanton begins his book the following way:

> I have been a psychotherapist in Washington, D.C., for over 25 years . . . This is what I have learned: We all lie like hell. It wears us out. It is the major source of human stress. Lying kills people. The kind of lying that is most deadly is withholding or keeping back information from someone we think would be affected by it. Psychological illness of the severest kind is the result of this kind of lying.

Adolescents spend much of their time playing this game of hide-and-seek. The better we get at playing hide-and-seek, the greater the sense of isolation and aloneness, the greater our unhappiness. Keeping secrets and hiding from others is a trap that keeps us from being who we are meant to be.

Psychopaths are so good at lying that they can look you directly in the eye and tell very convincingly lies. Yet, as Dr. Blanton writes, "Important secrets and all the plotting and cogitation that go with them are all bullshit." Dishonesty is separation. Hiding keeps us from knowing Self. It keeps us from the memory of God and it makes us unhappy.

Nations deliberately deceive other nations through espionage, spying, concealment, and secrecy. This deception is so much a part of international affairs—so much a part of business relationships, church politics, and computer games—that we don't even think it is unnatural.

Two Hollywood executives are talking to each other.
One says, "You're lying!"
The other responds, "I know. But hear me out."

> *The reason this course is simple is that truth is simple.*
> *Complexity is of the ego, and is nothing more than*
> *the ego's attempt to obscure the obvious.*

> T-15.IV.6:1–2

Guilt, Hiding, Fear, Truth

Psychologists use the word *complex* to describe complicated places in the psyche where we are hung up, attached, not free—that is, not truthful. Complexes are complicated, secret webs we weave, in which the ego unwittingly gets caught. The more "mythological" and complex the story spun by the ego, the more we can be sure it is not true. Truth, the Course tells us time and time again, is natural and simple (T-11.V.3:5).

> *Your "guilty secret" is nothing, and if you*
> *will but bring it to the light, the Light will dispel it.*

And then no dark cloud will remain between you
and the remembrance of your Father . . .

T-13.II.9:2–3

Your Guilty Secret

A friend of mine, fashion photographer Garry Gross (1937–2010), went
to one of Ken Wapnick's workshops and listened to him talk about
guilt. Garry could not think of anything about which he felt guilty and
said so, to which Ken responded, "You don't feel guilty? Shame on you!"
This brought, of course, an uproar of laughter. We each have more guilt
buried within than we are willing to acknowledge. Remember: Our first
defense is denial. When we say there is nothing about which we feel
guilty, we simply and conveniently overlook whatever we do not want to
see, because we believe that looking would be too difficult. Yet, only by
looking within can we be set free.

Under each cornerstone of fear on which we erect
our insane systems of belief the truth lies hidden.

T-14.VII.2:7

There is only one Mind. We are all part of that Mind. When we hide,
we shut ourselves off from wholeness, from communication with that
Mind and the Thinking of the Universe (W-52.5:7). Just as "As we give
so do we receive," so too, "What we hide is hidden from us." Lying, or
hiding, blocks awareness of inner guidance. The Holy Spirit is always
present. But we make ourselves absent to guidance by lying and then
we wonder why life seems to be lacking in meaning. What we call "life"
is actually sleepwalking when we are unaware of the inspiration that
literally gives life. The more we fortify ourselves with secrets, the deeper
our despair, isolation, aloneness, and unhappiness.

What is in fashion is not the truth. If you think your girlfriend is wearing an ugly dress, that's your opinion. It is not the truth. Opinions and beliefs are not truth. The cruel truth is not the truth. Telling someone what we think of him says more about who we are than who he is. We heal our brothers and sisters (and ourselves) by perceiving the truth (the innocence) within them. "God, who sees only our perfection, does not know of unholiness" (W-39.4:5).

You're only as sick as your secrets.

ALCOHOLICS ANONYMOUS

A Test for Truth

Those who have been through any of the "Anonymous" programs will tell you how free they felt once they were no longer hiding in the shadow of their addiction and, therefore, unhappily trapped by the ego and its many lies. At the end of the 2012 movie *Flight*, "Whip" Whitaker (the main character, played magnificently by Denzel Washington), finds himself in prison, giving a brilliant speech in which he describes himself as being free for the first time in his life because he is no longer hiding. We are happy to the degree to which we are free, and we are free to the degree to which we do not hide.

Search your mind carefully
for any thoughts you may fear to uncover.

T-13.III.7:5

Think honestly
what you have thought that God would not have thought,
and what you have not thought that God would have you think.
Search sincerely

for what you have done and left undone accordingly,
and then change your mind to think with God's.

T-4.IV.2:4–5

"Think honestly," "search sincerely," and look carefully.
Be willing to relinquish whatever impedes the journey.
Be willing to look at the ego with perfect honesty.
Be willing to see all brothers and sisters as sinless.
Be willing to exchange illusions for the truth.

If you imagine someone who is brave enough to
withdraw all his projections, then you get an individual
who is conscious of a pretty thick Shadow.
Such a man [can no longer say] they do this
or they must be fought against. . . .
Such a man knows that whatever is wrong in the world
is in him and if he only learns to deal with his own Shadow,
he is doing something real for the world.
He has succeeded in shouldering at least an infinitesimal part
of the gigantic, unsolved social problems of our day.

SWISS PSYCHOTHERAPIST CARL GUSTAV JUNG

To be free, we must be willing to dig deep and look at our guilty
secrets. We need not hang out our dirty laundry for the world to see, nor
offer up a public confession. That probably would not make anyone feel
better. We simply need to stop trying to hide from God and, therefore,
from ourselves. We need to look at our "secret sins" and "hidden hates."
By exposing them to the light, the light will shine them away.

Bring, therefore, all your dark and secret thoughts to Him,
and look upon them with Him.

He holds the light, and you the darkness.
They cannot coexist when both of You together look on them.
His judgment must prevail,
and He will give it to you as you join your perception to His.

T-14.VII.6:8–11

1. Take It to the Holy Spirit

The Holy Spirit holds the light that dispels the darkness. The Holy Spirit cannot bring the light to whatever we are hiding. We must be willing to look at our lives honestly. Unless we demonstrate our willingness to look at what is hidden in darkness, darkness remains and blocks our path to freedom.

My mind is like a bad neighborhood
I try not to go into alone.

AMERICAN AUTHOR ANNE LAMOTT (1954–PRESENT)

2. Take It to a Loving Friend or Therapist

Programs like Alcoholics Anonymous offer opportunities to look at our darkness in an atmosphere of unconditional acceptance. Such a process can be refreshing. I once counseled a woman who told me that she lied all the time about things that she did not even need to lie about. She didn't know why she did it. It had become a bad habit, her *modus operandi*—the way she made her way through the world. Living this way was making her sick. I was proud of her for telling me the truth, and it was a great relief for her. She later stated that she was making every effort to speak only the truth, even if it made her feel embarrassed. It's much better than living unhappily with shame and guilt.

Choosing to be truthful includes taking responsibility for all our actions. Being responsible means not blaming outside circumstances, other people, or past events for the conditions of our lives. When tempted to hide, think: Is hiding really necessary? What are we trying to keep secret? Why are we being deceptive and divisive? Why not just tell the truth? What would happen if we did? When tempted to lie, look at the lie. Be willing to speak the truth, even if it means being embarrassed. Be willing to be uncomfortable. It is so much better than the aloneness, isolation, guilt, and unhappiness that accompanies dishonesty.

> *The escape from darkness involves two stages:*
> *First, the recognition that darkness cannot hide.*
> *This step usually entails fear.*
> *Second, the recognition that there is nothing you want to hide*
> *even if you could. This step brings escape from fear.*
> *When you have become willing to hide nothing,*
> *you will not only be willing to enter into communion*
> *but will also understand peace and joy.*
>
> T-1.IV.1–4

3. Ask for Forgiveness and Relinquish Hiding

When we feel as though we've hurt someone, it's a good idea to ask for her forgiveness. "It is impossible to remember God in secret and alone" (T-14.X.10:1). We cannot experience "perfect" communication when we harbor secret sins and hidden hates.

> *God has no secret communications,*
> *for everything of Him is perfectly open*
> *and freely accessible to all, being for all.*

Nothing lives in secret, and what you
would hide from the Holy Spirit is nothing.

T-14.X.11:2–3

Looking at secret sins and hidden hates takes away their shadowy power and their unconscious dominance over us. Granting exposure to dark places loosens the ego's grip as we learn to use the Mind (Spirit), rather than being used by the mind (ego). Start by letting a little more truth in. We, thereby, create space for even greater truth. Honesty is a small thing. It just requires a little willingness to let what is true be true.

4. Drop Exaggerations, Embellishments, and Overstatements

The use of exaggerations, embellishments, overstatements, and understatements is completely useless, a waste of time, and it leads to guilt. We exaggerate or embellish only if we either want to impress or distress. How long it took to do something, how far we traveled, or how hard we had to work—none of these things matter.

5. Notice If You're Tempted to Lie about Small Things

When someone asks a question about a book we have read or how familiar we are with a certain idea, we may be a tempted to say, "Yes, I know about that" or "I read that." Admitting that we don't know is more refreshing than pretending that we do.

Unless we are enlightened, we're still on the way
and probably a student 'til our dying day.

Trust that telling the truth will be okay, because it will be okay.

When in doubt, tell the truth.

AMERICAN AUTHOR
MARK TWAIN (1835–1910)

The more truth we admit to, the easier life is and the less separation we experience. When we tell the truth, we feel better about ourselves, and destiny opens up in accordance with our greater happiness. When we are truthful, we are "ready" for miracles. Other people are likely to be more accepting of our truth than we may think. Honesty brings with it a self-absolution. Absolution is forgiveness. Absolution is pardon, release, freedom, and liberty. Absolution is peace.

Freedom cannot be learned by tyranny of any kind,
and the perfect equality of all God's Sons cannot be
recognized through the dominion of one mind over another.

T-8.IV.6:7

Once illusion (hiding, secrecy, dishonesty) is relinquished, truth must take its place. Ultimately, all truth is (or will be) known. *Ultimately* can mean now, tomorrow, or at the hour of death. To know the truth is to step into eternity and allow eternity to enter our lives. The little inadequacies that clutter our human lives are not who we are, and we cannot advance into the Kingdom by hanging onto petty concerns and little fears.

The only way to speak the truth is to speak lovingly.

AMERICAN TRANSCENDENTALIST
HENRY DAVID THOREAU

The Freedom and Peace of Truth

There isn't any choice about whether or not to tell the truth. All darkness will be brought to light, so it might as well be now. Truth is beyond our ability to destroy, but entirely within our ability to accept (T-5.IV.1:3–4).

> *This above all—to thine own self be true,*
> *and it must follow, as night the day,*
> *thou canst not then be false to any man.*

FROM *HAMLET*, BY
WILLIAM SHAKESPEARE

There is no pillow as soft as a clear conscience; the greater the transparency, the higher the level of integrity, the more peaceful the mind. Happiness is peace of mind, and peace of mind requires honesty. Ultimately, the practice of honesty is the process by which we reach the goal of Truth.

> *You will know the truth and the truth will set you free.*

JESUS, AS RECORDED IN JOHN 8:32

Truth is a constant. It cannot be permanently lost, only temporarily forgotten. It is there deep within, whether we can see it or not. By observing the law of honesty, we move ever closer to the Truth that is God. Defenses and deceptions are not necessary. We can be free right now. We can experience Heaven right now. Heaven is the Truth—the only Truth. At any moment, we may know the Truth and it will set us free. Being honest just means being who we are meant to be. We are all children of God. There is nothing we need to defend. Knowing I am a child of God, I cannot be conflicted.

The truth undoes what never was.
The peace of mind which the advanced teachers of God
experience is largely due to their perfect honesty.

M-4.II.2:1

The goal of truth has further practical advantages.
If the situation is used for truth and sanity,
its outcome must be peace.

T-17.VI.5:1–2

Remember:

If you tell the truth,
you don't have to remember anything.

AMERICAN AUTHOR MARK TWAIN

CHAPTER 14

The Major Addiction We All Share

TOLERANCE AND HAPPINESS

God's teachers do not judge.
To judge is to be dishonest,
for to judge is to assume a position you do not have.

M-4.III.1:1–2

"You're Judging Me!"

In the movie *Silver Linings Playbook* (2012), when the characters get "off balance," they start yelling at each other, "You're judging me!" "You're judging me!" No one wants to be judged. Judgment destroys honesty and shatters trust (M-4.III.1:10). Judgment is a function of the ego unknown to God. To be God-like, we must then give up all judgment.

We make up the world we judge until
we no longer judge the world.

The one major addiction we all share is judgment. Judgment happens easily; it slips into the mind and finds its home in the throat, waiting for permission from the mind and, once that permission is granted, it quickly moves to the tongue. Simply and quietly, it comes in the back door and stands in the shadows, waiting for some perturbation, some little disconcerting agitation, to come walking by. And, when it does, the trap springs shut, the mind closes, judgment jumps to the tongue, and, lickety-split with the slip of the lip, a judgment is made. The word is said, the deed is done, and both the judge and the judged are trapped.

The ego seeks to make us blind,
and, thus, is truth left far behind.

Heaven is—always and only—awareness of perfect oneness. After Adam and Eve ate of the fruit of the Tree of Knowledge of Good and Evil, a seeming split entered the mind. "Choice" presented itself and, thus, the separation. Eating the fruit symbolizes our usurping the ability to self-create. Without judgment, there is no separation.

Heaven is perfectly unambiguous.
Everything is clear and bright, and calls forth one response.
There is no interruption.
There is a sense of peace so deep that no dream in this world
has ever brought even a dim imagining of what it is.

T-13.XI.3:8–9&12–13

Tolerance Is Freedom from Judgment

Not judging does not mean "Am I having chicken or fish for dinner?" "Am I going to wear my blue or brown shirt?" "What movie shall we go see?" We are simply asked to give up all forms of condemnation.

If you did not feel guilty you could not attack, for condemnation
is the root of attack. It is the judgment of one mind by another

as unworthy of love and deserving of punishment.

T-13.IN.1:1–2

You have no idea of the tremendous release and deep peace
that comes from meeting yourself and your brothers
totally without judgment.

T-3.IV.3:1

Tolerance accepts all loving ideas, opinions, and practices. Tolerance does not mean allowing hurtful, unkind, or cruel behavior. It does not mean "to tolerate" in a judgmental way. We're talking about giving up all judgment. Judges sit on benches raised up from the ground. To judge is to place ourselves above our brothers and sisters, looking down. If I judge you as somehow lower than me, I put myself down.

The Basic Law of Judgment

When the Bible says "Judge not that ye be not judged,"
it means that if you judge the reality of others
you will be unable to avoid judging your own.
The choice to judge rather than to know
is the cause of the loss of peace.

Tolerance enjoys sharing ideas, interests, and commonalities. Being tolerant, we allow others to be who they are. Being tolerant, we also forgive ourselves for our mistakes.

Toleration is the greatest gift of the mind;
it requires the same effort of the brain

that it takes to balance oneself on a bicycle.

HELEN KELLER (1880–1968)

Helen Keller's blindness gave her focus. To be willing to suspend judgment and let people be who they are—these are the greatest of gifts.

Having just performed a wedding ceremony in Central Park in New York City, I walked out of the park at 81st street and Central Park West facing the Beresford, the building where Judy Whitson lived during the 1970s. It was either here or at Ken Wapnick's apartment that I would meet with Helen. As I gazed up, an older couple approached, arguing. The man said, "You are wrong!" His companion, whom I assumed to be his wife, replied, "No, you are wrong!" And he retorted, "No, you are wrong!" and he followed with a comment. They were each bitterly angry.

Removing Distorted Perception: To See Clearly, First, Remove the Beam

Let's reiterate two basic laws of the mind.

Projection makes perception (T-13.V.3:5).

And, perception is a choice (T-21.V.1:7).

The inappropriate use of perception occurs when we believe that some emptiness or lack exists within us and we can fill that emptiness with our own ideas. This process involves four steps:

First, you believe that what God created
can be changed by your own mind.
Second, you believe that what is perfect
can be rendered imperfect or lacking.

> *Third, you believe that you can distort*
> *the creations of God, including yourself.*
> *Fourth, you believe that you can create yourself,*
> *and that the direction of your own creation is up to you.*
>
> T-I.1:9–12

To project means to "hurl away." From the ego's point of view, the object of intolerance doesn't matter. We often project onto those closest to us. So there are many abused children, wives, husbands, and employees. We attack whomever we can make responsible for the unpleasantness we feel—the one who left the dirty dishes in the sink or the one who forgot to pick up a birthday gift. When God catches up with Adam and Eve, Adam says, "Eve made me do it," and Eve, says, "The serpent [that is, the devil] made me do it." Projection stands at the very beginning of the ego's development.

> *Man invented language to satisfy his deep need to complain.*
>
> AMERICAN ACTRESS AND COMEDIAN
> LILY TOMLIN (1949–PRESENT)

False Certainty and the Need to Complain

I went to dinner with a couple I had not seen in several years. Throughout the dinner, and then in conversation after, the woman in particular kept attacking the leadership in an organization where she worked. Her husband, his head bent over, mumbled and nodded in agreement. She was telling me all about her "frenemies." She was sharing the nightmare in which she lived. I did what I could to assuage her fear, though my voice found, it seemed, no receptive ear.

We hide our nightmares in the darkness of our false certainty and we refuse to see what we are doing (T-12.II.4:7). In a series of books

by Carlos Castaneda (1925–1998), reputedly describing his training
in shamanism, the teacher Don Juan tells his student, Carlos, that he
(Carlos) doesn't know anything because he is constantly rehashing his
problems with his family and friends. Rehearsing, rehashing, reviewing,
and revising our problems clouds our sight.

Sitting at a picnic table with a group of friends next to the Hudson
River one beautiful June day, the woman across from me told an awful
story of how she had been mistreated during a recent hospital stay.
When she finished, the woman next to her said, "You think that's bad?"
Thus it went around the table, each person singing a "Somebody Done
Me Wrong" song.

The world is not the problem!
Other people are not the problem!
Addicted to judgment?
Change teachers right away!

We've all been in situations like the ones I was in with my friends, or
we have been the one doing the carping. False certainty and projective
thinking is "not seeing." It is a nightmare. Only after Adam fell into a
deep sleep was it possible for him to experience nightmares (T-2.I.4:5).
Were we fully awake and holding in our minds the remembrance of
God, nightmares (like war) would be impossible. Awakening to the
truth, all nightmares end.

A dream of judgment came into the mind
that God created perfect as Himself.
And in that dream was Heaven changed to hell,
and God made enemy unto His Son.
How can God's Son awaken from the dream?
It is a dream of judgment.

So must he judge not, and he will waken.

T-29.IX.2:1–5

Perfect happiness comes in being perfectly awake and being perfectly awake means being judgment-free. Deny responsibility and back further into oblivion. Take responsibility and step forward into the light. Judgment implies a lack of trust. Without judgment, we are all equal.

> *It must be clear that it is easier to have a happy day*
> *if you prevent unhappiness from entering at all.*
> *But this takes practice in the rules that will protect you*
> *from the ravages of fear. When this has been achieved,*
> *the sorry dream of judgment has forever been undone.*

T-30.I.13:1–3

We are moving in the direction of giving up all judgment forever. We cannot judge and learn at the same time. Intolerance divides, separates, and rejects. The nature of the ego is to separate, segregate, compare, analyze, interpret, project, and judge. It is the nature of the ego to defend. The ego is fragile, volatile, and easily offended. It leads us to believe that we have the right (and should) correct others. If we just tell someone off, once and for all, he will "get it" and shape up. But that never happens! Attack simply creates more defensiveness. Miracle-mindedness contains no judgment. It does nothing. It waits and watches and judges not. God knows nothing of judgment (T-2.VIII.2:3).

True Perception and Perfect Judgment

Opinions and judgments are dreams. Projections keep us from true perception. True perception is innocence. All perceptions of the ego are distorted; therefore, true perception never comes from the ego. True perception is, however, the basis for knowledge and the affirmation of truth beyond all perceptions (T-3.III.1:10).

> *True perception is a remedy with many names.*
> **Forgiveness, Salvation, Atonement,**
> **True Perception all are one.**
> *They are the one beginning, with the end to lead to oneness*
> *far beyond themselves. True perception is the means*
> *by which the world is saved from sin, for sin does not exist.*
> *And it is this that true perception sees.*
>
> C-4.3:5 9

God Does Not Judge

The purpose of time is to "give us time" to achieve this perfect perception of our own perfect creations. Dreams end where knowledge, or perfect judgment, begins. Then, despite the seeming severity of our situation, we're okay. Even if the body is not okay, the mind is okay.

Story Time

The ninety-two-year-old, petite, poised, and peaceful lady is fully dressed by eight o'clock, with her hair well-combed and makeup nicely applied, even though she is legally blind. She is moving into a nursing home today. Her husband of seventy years recently passed away, making the move necessary. After many hours waiting patiently in the lobby, she smiles sweetly when told her room is ready.

As she maneuvers her walker to the elevator, the nurse provides a visual description of her tiny room, including the eyelet curtains that hang by her window. "I love it!" she says with the enthusiasm of an eight-year-old having just been presented with a new puppy. "But, Mrs. Jones," says the nurse, "you haven't seen the room yet . . . just wait." "That doesn't have anything to do with it," she replies. "Happiness doesn't depend on how the furniture is arranged . . . it's how my mind is arranged. I have already decided. *I love it!*"

The Big Lie

The Big Lie is that life is limited to a body trapped in space and time. It is that we are going to die—that is the end of the story and that is all there is to it. There is no God; there is no Heaven; there is no eternal truth. Workbook Lesson 10 from the Course says, "My thoughts do not mean anything" and the thoughts "we think we think," are not our real thoughts (W-10:1:2). They are not real because they are dreams, fantasies, judgments, illusions, wishes and worries, dramas, soap operas, and tragedies. Stopping the mind's miscreations, holy instances (little windows and doors) begin to enable vision. The memory of God cannot come to a conflicted mind (T-23.I.1:1–2). Being free of judgment does not mean not engaging in decision making or discernment. True discernment is wisdom and wisdom is the relinquishment of judgment (M-10.4:5).

Approach and Avoidance: Do Only This

A wise teacher tells us what we need to learn to increase our joy.

"Then you shall judge yourself," the king answered.
"That is the most difficult thing of all."
It is much more difficult to judge oneself than to judge others.
If you succeed in judging yourself rightly,

you are indeed a man of true wisdom.

FROM *THE LITTLE PRINCE*,
BY ANTOINE DE SAINT-EXUPÉRY

Correct judgment lies in the recognition that as a child of God I am like my Father, incapable of judging others with whom I share one perfect Mind. I shall, therefore, not judge myself as well.

Waking Up

Here is how English mystic Douglas Harding (1909–2007) described his awakening:

> What actually happened was something absurdly simple and unspectacular: I stopped thinking. A peculiar quiet, an odd kind of alert limpness or numbness, came over me . . . Past and future dropped away. I forgot who and what I was, my name, manhood, animal-hood, all that could be called mine.

HAVING NO HEAD, BY DOUGLAS HARDING,
INNER DIRECTIONS PUBLISHING, CARLSBAD, CA, 1961.

Stop Thinking

A therapist friend told the following story about one of her clients:

> A man was living a nightmarish life. His business was failing, he was battling alcoholism, he was in deep trouble with the IRS, and his wife was threatening to leave him. Overwhelmed with the burden of life and seeing no way out, he decided to commit suicide. He raised a gun to his head. Realizing he would be dead in a few seconds, he decided to give his mind a moment's rest before he pulled the trigger and left this world forever. He would soon be dead, so why worry? The IRS couldn't bother him where he

was going. And then, "Wait a minute . . ." He put the gun down. Free for the first time in years from his anger, his projections, his judgments, and his nightmarish dreaming of the world, he found himself in a state of bliss and he heard a voice say, "I'm here to help you."

His wife left him. He sold his McMansion to pay off his bills, and he sold his business to his son. A lawyer friend helped him work things out with the IRS. They even forgave part of his debt. He got a small condo on the ground floor with a patio and a sliding-glass door facing to the west, where the sun set, onto a lawn overlooking a small human-made lake. Here each evening neighbors gathered to share the joy of watching their dogs chasing each other around the small lake.

He joined Alcoholics Anonymous, and gave up drinking, smoking, junk food, and ice cream. He began walking around the lake every day. Over time, he lost thirty pounds. His health improved. He was free of his addictions, a wife who badgered him, a home that had become a money pit, and a business he no longer enjoyed. He found himself feeling miraculously free, joyful, and unburdened.

He got a part-time job as a greeter at Walmart and with a big smile and a happy, "Good morning," he found himself making new friends every day. Soon, a new lady friend he met at Walmart joined him on his patio to sip a glass of tea while they held hands, watching the dogs joyfully running after each other as the sun set.

> *God's teachers do not judge. To judge is to be dishonest,*
> *for to judge is to assume a position you do not have.*
>
> M-4.III.1–2

The Wish to Be Victimized

The ego enjoys being abandoned and betrayed; that is proof of its reality. Suffering is "proof" that somebody can hurt us. We did not do it to ourselves; somebody did it to us. Perceiving ourselves as victims alludes to our dreaming. It speaks of illusion. We cannot be unfairly treated. Jesus is hanging on a cross, a crowd jeering and insulting him, and yet, he does not see himself betrayed. "Father," he says, "Forgive them. They know not what they do." He did not say that so God would know what to do. He said it so we would know what to do in much less severe circumstances.

When Jesus says, "A man's enemies are those of his own house" (Matthew 10:30), he is not talking about our brother or sister. He is talking about ourselves. If we tell the world how badly we've been treated and how much we have suffered at the hands of others, we make ourselves sick, emotionally and/or physically, and we back further into guilt through our projections.

> Only my condemnation injures me.
> Only my own forgiveness sets me free.
>
> W-P1.198.9:3–4

Fearful Dreaming and Suffering

Notice how many dreams involve trying to get away from some shadowy figure. We may dream that something is to be found out that we do not want known. We are often victims in our dreams. We are being pursued, someone is after us; therefore, we have a right to be paranoid, don't we?

Mr. Blackman goes to a psychiatrist. He says, "Doc, I have this terrible feeling that everybody's trying to take advantage of me."

The psychiatrist says, "Relax, Mr. Blackman. It's a common thing. We all think that people are trying to take advantage of us."

Mr. Blackman says, "Doc, that's such a relief. How much do I owe you?"

The psychiatrist replies, "How much have you got?"
When we believe that we are victims, all we "know" is what we
believe has been done to us. It's also likely that we will spend a good deal
of our time telling the world exactly how unfairly we've been treated.

> The "reasoning" by which the world is made,
> on which it rests, by which it is maintained,
> is simply this: "You are the cause of what I do.
> Your presence justifies my wrath,
> and you exist and think apart from me.
> While you attack I must be innocent.
> And what I suffer from is your attack."
> No one who looks upon this "reasoning" exactly as it is
> could fail to see it does not follow and it makes no sense.
> Yet it seems sensible,
> because it looks as if the world were hurting you.

> T-27.VII. 3:1–6

The Escape from Victimhood

To be happy, we must stop living according to the nonsensical, insane
dictates of the ego and start living according to the certainty of God's
perfect law.

> There is a way of finding certainty right here and now.
> Refuse to be a part of fearful dreams whatever form they take,
> for you will lose identity in them.

> T-28.IV.2:1–2

All thoughts have their consequences. We may apologize by saying,
"I'm sorry. I wasn't thinking." And, literally, we weren't thinking. We are,

at all times, prisoners to our thoughts. Wallowing in gossip, rumors, and lies, it is easy to get stuck in time. Forgiveness is the only road that leads us out of victimhood. By forgiving, we stop living in the past. Forgiveness brings us closer to the end of time.

The Law of Extension and the Law of Deprivation

Just as there is a correct form of denial—namely, the denial of error—so, too, is there a right-minded form of projection, which the Course calls extension.

> *We have said that without projection there can be no anger,*
> *but it is also true that without extension there can be no love.*
>
> T-7.VIII.1:1

> *To the Holy Spirit, it is the fundamental law of sharing,*
> *by which you give what you value*
> *in order to keep it in your mind.*
> *To the Holy Spirit it is the law of extension.*
> *To the ego it is the law of deprivation.*
> *It therefore produces abundance or scarcity,*
> *depending on how you choose to apply it.*
>
> T-7.VIII.1:7–9

Nonjudgment Day

Intolerance is unhappiness. We can project fear and pain, or extend love and comfort. We cannot project fear and pain and be happy at the same time. We experience true happiness by letting others be who they are without trying to fix them. Projecting our dissatisfaction, judgment, annoyance, and anger doesn't satisfy or bring us happiness.

Condemn and we become prisoners of guilt. Forgive and we are set free (T-27.VIII.13:1). It's a simple basic law: As I do unto others, so is it done unto me.

A couple went to church one Sunday. When they returned home, the wife said, "Did you see how the Jones girl was dressed today? Where did she think she was—at church . . . or at a cocktail party?

"No," said the husband, "I didn't notice."

"Did you see what Mrs. Hacket was wearing? That blouse was cut way too low."

"No," said the husband, "I didn't notice."

"Oh," said the wife with exasperation, "A lot of good it does for you to go to church!"

Deliberately sit in a restaurant, a shopping mall, a house of worship, or at work. Look around and love everyone you see. The way people dress, what they may do for a living—none of that matters. When we give up judgment, we give up illusion. To give up judgment is to give up something we never had. Once we let God take the reins, the path ahead is more clearly seen. This judgment is neither "good" nor "bad." It is the only judgment there is, and it is only one: "God's Son is guiltless, and sin does not exist" (M-10.2:7–9).

Forget It

If you see a tall fellow ahead of the crowd,
A leader of the group, marching fearless and proud,
And you know of a tale whose mere telling aloud
Would cause his proud head in anguish be bowed,
It's a pretty good plan to forget it.

If you know of a skeleton hidden away in a closet,
Guarded and kept from the day in the dark,
Whose showing, whose sudden display,

Would cause grief and sorrow and life long dismay,
It's a pretty good plan to forget it.

If you know of a spot in the life of a friend,
We all have spots concealed world without end,
Whose touching his heartstring would hurt or rend,
'til the shame of the showing no grieving could mend,
It's a pretty good plan to forget it.

If you know of a thing that would darken the joy
Of a man or a woman, a girl or a boy,
That will wipe out a smile, or the least way annoy
A fellow or cause any gladness to cloy,
It's a pretty good plan to forget it.

ENGLISH ARCHITECT
MORTIMER LEWIS (1796–1879)

CHAPTER 15

The Strength of Gentleness

Then the King will say to those at his right hand,
"Come, O blessed of my Father, inherit the
Kingdom prepared for you from the foundation of
the world;
for I was hungry and you gave me food,
I was thirsty and you gave me drink,
I was a stranger and you welcomed me,
I was naked and you clothed me,
I was sick and you visited me,
I was in prison and you came to me."

Then the righteous will answer him,
"Lord, when did we see thee hungry and feed thee,
or thirsty and give thee drink?
And when did we see thee a stranger and welcome thee,
or naked and clothe thee?
And when did we see thee sick or in prison
and visit thee?"
And the King will answer them,
"Truly, I say to you, as you did it to one of the least
of these my brethren, you did it to me."

MATTHEW 25:34–40

The Call for Love

Eleanor Callahan went to the post office to buy stamps just before Christmas. The lines were particularly long, and someone pointed out to Eleanor that there was no need to wait in line because there was a stamp machine in the lobby. "I know," said Eleanor, "but the machine won't ask me about my arthritis."

> *. . . where there is a call for love,*
> *you must give it because of what you are.*
>
> T-14.X.12:3

From the beginning of the section on gentleness in the Course's *Manual for Teachers*, we read:

> *Harm is impossible for God's teachers.*
> *They can neither harm nor be harmed.*
> *Harm is the outcome of judgment.*
> *It is the dishonest act that follows a dishonest thought.*
> *It is a verdict of guilt upon a brother,*
> *and therefore on oneself.*
>
> M-4.IV.1:1—5

The Ego Is Neither Gentle nor Kind

He who finds fault with his brother finds fault with himself. Punishment is unknown to God and, thus, unknown to right-mindedness. God literally cannot think an unkind thought and in truth, neither can you. The Course asks, "Are thoughts, then, dangerous? To bodies, yes!" (T-21.VIII.1:1–2) A judgment having been made, the judge (ego) decides that punitive measures are called for. God's teachers, however, are wholly gentle.

Who would choose the weakness that must come from
harm in place of the unfailing, all-encompassing
and limitless strength of gentleness?

M-4.IV.2:7

Gentleness and *kindness* are synonyms, and the Course uses the words interchangeably, though *kindness* is used more frequently than *gentleness*. Gentleness is patient, steadfast, and the very opposite of harm.

The might of God's teachers lies in their gentleness,
for they have understood their evil thoughts
came neither from God's Son nor his Creator.

M-4.IV.2:8

I always experienced Helen Schucman as being wholly gentle and kind. Likewise, I always experienced Ken Wapnick as being wholly gentle and kind, even when he disagreed with me. In *A Course in Miracles and Christianity*, he writes: "I have frequently made the public comment that one of the most important lessons a student of *A Course in Miracles* can learn is how to disagree with someone (whether that person be on another spiritual path or a student of the Course) without it being an attack."

It takes gentleness to be a parent, teacher, minister, doctor, shop owner, grocery store clerk—human being. Can it be done consistently and with unconditional love? How do we correct a poorly performing employee, a child who misbehaves, a selfish or lazy partner? Can it be done gently and without spite or do we prefer a sharp tongue? Learning to live with spiritual principles requires ever-increasing awareness and great discipline.

You want to be happy. You want peace.
You do not have them now,
because your mind is totally undisciplined . . .

W-20.2:4–6

In the gospels, Jesus says that he is gentle and humble in heart. His yoke is easy, his burden light. Jesus, as an expression of the Christ Mind, did not become stressed when the world around him went crazy. Perfect happiness calls for the maintenance of sanity and gentleness in a harsh and sometimes insane world.

God's teachers are wholly gentle.
They need the strength of gentleness, for it is
in this that the function of salvation becomes easy.

M-4.IV.2:1–2

Just as peace is stronger than war, nothing is stronger than gentleness. Gentleness, like an ever-flowing stream, can wear away the roughest edges. Loving-kindness and gentleness are stronger than anger and attack. Even bullies and tyrants melt in the presence of loving-kindness!

American spiritual teacher Ram Dass (1931–present) tells a story in his book *How Can I Help?* about a "big, drunk, and dirty" man who terrorizes a train car in Tokyo. An expert martial arts student happens to be on that train, and he begins to think about taking down the drunk before the man hurts anyone. As the martial arts student is about to attack the drunk, a little old Japanese man intervenes politely, addressing the drunken man, disarming him with gentle words. As the little old man engages the drunken man in conversation, the drunk breaks down and begins to sob, saying that he has no wife, no home, no job, and is so ashamed of himself. Before long the old Japanese man begins gently stroking the dirty, matted hair of the sobbing man, who is sprawled at his side with his head in the old man's lap.

> *Who would choose the weakness that must come from*
> *harm in place of the unfailing, all-encompassing*
> *and limitless strength of gentleness?*

M-4.IV.2:7

Saint Francis of Assisi, perhaps the most revered of all Catholic saints and the man Pope Francis chose to name himself after, was admired for the kindness he showed to every living thing. He was gentle to animals, plants, and those who were hurt, weak, or poor. He is remembered for his sermons to the animals and his love for all of nature.

Selflessness and the Self-Fullness of Spirit

Tenzin Gyatso, the 14th Dalai Lama, has said that his religion is kindness. Kindness is the "law" he lives by. Kindness is the very opposite of selfishness. Selfishness is dishonest and withholding, while kindness is truthful and sharing. It is literally "doing unto others as we would have them do unto us."

> *If you want others to be happy, practice compassion.*
> *If you want to be happy, practice compassion.*

THE DALAI LAMA (1935–PRESENT)

There is no God but God. God has a job for us. He would like to put us in his employ. He needs our help in transforming this world into a place of gentleness and joy (T-25.III.8:1). Simply be gentle with everyone. No attachments, no aversions. Don't hold on to hurt feelings. Better yet, don't create them. Forgiveness is a demonstration of gentleness. In

The Song of Prayer pamphlet, Jesus speaks of "forgiveness kindness" (S-2.I.1:4). It is a kindness to forgive.

> *It is one of the beautiful compensations of life that no one*
> *can sincerely try to help another without helping himself.*
>
> CHARLES DUDLEY WARNER (1829–1900),
> COAUTHOR WITH MARK TWAIN OF *THE GILDED AGE*

The only way to give anything is to do so expecting nothing in return. Gentleness is not a loan. I had a friend with a rough exterior, a hard man, not easy to get to know. He had a stroke; afterward he became childlike and emotional. Knowing perhaps that death was near, he cried often and told all the members of his family and his circle of friends how much he loved them. The love had been inside him all along; it was merely covered by a mask.

> *Sometimes, only a thin veneer,*
> *keeps our sight from being clear.*

> *I shall pass through this world but once.*
> *Any good that I can do, or any kindness that I can show*
> *to any human being let me do it now and not defer it.*
> *For I shall not pass this way again.*
>
> FRENCH-BORN AMERICAN QUAKER
> STEPHEN GRELLET (1773–1855)

> *The Maker of the world of gentleness*
> *has perfect power to offset the world of violence*
> *and hate that seems to stand between you and His gentleness.*
>
> T-25.III.8:1

See no one as a body. Greet everyone as the son or daughter of God. If something troubles me about my brother, I want to look carefully and see what it is. Why am I disturbed? Can I not let this piece of insanity go? Can I opt for "reasonableness" instead? Meeting anyone is a holy encounter and an opportunity to offer a demonstration of our love. What we think about others, we think about ourselves (T-8. III.4:1–3). The compassionate are loving unto themselves and all others. It is a blessing to be moved to help, whether the other ever knows of it or not.

> *The grace of God rests gently on forgiving eyes,*
> *and everything they look on speaks of Him to the beholder.*
> *He can see no evil; nothing in the world to fear,*
> *and no one who is different from himself.*
> *And as he loves them, so he looks upon himself*
> *with love and gentleness.*
>
> T-25.VI.1:1–3

> *The only safety lies in extending the Holy Spirit,*
> *because as you see His gentleness in others*
> *your own mind perceives itself as totally harmless.*
>
> T-6.III.3:1

Guiltlessness

In Heaven, (the only reality there is), everyone is guiltless. Heaven is the experience of gentleness. God is wholly gentle, and the Holy Spirit sees only guiltlessness.

> *You know not what you do, but He Who knows is with you.*
> *His gentleness is yours, and all the love you share with God*

He holds in trust for you. He would teach you nothing
except how to be happy.

T-14.V.2:6–8

There is such need for gentleness in this world! Looking into the eyes of the waitress who used to serve me breakfast, I could see much loneliness, pain, and need for support. A heavy smoker, she did not look well. She lived alone; her children had moved far away. No one ever invited her to visit. She could not afford to travel. Her only income was the little that a breakfast waitress earns. She wanted to talk. She needed a kind word and a generous tip.

As I looked about me at people turning evil, shrunken,
colorless, old and weird, I suddenly thought,
"Well, what did you think it was that needed to be loved?"
And just like that, the doors opened, and I was in paradise.

—FROM *THE LAZY MAN'S GUIDE TO ENLIGHTENMENT,*
BY THADDEUS GOLAS

Everyone is going through something. Everyone is lonely. Everyone is isolated. Everyone needs to be seen for who they are—a perfect child of God. Choosing to see the face of the Christ in my sister or my brother, I thereby open the door for each of them to the Kingdom of Heaven.

The Sunday Morning Kiss

Mildred Byrnes was a tiny woman in my parish in Central Valley, New York. Every Sunday morning, along with a number of other older ladies, Mildred stood in a little processional line in the church vestibule. Each one waiting for me to give her a hug, a "How are you?" and a kiss on the cheek. This was the only real affection she experienced coming from a man—this little peck of a kiss on Sunday morning. There are many "Mildred Byrnes" in the world. We need their love and they need ours.

> *Happiness is an attribute of love.*
> *It cannot be apart from it.*
> *Nor can it be experienced where love is not.*
> *Love has no limits, being everywhere.*
> *And therefore joy is everywhere as well.*

W-103.1:1–5

Nice Guys Finish First: The Fair Play Trophy

Leo Durocher (1905–1991), nicknamed "Leo the lip," was a famous baseball manager who is remembered for saying, "Nice guys finish last." Cyclist Lance Armstrong (1971–present) apologized for using performance-enhancing drugs, saying it came from his "determination to win at all costs." Nothing makes us unhappier than guilt and the feeling that we have "hurt" others and thus, ourselves. Nice guys may finish last, but they finish with a clear conscience.

The Committee for International Fair Play of the International Sports Press Association annually awards trophies for gestures of fair play. The first trophy went to an Italian bobsledder named Eugenio Monti (1928–2003). In the two-man bobsled event at the 1964 Innsbruck Olympics, Monti was the leader after his final run. The only one who had a chance to beat him was Tony Nash of Great Britain. As Nash and his teammate got ready for their final run, they discovered that a bolt on their sled had broken. Monti was informed of the problem and had his extra bolt sent to Nash. Thanks to Monti's generosity, Nash fixed his sled and came hurtling down the course to set a new record and win the gold medal. Monti was awarded the International Fair Play Award.

In a marathon tandem kayak racing event at the world championships in Copenhagen, Danish paddlers were leading when their rudder was damaged. British paddlers, who were in second place, stopped to help the Danes. The Danes went on to defeat the British by one second, but the British kayakers received the International Fair Play Award.

In the 1992 Olympics, Henry Pearce of Australia was competing in the single-scull rowing event. He was leading when a duck and her string of ducklings came into his path up ahead. They were on a collision course, and Pearce reckoned that his scull would cut the string of ducklings in two and sink a few ducklings in the process, so he pulled in his oars. When the ducks passed, Pearce again bent his back to the task. He set no record but he still won the race and the International Fair Play Award.

The memory of God comes to the quiet mind.
It cannot come where there is conflict, for a mind
at war against itself remembers not eternal gentleness.
The means of war are not the means of peace,
and what the warlike would remember is not love.
War is impossible unless belief in victory is cherished.
Conflict within you must imply that you believe
the ego has the power to be victorious.

T-23.I.1:1–5

Creation's Gentleness

Projection makes perception and extension creates love. The images we see reflect our thoughts. We cannot understand the world when we place our projections upon it. Perfect vision heals all the mistakes that any mind has made at any time or place. Perfect vision sees creation's gentleness.

If you will sit quietly by and let the Holy Spirit relate
through you, you will empathize with strength,
and will gain in strength and not in weakness.

T-16.I.2:7

There is no cruelty in God and none in me.

W-170

That old fellow on the subway, the man with the wrinkled clothing and uncombed hair—he's been standing on his feet all day, helping people in a deli. He is very tired. All he can think about is getting home, taking off his shoes, pouring himself a glass of wine, and watching TV. There is great gentleness in this old man. He'll be praying for you in church on Sunday morning.

Lesson 67 from the workbook is "Love created me like Itself." Take a moment and repeat these lines from Lesson 67.

Holiness created me holy.
Kindness created me kind.
Helpfulness created me helpful.
Perfection created me perfect.

W-PI.67.2:3–6

CHAPTER 16

The Constancy of Joy

The constancy of joy
is a condition quite alien to your understanding.
Yet if you could even imagine what it must be,
you would desire it although you understand it not.
The constancy of happiness has no exceptions;
no change of any kind.

T-21.VIII.2:1–3

The whole glory and perfect joy that "is" the Kingdom
lies in you to give. Do you not want to give it?

T-7.V.9:10–11

Joy—like trust, honesty, tolerance, and gentleness—is our natural state. My friend George Robinson, a Course teacher from Charlottesville, Virginia, shared his experience of going to see an ophthalmologist when a case of shingles spread to his left eye. The ophthalmologist was describing all the terrible things that could happen to George, including blindness. George, who exudes calmness, said, "All is well." The doctor hit his fist on the table and exclaimed, "All is not well!"

George replied, "Doctor, you are talking about the body. I am talking about the mind." Despite the potentially dire diagnosis of his body,

George's mind remained free. Some bodies are disabled from birth, from accidents, from old age. On the physical level, there may not be much that can be done. On the attitude level, incredible strides are possible. Blind and deaf Helen Keller said that it was through her handicaps and her mind alone that she found God. She saw and heard nothing of the world. She knew what she knew by being loved to life by her teacher, Anne Sullivan (1866–1938).

> *Even in Heaven does this law obtain.*
> *The Son of God creates to bring him joy,*
> *sharing his Father's purpose in his own creation,*
> *that his joy might be increased, and God's along with his.*

T-25.IV.2:6–7

Joy is unified purpose (T-8.VII.15.1). Life is joyful when we know we are at all times being directed by the voice of God. The more we awaken, the more amazing are the ways of God. There is less and less reason for despair.

> *The Holy Spirit's curriculum is never depressing,*
> *because it is a curriculum of joy.*

T-8.VII.8:5

I can love and be joyful but I cannot be joyful and hold grievances. To let go of anger and grievance means that the ego no longer exists. If there are no attack thoughts, there is no guilt and there is no home for the ego. The Holy Spirit sees everything as an expression of love or a call for love. All that the Holy Spirit knows is love. To see only love is to know only love. Joy accompanies tolerance as:

Minds that are joined and recognize they are,
can feel no guilt. For they cannot attack,
and they rejoice that this is so,
seeing their safety in this happy fact.
Their joy is in the innocence they see.

T-25.IV.1:1–3

Misery is of the ego and joy comes from the spirit (T-4.IV.5:6). Joy from the ego's point of view means getting what the body wants—all the toys, the money, and the stimulants possible. Joy for Spirit comes in the abundance of sharing, uniting, and remembering Oneness.

The Call to Joy

The whole of Las Vegas is a show. It is so mythological, so over the top. It is clearly a fantasy and not to be taken too seriously. A friend told me how her husband, having gone to a convention in Las Vegas, called her within twenty-four hours of arrival and said, "Help! It's all artificial. I need to get out of here." It's all on the outside. Such excitement, while temporarily exhilarating, does not bring peace of mind, nor does it provide lasting happiness.

Go to Las Vegas and look. It's all about stimulation of the senses—more and more bling-bling; more and more lights; more and more glitz, glamour, and glitter; more sex; more food, more drink, more sound, more 3D everything. From an objective point of view it may be fun. Still, it's all about the outside. A clip on *America's Funniest Home Videos* shows a little boy sitting in the backseat of a car. He looks into the camera and says with all sincerity, "Is this a real world?"

We will always be building a Las Vegas somewhere and ever more spectacular shows. The ego "lives" in a fantasy world. It looks for a quick fix, an easy solution, a shot, a relief—something from the outside, a pill perhaps. The inside is never found on the outside and we're not surprised to hear that the highest suicide rate in the United States is in Las Vegas, "sin city" USA. I have several friends in Las Vegas. Knowing that it is all a show, they have taken an objective view and look more deeply within.

> *The rituals of the god of sickness*
> *are strange and very demanding.*
> *Joy is never permitted,*
> *for depression is the sign of allegiance to him.*
> *Depression means that you have forsworn God.*
>
> T-10.V.1:1–3

To forswear is "to reject," "to renounce," "to deny," or "to abjure." To "fall" into ego and the idea of a separate self is to wander away from home, away from God's protection. To be depressed means not following GPS. It means being off track—lost without a sense of direction. God is always there and always available. It is up to us to respond. If we do not, if we make the decision to be angry, to attack a brother or sister, we separate ourselves from Oneness and separation from Oneness is depressing.

> **The opposite of joy is depression.**
> *When your learning promotes depression instead of joy,*
> *you cannot be listening to God's joyous Teacher*
> *and learning His lessons.*
>
> T-8.VII.13:1–2

Joy is the opposite of depression. Joy comes in joining. Depression comes in isolation and aloneness—alone within our own mind, alone in a place where we are unable to share, alone in our experience of guilt. No one enters Heaven by himself (W-13417:7).

> *You are indeed essential to God's plan.*
> *Just as your light increases every light that shines in Heaven,*
> *so your joy on earth calls to all minds to let their sorrows go,*
> *and take their place beside you in God's plan.*
> *God's messengers are joyous, and their joy heals sorrow and*
> *despair. They are the proof that God wills perfect happiness for*
> *all who will accept their Father's gifts as theirs.*
>
> W-100.4:1–4

Depression comes when we are not fulfilling our destiny. Jesus followed God's guidance so clearly he could say, "I and the Father are one." There was no difference between His will and the will of His Father. We have the same Father and just as Jesus remembers His identity, so may we. Teachers of God learn to progressively turn their will over to God. Only in this way is perfect happiness possible.

Joy is a decision we make about how we want to see. Where do we look for a confirmation of reality? When we let our minds be drawn to bodily concerns, to things we buy, to prestige as valued by the world, we are asking for sorrow not for happiness (W-133.2:2).

A study by a group of social psychologists concluded that close sympathetic and intimate connections with others were the most important ingredient in happiness. If I could coin a word to describe our sorrowful, isolated, separated, and broken state, it might be *alonement*. Alonement is unhappiness and depression. God is love. What makes for happiness is giving and receiving love.

Depression is an inevitable consequence of separation.
So are anxiety, worry, a deep sense of helplessness,
misery, suffering and intense fear of loss.

W-41.1:2–3

Selfishness Is Unhappiness

What makes us more depressed than anything is the consequences of selfishness—the choices to lie, to eat too much, to drink too much, to spend too much, or choices we make to judge.

Only the healed mind can experience revelation with lasting
effect, because revelation is an experience of pure joy.
If you do not choose to be wholly joyous,
your mind cannot have what it does not choose to be.
Remember that spirit knows no difference
between "having" and "being."

T-5.I.1:3–5

Real joy comes in knowing that we are never alone. The Holy Spirit is always with us; God is always with us. The deeper I know this, the deeper my peace and tranquility.

Morning is when I am awake and there is a dawn in me.

AMERICAN TRANSCENDENTALIST
HENRY DAVID THOREAU

My mother, Milly, sat each morning at her kitchen table reading her daily Unity devotionals. A quiet contentment and connection can come during the early morning hours—alone in our bedroom, our living room, study, den, or kitchen with just the Course as a companion, quietly communing with the unseen but known. Sometimes when the body is most alone, we are the most connected.

> *The Holy Spirit is invisible, but you can see the results of His*
> *Presence, and through them you will learn that He is there.*
>
> T-12.VII.3:1

Mystics are lovers of God. When God fills our being, we are God. We are in love.

> *Grief can take care of itself, but to get the full value of a joy,*
> *you must have somebody to divide it with.*
>
> AMERICAN AUTHOR MARK TWAIN

Oh, Honey, Look!

In 2009, I went to San Francisco to *A Course in Miracles* conference. After the conference, I was going to go see Judy and her husband Bill (Whit) Whitson, who live just across the Golden Gate Bridge in Belvedere, California. After crossing the bridge, there is a pull-off that provides a beautiful view of San Francisco in the background. Many pictures are taken from this spot. I pulled over, wanting to share the moment, I got out my old flip top cell phone, called Dolores, and said, "Honey, you should see what I'm seeing right now," and I tried to describe it. She said, "I'm sure it is beautiful but I'm not there. Unfortunately, I can't see it."

> *God, Who encompasses all being,*
> *created beings who have everything individually,*
> ***but who want to share it to increase their joy.***
> *Nothing real can be increased except by sharing.*

That is why God created you.
Divine Abstraction takes joy in sharing.
That is what creation means.

T-4.VII.5:1–5

Two years later, in 2011, I was back in San Francisco for the biannual conference. This time Dolores came along and we allotted extra time to drive up Highway 1, north out of San Francisco. If you've ever taken this drive, you know there are many points at which you will come around a bend and there in front of you is a magnificent sight of big waves crashing up against huge rocks and boulders protruding up out of the ocean. Each time we would round one of these bends and a new sight would open up before us, Dolores would say, "Oh, Honey, look!" Nothing could have brought more joy to my heart than hearing Dolores say, "Oh, Honey, look!"

It is impossible to remember God in secret and alone.
For remembering Him means you are not alone . . .
Everyone seeks for love as you do,
but knows it not unless he joins with you in seeking it.

T-14.X.10:1–2&5

When you have learned that your will is God's,
you could no more will to be without Him
than He could will to be without you.
This is freedom and this is joy.

T-8.II.6:4–5

Joy and Freedom

When we judge our brothers and sisters we "hear no song of liberation for ourselves." (T-26.I.6:4) Addicts who find freedom from addiction discover a whole new life opening up to them. Think of any moment when you've experienced some real joy and I'll bet it was some time when an "opening" came your way, perhaps a "revelation," some kind of "insight." Certainly some kind of freedom—some "good news"—came your way and the love of God filled your heart. Revelation is a joyful experience because of the "newness" of the insight, freedom from fear and the relief it brings to the entrapped mind. Miracle-mindedness makes room for revelation.

> *Only the healed mind can experience revelation with lasting effect, because revelation is an experience of pure joy.*

T-5.I.1:3

During the summer of 1975, I took a wilderness survival training course. Along with four new acquaintances from New York City, I drove my Volkswagen camper up into the Adirondack Mountains in upstate New York, where we joined five others and two leaders in a seven-day Backwoods Training Program, followed by three days and two nights when we were left alone in the woods. The program was educational and fun. We learned how to live off the land, and we enjoyed socializing with our fellow participants.

We had two trainers, a young man and a young woman. I remember very little about the young man, but the woman left an impression on all of us. She seemed to be out to prove herself and laid down the law like a drill sergeant. Everyone was very stoic and polite and no one complained about the way she treated us. For some reason, we also never talked to each other about her, although there were occasional raised eyebrows and sideways glances.

On the day we left, we piled into my VW camper and as we pulled out of the parking lot onto the road, everyone in the van burst out laughing. For the next five minutes or more, we couldn't stop laughing. It was an interesting moment of nonverbal mind-to-mind communication. No one said anything about why we were laughing. No one had to say anything. We were all laughing from the sheer joy of being free of tyranny, and we all knew it.

Many folks are afraid that death will mean the end of them, and, yet, it is nothing more than a beginning and in that there is great joy. To be afraid of death is to be afraid of life.

Only joy increases forever,
since joy and eternity are inseparable.
God extends outward beyond limits and beyond time,
and you who are co-creator with Him
extend His Kingdom forever and beyond limit.
Eternity is the indelible stamp of creation.
The eternal are in peace and joy forever.

T-7.I.5:3–6

Revelation and Rebirth

Joy comes in freedom and in revelation. Revelation is a kind of waking up, a kind of rebirth. It comes when we are healed; it comes in knowing we are forgiven. Joy might come in some practical way—an increase in salary or the move to a nicer home, away from crowded conditions, to a more open space. It may come in the start of a new job. Nothing beats a new love. And there is no reason why our present love cannot forever be new. There is more depth in the other person than we will ever get to know, so dig deeper: Intimacy is joyful, communication is joyful. Joy comes in opening the heart that makes room for ever more love. Love is endless joy.

> *I said before that you must learn to think with God.*
> *To think with Him is to think like Him.*
> *This engenders joy, not guilt, because it is natural.*
>
> T-5.V.4:5–7

To be joyful is to be natural. To be natural is to be joyful. Why does a bird sing? Because it is the most natural thing in the world for it to do. According to the Course, learning is joyful as it leads us along our natural path, and facilitates the development of the people we already are (T-8.II.2:7).

To be joyful is to extend freedom. Joy means holding on to nothing. There is no freedom as wonderful as freedom from guilt and fear. Freedom from guilt comes in knowing the truth. Knowing the truth dispels illusion.

> *Take this very instant, now,*
> *and think of it as all there is of time.*
> *Nothing can reach you here out of the past,*
> *and it is here that you are completely absolved,*
> *completely free and wholly without condemnation.*
>
> T-15.I.9:5–6

Freedom from guilt is pure joy, true joy. The truth is joyful because it is a freeing experience. Joy comes not in the temporal; it comes in knowing who we are—not automatons limited to bodies that will die. Real joy comes in knowing that our bodies are not eternal.

Joy calls forth an integrated willingness to share it,
and promotes the mind's natural impulse to respond as one.

T-5.IN.1:6

Joy comes in letting go of everything that would hurt and harm us. Only those who attack know guilt. Joy comes in the release from all guilt. Joy comes in knowing you are a child of God—a wonderful, blessed, eternal child. We become progressively happy as we grow in this awareness. Not having an agenda, carrying no preconceptions about the way things are supposed to be, just observing life can be wonderfully joyful and freeing.

Joy is the inevitable result of gentleness.
Gentleness means that fear is now impossible,
and what could come to interfere with joy?

M-4.1:1–2

Joy comes in being free.
Joy comes in the release from pain.
Joy comes in knowing who made us.
Joy comes in knowing our reality as children of God.
Joy comes in doing His will and no other. It is the joyous discovery that His Voice is our voice and we are all one with God.

. . . joy is our function here.
If you are sad, your part is unfulfilled,
and all the world is thus deprived of joy, along with you.
God asks you to be happy, so the world can see how much
He loves His Son, and wills no sorrow rises to abate his joy;
no fear besets him to disturb his peace.
You are God's messenger today.

You bring His happiness to all you look upon;
His peace to everyone who looks on you and sees
His message in your happy face.

W-100.6:1–5

She gives most who gives with joy.
The best way to show our gratitude to God
and His people is to accept everything with joy.
A joyful heart is the inevitable result
of a heart burning with love.
Never let anything so fill you with sorrow
as to make you forget the joy of the Christ risen.

MOTHER TERESA

CHAPTER 17

In Defenselessness My Safety Lies

God's teachers have learned how to be simple.
They have no dreams that need defense against the truth.
They do not try to make themselves.
Their joy comes from their understanding Who created them.
And does what God created need defense?

M-4.VI.1:1–5

Psychological research has shown that as we get older we either become milder, softer, more laid-back, and, thus, happier, or we become harsher, harder, more uptight, and, thus, unhappier. Which way do you want to go? Just as our choice of food, exercise, and lifestyle habits determines the physical shape we're in as we grow older, our attitude determines our mental state.

The aim of all defenses is to keep the truth from being whole.

W-136.2:4

The Dishonesty of Defensiveness

Truth is always defenseless and it has no reason to hide. Defenses are thus the plans we make against the truth. A lie needs a defense; truth needs none. Defensiveness requires dishonesty to support its claims. Defenses are:

. . . secret, magic wands you wave when truth
appears to threaten what you would believe.
They seem to be unconscious but because of the
rapidity with which you choose to use them.

W-136.3:2–3

Since it is the function of the ego to project, it sees nothing but its own seemingly justified attack thoughts hurled back its way. The ego is always on the defensive. Most of "Reality TV" is not about happy people. It's about people fighting others. It's about attacking, defending, attacking, defending.

I was in Daytona Beach, Florida, driving down a highway I had never been on before. Suddenly I realized that the lane I was in had turned into a left-hand turning lane only. Not wishing to turn left, I put on my right blinker, so I could move back to the through lane. There was a car on my passenger side's "blind spot" and a young man started honking his horn, loudly and repeatedly. He then moved up alongside my car, rolled down his window and started screaming obscenities at me, letting me know exactly what kind of idiot I was. I should have looked more carefully. I just didn't see him.

He then pulled in front of me and began driving very slowly, giving me the finger over his right shoulder. Every car behind us was now forced to drive more slowly and they, too, began honking their horns. Since he seemed inclined to continue his behavior, I turned off the road to escape.

Here is the world's demented version
of salvation clearly shown.
Like to a dream of punishment, in which the dreamer is
unconscious of what brought on the attack against himself,
he sees himself attacked unjustly and by something not himself.

T-27.VII.1:2–3

Reprisal and Revenge, Despair and Unhappiness

The ego seeks joy in reprisal and revenge. This upside-down, backward thinking leads to great unhappiness. To hold a grudge is to let the ego rule. To let go of a grievance would mean the "I" that holds the grievance would no longer exist. The ego then must defend itself or disappear. The young man's actions were based on the need to be right. To have been upset with him would have been as much an error as his unwillingness to forgive my blunder.

> *Both the separation and the fear are miscreations*
> *that must be undone for the restoration of the temple,*
> *and for the opening of the altar to receive the Atonement.*
> *This heals the separation by placing within you the one*
> *effective defense against all separation thoughts*
> *and making you perfectly invulnerable.*
>
> T-2.III.2:3–4

The Defense of Forgiveness

Forgiveness comes in our ability to rise above the battlefield and see it for what it is, rather than striking back. See the error for the silliness that it is and let it go. If I had attacked the young man by honking my horn at him, I would have been as insane as he was at that moment. Perfectly aware of the right defense, perfect vision passes over all defense and looks past error to truth.

> *"As you teach so shall you learn."*
> *If you react as if you are persecuted,*
> *you are teaching persecution.*
> *This is not a lesson a Son of God should want to teach*
> *if he is to realize his own salvation.*

Rather, teach your own perfect immunity, which is
the truth in you, and realize that it cannot "be" assailed.

T-6.I.6:1–4

To choose a miracle is to allow Spirit to guide. To hold a grievance is to "forget" who we are. If we let a miracle replace a grievance, we reawaken the memory of who we truly are: We replace fear with love and the result is happiness. I cannot hold a grievance and be happy. I cannot hold a grievance and know myself. To hold a grievance is to see myself as a body. To hold a grievance is to forget who I am.

To conceive of the body as a means of attack
and to believe that joy could possibly result,
is a clear-cut indication of a poor learner.

T-8.VII.14:5

A student once said, "You need an ego to drive a car. After all, we call it defensive driving." You do not need an ego to drive a car. What *is* needed is lots of awareness. We need to know what's going on in front of us. We need to know what's going on behind us, to the right, and to the left of us. Egos have horns and they know how to use them. Psychologists sometimes say you need ego defense; otherwise, you will go insane. The opposite is true. Without ego defense, we find sanity, we find Self, we find God.

God does not believe in retribution.
His Mind does not create that way.
He does not hold your "evil" deeds against you.

T-3.I.3:1–6

Undoing Blame

In order to know perfect happiness, all attack, all blame, all projection must be undone. There is literally no one to blame—not even ourselves. We blame ourselves the most and the result is guilt and depression. The solution is forgiveness of ourselves, which can only happen from a higher perspective.

> *If your brothers are part of you and you blame them*
> *for your deprivation, you are blaming yourself.*
> *And you cannot blame yourself without blaming them.*
> *That is why blame must be undone, not seen elsewhere.*
> *. . . Self-blame is ego identification,*
> *and as much an ego defense as blaming others.*
> *"You cannot enter God's Presence if you attack His Son."*
>
> T-11.IV.5:1–4&6

The National Geographic Channel once ran a series on *Doomsday Preppers,* folks who hoard guns, ammunition, food, medicine, gasoline, and more against a wide variety of end-time scenarios. Preparations are being made for the collapse of the world's economy, a nuclear explosion, a catastrophic earthquake, an asteroid hitting the earth, the shift of the earth's magnetic poles, or the eruption of the volcano underneath Yellowstone National Park. A host of possibilities present themselves.

> *You who feel threatened by this changing world, its twists of*
> *fortune and its bitter jests, its brief relationships*
> *and all the "gifts" it merely lends to take away again;*
> ***attend this lesson well.***
> *The world provides no safety. It is rooted in attack,*
> *and all its "gifts" of seeming safety are illusory deceptions.*
> *It attacks, and then attacks again.*

No peace of mind is possible where danger threatens thus.

W-153.1:1–5

Rather than enjoying their remaining days with friends, reading, bicycling, playing golf, traveling, or whatever usually interests retirees, one retired "prepper" couple spend each day storing more and more food and building greater and greater stockpiles of armaments against anyone who might attack their home, which is slowly becoming a fortress.

One doomsday prepper said he would use whatever means necessary to stop intruders. He was training his German Shepherds to be attack dogs, teaching his children how to siphon gasoline from parked cars, and showing them how to "hot-wire" cars so they can start them without keys. He was teaching his children how to make gunpowder and taking them to target practice.

Fear cannot be controlled by me but it can be self-controlled.
Fear prevents me from giving you my control.
The presence of fear shows that you have raised
body thoughts to the level of the mind.
This removes them from my control,
and makes you feel personally responsible for them.
This is an obvious confusion of levels.

T-2.VI.1:4–8

In traditional Hindu spirituality, the final stage of life is known as *vanaprastha,* or "forest dweller." At a certain age, a man would (with or without his wife) retire from worldly attachments and move into the forest to lead a life of contemplation. His (or their) remaining days were then to be spent in meditation and in becoming "one who neither hates nor loves." Thus, they joyfully prepare to deepen their peace before they leave this world.

Learning to Die is the title of the first book I wrote. Would that we could spend our final days learning to die, to let go of the illusion of the world, rather than grasping for some form of nothingness.

> *Lay not up for yourselves treasures upon earth, where moth*
> *and rust corrupt, and where thieves break through and steal but*
> *lay up for yourselves treasures in Heaven, where neither moth*
> *nor rust corrupt and where thieves do not break through and*
> *steal for where your treasure is, there will your heart be also.*
>
> MATTHEW 6:19–21

> *You can defend truth as well as error.*
> *The means are easier to understand after the value of the*
> *goal is firmly established. It is a question of what it is "for."*
> *Everyone defends his treasure, and will do so automatically.*
> *The real questions are, what do you treasure,*
> *and how much do you treasure it?*
>
> T-2.II.3:1–5

Soldiers are taught to refer to their opposition as the "enemy." During World War II, U.S. soldiers called the Germans *krauts.* In Vietnam they were called *gooks.* Soldiers must dehumanize the enemy in order to make the "kill."

> *You've got to be taught to hate and fear,*
> *You've got to be taught from year to year,*
> *It's got to be drummed in your dear little ear,*
> *You've got to be carefully taught.*
>
> FROM THE MUSICAL *SOUTH PACIFIC* (1949),
> BY ROGERS AND HAMMERSTEIN

One doomsday prepper devised a plan whereby he would hide and allow intruders to enter his home. He called those folks the "bad guys." When the "bad guys" (perhaps children) thought they were safe, he would pop out and kill them. "The last people standing," he said, "will be the good people who have killed all the bad people."

> *No one can become an advanced teacher of God until he fully*
> *understands that defenses are but*
> *foolish guardians of mad illusions.*
> *The more grotesque the dream, the fiercer*
> *and more powerful its defenses seem to be.*
>
> M-4.VI.1:6–7

One woman had amassed over five thousand pounds of food. She had food stored in every room of her house. Her bed was built on top of drums of water. The hallways in her home and the whole of her basement were full of supplies. "When the world goes to hell," she said, "I'll still be here."

> *The "here" that we are in is not the body.*
> *The "here" that is the real cause of the pain*
> *is in the ego's thought system.*
>
> DR. KEN WAPNICK

The belief in hell is unavoidable if we see ourselves as bodies only. The sacrifice of the truth of our being as Spirit is hell (M-13.6:11). If people start killing each other over food supplies, what a hell of a world this would be. How would you like to look out your window and see your neighbor's body lying there dead and you were the one who pulled the trigger?

Is not this picture fearful?
Can you be at peace with such a concept of your home?
It is your mind which gave the body all the functions
that you see in it, and set its value far beyond
a little pile of dust and water.

W-135.6:1—2&4

Where would you like to place your bet—on an ephemeral body or an eternal spirit? It is no doubt a good idea to have insurance for our cars, our homes, and our bodies. It's probably a good idea to have some money saved up in case of an emergency. It might be a good idea to have batteries, water, and extra food supplies put aside, but, needing to defend one's stockpile of five thousand pounds of food is quite a burden and it provides little in the way of true security or happiness.

The body is the ego's idol;
the belief in sin made flesh and then projected outward.
This produces what seems to be a wall of flesh around the mind,
keeping it prisoner in a tiny spot of space and time,
beholden unto death, and given but an instant in which to sigh
and grieve and die in honor of its master.

T-20.VI.11:1—2

Where shall we place our faith—in increasing stockpiles of armaments and ammunition so we can kill our neighbors should they come asking for help? If your neighbors come to you and ask you for help, do whatever you can to help them.

A major source of the ego's off-balanced state is its lack of
discrimination between the body and the Thoughts of God.

Thoughts of God are unacceptable to the ego,
because they clearly point to the nonexistence of the ego itself.

T-4.V.2:1–2

The end of the world will not be its destruction. The world will not be destroyed, nor attacked, nor even touched. When not one thought of sin remains, the world will be over (M-14.2:10). The illusion—held together by the ego—will cease to seem to be, then will the earth be transformed into Heaven and knowledge will replace perception.

The ego says, "In defensiveness my safety lies."
The Course says, "In defenselessness my safety lies."

Defenses are the costliest of all the prices which the ego would
exact. In them lies madness in a form so grim that hope of
sanity seems but to be an idle dream, beyond the possible.
The sense of threat the world encourages is so much deeper,
and so far beyond the frenzy and intensity
of which you can conceive, that you have no idea
of all the devastation it has wrought.

W-153.4:1–3

It is not danger that comes when defenses are laid down.
It is safety. It is peace. It is joy. And it is God.

M-4.VI.1:11–15

Finally, the day comes when we awaken, realizing that there never was anything to be afraid of.

The body they may kill, God's truth abideth still.

His Kingdom is forever.

FROM THE HYMN "A MIGHTY FORTRESS," BY MARTIN LUTHER (1483–1546),
FOUNDER OF THE PROTESTANT REFORMATION

The Kingdom is perfectly united and perfectly protected,
and the ego will not prevail against it. Amen.

T-4.III.1:12

CHAPTER 18

The Fundamental Law of Sharing

We have said that without projection there can be no anger,
but it is also true that without extension there can be no love.
These reflect a fundamental law of the mind,
and therefore one that always operates.
It is the law by which you create and were created.
It is the law that unifies the Kingdom,
and keeps it in the Mind of God.
To the ego, the law is perceived as a means of
getting rid of something it does not want.
To the Holy Spirit, it is the fundamental law of sharing, by
which you give what you value in order to keep it in your mind.

To the Holy Spirit it is the law of extension.
To the ego it is the law of deprivation.
It therefore produces abundance or scarcity,
depending on how you choose to apply it.
This choice is up to you, but it is not up to you to decide
whether or not you will utilize the law.
Every mind must project or extend,
because that is how it lives and every mind is life.

T-7.VIII.1:1–11

Let's Review Briefly

PROJECTION (CONDEMNATION) IS THE REALM OF THE EGO

When we project, we offer our judgments, interpretations, evaluations, criticism, analysis, complaints, and disparagements to the world. In so doing, we circumscribe and diminish our lives.

EXTENSION (LOVE) IS THE REALM OF SPIRIT

When we extend, we offer our love, support, appreciation, gentleness, gratitude, understanding, affection, friendship, tenderness, devotion, and kindness to the world. In so doing, we experience abundance.

The ego is delusional, unstable, and temporal.
Spirit is reasonable, stable, and everlasting.

The full appreciation of the mind's Self-fullness
makes selfishness impossible and extension inevitable.
That is why there is perfect peace in the Kingdom.
Spirit is fulfilling its function,
and only complete fulfillment is peace.

T-7.IX.4:6–8

We are being asked to exchange the wrong-minded (illusory) point of view—the projective view—of the ego for the truly natural extension of Spirit. We live in a "go for it," ego-driven world. A popular book of the early 1990s was titled, *Go for It*. If you want to have something, you get it, you take it, you buy it—it is yours. Scarcity is based on mistrust and the illusion of needs. The sense of separation from God is, however, the only "need" we need to correct. As it is, our "needs" are based on our belief in the ego-body. Generosity is based on trust. In times of war, everyone suffers. In times of peace, everyone prospers.

There is a light that this world cannot give.
Yet you can give it, as it was given you.
And as you give it, it shines forth to call you
from the world and follow it.
For this light will attract you as nothing in this world can do
And you will lay aside the world and find another.

T-13.VI.11:1–5

THE LAW OF EXTENSION AND THE LAW OF DEPRIVATION

To the ego, if I give what I have to you, I do not have it; you do. To Spirit, giving and receiving are the same. If you are not getting enough (love, for example), start giving more.

If paying is associated with giving it cannot be
perceived as loss, and the reciprocal relationship
of giving and receiving will be recognized.

T-9.II.10:3

WHAT WE PROJECT, WE BELIEVE

The abundance of Christ is the natural result of choosing to follow Him (T-1.V.6:2). How can you want anything if you already have everything? Perfect happiness is abundance—not of things but an abundance of love coming from inside.

What we project, we "give" reality to by believing it to be true (T-7.II.3:1). One of the doomsday preppers was so convinced that a major catastrophe was going to occur on that ominous 12/12/12 date that despite the protestations of his family, he moved them from their suburban home in Florida to a well-fortified, highly armored position high up on a mountaintop in Tennessee.

Belief is an ego function,
and as long as your origin is open to belief
you are regarding it from an ego viewpoint.
When teaching is no longer necessary
you will merely know God.
Belief that there is another way of perceiving
is the loftiest idea of which ego thinking is capable.
That is because it contains a hint of recognition
that the ego is not the Self.

T-4.II.4:8–11

Mormons believe that those of their faith who are worthy and make it to Heaven will have bodies identical to the bodies they had in this world. Hindus and Buddhists believe in reincarnation. Catholics believe in purgatory and different levels of Heaven and hell. The ego can believe all sorts of things, but belief does not create reality. Belief is fantasy. Belief is dreaming. Belief is illusion. Beliefs can change. Truth remains forever constant.

To the world, generosity means "giving away"
in the sense of "giving up." To the teachers of God,
it means giving away in order to keep.

M-4.VII.1:4–5

When God's love is expressed through us, there is no such thing as a winner or a loser. By giving love, we know (that is, experience and understand) what love is. The more we give love away, the more we know it ourselves. To the ego (which knows only projection), to give means to lose. We are either projecting our interpretations (or beliefs) onto the world or extending love. This basic law of the mind working in the world of the ego or the world of Spirit produces scarcity or abundance. The more love we give away, the more love comes back our way. The more we project onto the world, the more guilt we push onto the world, the guiltier we feel, The greater our scarcity, the greater our greed.

There are two major drawbacks when projecting judgments:

1. Conflict separates and cannot be shared.

No one wants to be conflicted.

A conflicted teacher is a poor teacher and a poor learner, and the transfer value of such a teacher is limited (T-7.VIII.3:4).

> *Thoughts increase by being given away.*
> *The more who believe in them the stronger they become.*
> *Everything is an idea.*
> *How, then, can giving and losing be associated?*
>
> T 5.I.2:2–5

2. What we give away comes back.

All projections boomerang. They may come back immediately or it may take a little time, but whatever we give comes back. Dishonest acts return to their maker; all false systems eventually implode, while acts of generosity bless the giver and the receiver. The ego believes that we can get rid of guilt by throwing it away. Projecting is how we keep something. Throwing judgments onto the world is how we keep them. Much of "casual" conversation consists of confirming prejudices.

> *The game of life is the game of boomerangs.*
> *Our thoughts, deeds and words return to us*
> *sooner or later, with astounding accuracy.*
>
> AMERICAN ARTIST AND AUTHOR
> FLORENCE SCOVEL SHINN (1871–1940)

A Blessing or a Bother?

On six occasions the Course says, "Ideas leave not their source." We cannot perpetuate an illusion about others without perpetuating an illusion about ourselves (T-7.VIII.4:1). If we think someone is unworthy of God's love, we must feel deep within that we, too, are unworthy.

I was on line at a grocery store when an older lady ahead of me, realizing she didn't have enough money to pay for the groceries she had placed on the checkout counter, asked the clerk to start putting back some of her items. She was trying to decide what was most essential and what she could do without. Reluctantly, she removed the cheese from her intended purchases, and I thought, "I'll bet she really likes cheese." Then the man behind her handed her a $20 bill and said to the clerk, "Put those items back in her bag."

That man walked out of the store happily, having done the right thing. How could you do something like that and not be happy? The man was enriched, as was the lady who had some of her groceries paid for. The enrichment wasn't the cheese. The enrichment was in the act of generosity. Truth sets us free and so does generosity of Spirit. We are truly generous when we do something for someone we don't know.

*Only those who have a real and lasting sense of abundance can
be truly charitable. This is obvious when you consider
what is involved.
To the ego, to give anything implies that you will have to do
without it. When you associate giving with sacrifice, you give
only because you believe that you are somehow
getting something better,
and can therefore do without the thing you give.*

T-4.II.6:1–4

Happiness comes in doing something without the need for reimbursement. When we give, needing nothing in return, it costs us nothing, while enriching us greatly. We are always giving our thoughts away. We are always projecting or extending. If we project our guilt, we experience more guilt. If we extend love, we experience more love. Whatever we give, we get, and we receive more than we give. This is the way guilt grows. This is the way love grows.

Sacrifice and Abundance

Traditional Christianity says it is necessary to sacrifice (that is, pay for) or atone for sins. Giving to get is not truly giving. Giving grudgingly is not truly giving.

> *"Giving to get" is an inescapable law of the ego,*
> *which always evaluates itself in relation to other egos.*
>
> T-4.II.6:5

One of many techniques of psychopaths is the use of generosity as a means of "giving to get." They offer us their praise to get on our good side and give in order to place us in their debt.

> *The gift of life is yours to give, because it was given you.*
> *You are unaware of your gift because you do not give it.*
> *You cannot make nothing live,*
> *since nothing cannot be enlivened.*
> *Therefore, you are not extending the gift you both "have"*
> *and "are," and so you do not know your being.*
>
> T-7.VII.5:1–4

We can give the Light the world cannot give; because it has been given to us, it is also ours to give. As we give our Light it shines. It glows! Stand in the sunlight. While the sun is warming your body, it is warming billions of other bodies in that same moment. In the same way the love of God, as reflected by the Holy Spirit, flows forth into the minds of all who are willing to receive it. Jesus, at the age of twelve, said to his parents, "Don't you understand? I have to be about my Father's business." The search for God is the ultimate business we are all called to "be about." It's gratifying business. It's good business.

> *"Many are called but few are chosen"*
> *should be, "All are called but few choose to listen."*
> *Therefore, they do not choose right. The "chosen ones"*
> *are merely those who choose right sooner.*
> *Right minds can do this now and they will find rest unto their souls.*
> *God knows you only in peace, and this is your reality.*
>
> T-3.IV.7:12–16

Abundance

One day while working as a parish minister, I went to call on Amy Clark, an older member of our church. Amy was going into the hospital the next day for an operation. While I was there, she received a call from someone offering her a ride to the hospital. "Two others," she said, "had called to make the same offer." This is a perfect example of abundance. Amy was offered more than enough help because she was a lovely lady people wanted to help. You couldn't help being in love with Amy. She had no need to worry about logistics.

One day Dolores and I met a remarkable lady at the checkout counter at a Walmart store. She was bright and cheery, with a "Hello!" and a positive affirmation about our good taste in having chosen such treasures. She said she loved retail and had been doing it for thirty-six years. She virtually lit up the place. I commented on her cheery nature, and a supervisor standing nearby turned and said that a customer had recently "written her up" for being the best sales clerk she had ever seen. I offered her my congratulations. Her job was not glamorous and she probably earned little, but she had an abundance of love to share, and everyone she met was the richer for it.

The Principle of Jen

Our task is not just to do good; it is also to acknowledge the good in our brother and sisters, simply because it is there. Confucians believe in the principle of *Jen*—at heart, everyone is fundamentally good. Just as "Everyone already knows," "Everyone is already good." There is a light in everyone, even the psychopaths who hide it so well within their dreams. There is no one in whom the light has gone out completely.

> *In spite of everything I still believe*
> *that people are really good at heart.*
> *I simply can't build up my hopes on a foundation*
> *consisting of confusion, misery and death.*
>
> HOLOCAUST VICTIM ANNE FRANK (1929–1941)

In the 1991 movie *Regarding Henry,* Harrison Ford plays the part of a tough, unprincipled lawyer who gets shot in the head. Slowly, he regains his memory and ability to work, but he comes back from his injury a changed man. Having forgotten the training the world gave him, he comes back innocent. He is no longer clever, cold, and calculating. When he discovers the underhanded practices of the law firm he works for, he goes for the truth and undoes the injustices he previously wrought in exchange for wealth.

Today I learn the law of love;
that what I give my brother is my gift to me.

W-344

Something is needed to awaken us from the ego's insane dream. Although everyone has a natural impulse to do good, the right-minded part of us can become so buried by wrong-minded thoughts of sin, guilt, and fear that we have a hard time accessing, or remembering, our true Self. To remember who we are, we must look at the dark side of the ego-self and let it go in order to remember our innocence.

When a brother acts insanely,
he is offering you an opportunity to bless him.
His need is yours.
You need the blessing you can offer him.
There is no way for you to have it except by giving it.
This is the law of God, and it has no exceptions.
What you deny you lack, not because it is lacking,
but because you have denied it in another
and are therefore not aware of it in yourself.

T-7.VII.2:1–6

We have the power to remember Heaven, and we claim this power for ourselves and others as we become vigilant for God's Kingdom, blessing both our brothers and ourselves.

You were given everything when you were created,
just as everyone was.

T-1.IV.3:7

The Light of Love

When we are "in love," we have a deeper awareness of our loved one's needs, and we find it easy to be generous. We give our love away, and more love comes back our way. The more love we extend, the greater our capacity for love grows. Marriages fail when one or both partners stop giving, stop nurturing, stop extending love. If each partner gives 100 percent to the relationship, there is an abundance of what's needed to sustain the relationship.

To know the light of love is to be the light of love. The more we give love, the more love's presence can come into the mind as evident in my friend Dr. Rod Chelberg's experience with "light." Rod is in charge of 184 patients in four nursing homes in Bangor, Maine.

When I was doing my rounds on the dementia unit, I saw all the patients in my mind. They were all trapped in their bodies and they could not let go. They had sort of a feedback loop that kept them trapped here with no way to communicate. I stood there and was filled with love and compassion for all that I saw. We were all connected via our mind.

I allowed the love to flow and it was so beautiful. We were all deeply touched. The noisiness of the place settled down for a while as the blanket of peace and love settled on us. I stood there in awe. In a holy instant, we were all blessed. I love these events. It was beautiful and amazing at the same time. Here is where the white light shined. I am a lucky man.

Giving Our Forgiveness

There is nothing the world needs more than our forgiveness: Only as we forgive do we understand forgiveness. For-give-ness, like all giving, is always reciprocal. Freely giving, without letting the left hand know what the right hand is doing, we receive in ways immeasurable in ordinary terms.

The teacher of God is generous out of Self-interest.
This does not refer, however,
to the self of which the world speaks.
The teacher of God does not want anything he cannot give away,
because he realizes it would be valueless to him by definition. What would he
want it "for"? He could only lose because of it.
He could not gain. Therefore he does not seek what only he
could keep, because that is a guarantee of loss.
He does not want to suffer. Why should he ensure himself pain?
But he does want to keep for himself all things that are of God,
and therefore for His Son.
These are the things that belong to him.
These he can give away in true generosity,
protecting them forever for himself.

M-4.VII.2:1–12

CHAPTER 19

Patience and Happiness

Some say that my teaching is nonsense.
Others call it lofty but impractical.
But to those who have looked inside themselves,
this nonsense makes perfect sense.
And to those who put it into practice,
this loftiness has roots that go deep.

I have just three things to teach:
simplicity, patience, compassion.
These three are your greatest treasures.
Simple in action and in thoughts,
you return to the source of being.
Patient with both friends and enemies,
you accord with the way things are.
Compassionate toward yourself,
you reconcile with all beings in the world.

FROM THE *TAO TE CHING*, BY LAO TZU

Patience is natural to those who trust.
Sure of the ultimate interpretation of all things in time,
no outcome already seen or yet to come can cause them fear.

M-4.VIII.1:9—10

A man's car stalled in heavy traffic just as the traffic light turned green. All his efforts to start the engine failed, and a chorus of honking behind him made matters worse. He finally got out of his car, walked back to the driver behind him, and said, "I'm sorry, but I can't seem to get my car started. Could you do me a favor? Go up and give it a try, and I'll stay here and blow your horn."

Patience, like trust, honesty, gentleness, and joy, is a "state of mind." The ego "lives" in a story, a drama, a soap opera. "Happily ever after" does not work in a soap opera or in reality TV. The ego must worry or face certain death. "Happily ever after" only works in eternity. God has no ego . . . therefore, no problems.

> *Tribulation does not make people impatient,*
> *but proves that they are impatient.*
>
> GERMAN PROTESTANT REFORMER
> MARTIN LUTHER

Simplicity, Patience, Compassion

I knew a man who worked in a global shipping company on one of the upper floors of the Empire State Building in New York City. Each day he talked with people all over the world. He dealt with millions of dollars in sales and had many employees who worked for and with him. One day at a party, we were sitting on a couch together talking and he told me that his dream was to be a small-town librarian He dreamed of living a simple life, someplace where he could walk to work down a tree-lined street. "Ah, that," he said, "that would be the life." Later I wondered, if he were a librarian in a small town, would he start dreaming of working in the Empire State Building?

> *The Holy Spirit, seeing where you are but knowing you*
> *are elsewhere, begins His lesson in simplicity*

with the fundamental teaching that truth is true.
This is the hardest lesson you will ever learn,
and in the end the only one.
Simplicity is very difficult for twisted minds.

T-14.II.2:1–3

The hardest lesson we will ever learn is this: What was never true is not true now. There are thousands of philosophies, psychologies, and religious systems designed to "figure things out." The closest I've come to truth is in mysticism, Buddhism, and, of course, the Course. Recognizing that truth is true brings the incredible realization that the so-called "error" (guilt) never occurred.

I have said that the last step
in the reawakening of knowledge is taken by God.
This is true, but it is hard to explain in words
because words are symbols,
and nothing that is true need be explained.
However, the Holy Spirit has the task of translating the useless
into the useful, the meaningless into the meaningful,
and the temporary into the timeless.

T-7.I.6:3–5

In a state of timelessness, things just are and they are fine. We made time to take the place of timelessness, and then we began making ourselves not as we are, but, rather, as we wished ourselves to be. Atheism is a dead end, since all hope is ours because of God. As much as the ego might try, there is no getting away from God and, in the end, the ego knows it.

Those who are certain of the outcome
can afford to wait, and wait without anxiety.

M-4.VIII.1:1

Patience rests on trust and certainty of the outcome. To be impatient is to be a victim of time. When we lack patience, we believe peace of mind depends on something external.

Someone once said that the secret of patience is doing something else in the meantime. Waiting in line is a good time to "do something else," such as meditate. The moment we notice we're becoming impatient, we can say to ourselves, "I could practice patience now! This line isn't going to move for a while. I can wait with a peaceful mind or with a distressed mind." While waiting, observe your own serenity and calmness. Patience enables awareness and attention. Many things can be seen with patience. Take time. Look around. Patience is not lifeless waiting. We can see and be One-minded with the other folks in line, our brothers and sisters. Remember that every loving thought held in any part of the Sonship belongs to every part of the Sonship.

Being patient does not mean being irresponsible, ignoring time, being lackadaisical, arriving late for work, or missing appointments. Living within time, we obey the laws of time, just as we obey the laws of physics or the laws of the society of which we are a part—" . . . giving to Caesar that which is Caesar's and to God that which is God's."

There is no stress or anxiety in patience. If the cat doesn't go out when the door is opened or a child takes a long time to get ready, I can put a foot behind the cat and gently push him out the door or tell the child that we're ready to go without being the least bit upset or angry.

Complaining is nothing, fame is nothing.
Openness, patience, receptivity, solitude is everything.

BOHEMIAN-AUSTRIAN POET RAINER MARIA RILKE (1875–1926)

When we drive with a GPS and happen to go off course or make a wrong turn, the GPS simply informs us that it is "recalculating." In the same way, no matter how many times we go off course, God never scolds or shames us. The Holy Spirit never says, "What are you doing? I told you to go right and you went left." Instead, the Holy Spirit gently and consistently continues to offer us the right guidance. He knows, after all, we'll eventually return home, because:

Ideas leave not their source.
We cannot help but do the Course.

God is infinitely patient. We wander about doing all sorts of things other than our Father's will, yet God does not desert us. The introduction to the Course says it is a required course, but the time we take to do it is voluntary. If God is infinitely patient with us, can't we be a bit more patient with our brothers and sisters?

Your patience with your brother is your patience with yourself.
Is not a child of God worth patience?
I have shown you infinite patience because my will is that of our
Father, from Whom I learned of infinite patience.
His Voice was in me as It is in you, speaking for patience
towards the Sonship in the Name of its Creator.

T-5.VI.11:4–7

No matter how long it may take us to come around and pay attention, no matter how far we may wander, no matter how much we may block our ears, the Holy Spirit's voice gently calls us to "choose once again." There is great power in the acceptance, patience, perseverance, and consistency that enables us to break through the illusions that seemingly bind us.

Only infinite patience produces immediate effects.
This is the way in which time is exchanged for eternity.
Infinite patience calls upon infinite love,
and by producing results now it renders time unnecessary.

T-5.VI.12:1–3

It is possible to be awake now. Not for a single second do we need to wait. To be impatient is to be in a hurry. Living in the present, there is nothing to be in a hurry for. There is nowhere else to be. After all, no matter where you go— there you are. What matters is where the mind is. British Prime Minister Benjamin Disraeli (1804–1881) held that the secret of accomplishment consisted in mastering your subject. Such mastery was attainable only through continual application and study. Mastery of the Course comes with consistent, patient application and study. The complexities that bind us in knots have taken a lifetime to develop; letting them go is often a slow process. The miracle, however, speeds up that process by transcending time.

Answers are available to us now, but we need patience to see the results. Success with the Course, as with most things, requires that we "hang in there," and be quiet long enough to hear the still, small voice of God. Why do we say that someone has the patience of a saint unless patience is saintly? Only when the mind is nonprojective can we experience the peace of God.

Face your deficiencies and acknowledge them;
but do not let them master you.
Let them teach you patience, sweetness, insight.

HELEN KELLER

Patience waits for the right time, the right principle, and the right way to act. It understands that everyone fails, and it sees no benefit in rushing. When a mistake is made, patience allows us more time to correct the error. Patience gives us the ability to hold on in difficult times. The Kingdom of Heaven quietly, patiently awaits our return.

Patience is not a virtue. It is an achievement.

RUSSIAN AUTHOR VERA NAZARIAN
(1966–PRESENT)

Time, like the body, is a "learning device" and time teaches patience. The older we are, especially after we are retired, the more time we have to be patient. Ultimately time has no meaning. Only love endures forever.

Focus

According to a study on happiness, conducted by a group of psychologists, one of the traits that characterizes happy people is their ability to focus. Happy people live in the moment, without dwelling on the past or worrying about the future. Being focused enables one to be "in the flow." I once heard Ken Wapnick say that he had a good ability to focus, and I'm sure that's so; otherwise, he could not accomplish all that he does.

There's so much to do in a day,
if I didn't pray two hours a day,
I don't know how I would get it all done.

AMERICAN CIVIL RIGHTS LEADER
DR. MARTIN LUTHER KING JR. (1929–1968)

Eternity and peace are as closely related as are time and war.

T-5.III.8:13

Wars can only take place in time where there is "time" to plan for war. God does not attack. Attack can only be of the ego.

The word "jihad" has nowhere been used in the Qur'an to mean war....
It means "struggle." The action most consistently called for
in the Qur'an is the exercise of patience.

MAULANA WAHIDUDDIN KHAN (1925–PRESENT)

Let nothing disturb you, Let nothing frighten you,
All things are passing away: God never changes.
Patience obtains all things: Whoever has God lacks nothing;
God alone suffices.

—SAINT TERESA OF ÁVILA

CHAPTER 20

Where Is Your Faith?

The truth is true.
Nothing else matters, nothing else is real,
and everything beside it is not there.
Let Me make the one distinction for
you that you cannot make, but need to learn.
Your faith in nothing is deceiving you.
Offer your faith to Me,
and I will place it gently in the holy place where it belongs.
You will find no deception there, but only the simple truth.
And you will love it because you will understand it.

T-14.II.3:1–9

The Epileptic Boy

As they were rejoining the crowd, a man came up to him
and went down on his knees before him. "Lord," he said, "take
pity on my son: he is a lunatic and in a wretched state; he is
always falling into the fire or into the water. I took him to your
disciples and they were unable to cure him."
Jesus said in reply, "Bring him here to me."
And when Jesus rebuked it, the devil came out of the boy,
who was cured from that moment.

Then the disciples came privately to Jesus.
"Why were we unable to cast it out?" they asked.
"Because, you have little faith. I tell you solemnly, if your
faith were the size of a mustard seed you could say to this
mountain, "Move from here to there," and it would move;
nothing would be impossible for you."

MATTHEW 17:14–20

The disciples couldn't cure the epileptic boy because they didn't believe that they could, and the boy knew it. Often when Jesus effects a cure, before the healing occurs the Gospel says, "and Jesus looked at him and loved him." Everyone was afraid of the epileptic boy because no one knew when he might have a seizure. Jesus looked at him not with fear in his eyes but with love. He saw the innocence within and the boy for the first time saw that indeed he could be seen as whole.

Healing reflects our joint will.
This is obvious when you consider what healing is for.
Healing is the way in which the separation is overcome.
Separation is overcome by union.
It cannot be overcome by separating.
The decision to unite must be unequivocal,
or the mind itself is divided and not whole.

T-8.IV.5:1–6

In Jesus's day, illness such as epilepsy was considered the work of the devil. What other possible explanation could there be? People who were otherwise normal would suddenly change and do things contrary to their everyday behavior. It had to be explained somehow, and who knew anything about misfirings in the cerebral cortex? It was easy to blame an external source: it seemed as though he were possessed by a demon.

The father in this story was particularly concerned about his son, because the boy would hurt himself by falling into a fire or water. The disciples tried to cure him but were unsuccessful. When they wondered about the reason for their failure, Jesus told them it was because they lacked faith.

> *I have asked you to perform miracles, and have made it clear*
> *that miracles are natural, corrective, healing and universal.*
> *There is nothing they cannot do,*
> *but they cannot be performed in the spirit of doubt or fear.*
>
> T-2.II.2–3

Faithfulness means *knowing* that God's voice is true. God knows it, but we, too, must know it; otherwise, we will not effect a cure. Before we can "give" faith, we must have faith.

Turning Again for Home

In the story of every hero or heroine, there occurs an inevitable turning point. The hero begins to head for home after a long, arduous, possibly futile journey, when, at the point of greatest despair, he says, "I will no longer run away. I will do what God is asking."

Eventually, everyone begins to see the world as a dream. However, rather than become defensive and complain about the dream, we resist the urge to go back to sleep and we struggle to awaken. To know perfect happiness, we need not only awaken but we need to stay awake. We need to head for home. The body was purposely created so that we would be so distracted by it, and forget we had a mind that could remember God.

Faith is implicit in the acceptance of the Holy Spirit's purpose.

T-17.VI.6:2

Depression occurs when Spirit is ignored. Then only the tyrannical ego rules. The ego is nonexistent, even though it appears to be real and cruel, beating us up, persuading us that we are no good, and convincing us that there is no hope of happiness or release from the misery of our sins.

I am teaching you to associate misery with the ego and joy with the spirit. You have taught yourself the opposite.

T-4.VI.5:6

To say "I am under no laws but God's" (W-76) is a statement of freedom from tyranny. It is an acknowledgment that God has given us a way to get home. Forgetfulness, sleep, and death are the ego's mechanisms of dealing with the punitive pressures of guilt. "Go unconscious, have another beer, take another Xanax, pour another glass of wine." As British musician John Lennon said, "Living is easy with eyes closed." Whatever you do, "Don't look at what you've buried."

The theme song of the ego is "I'll Do It My Way," but "my way" can be very lonely and unfulfilling. Accepting our part in God's Plan for Salvation, life opens up. All that is required is faithfulness and willingness to do it God's way. Don't resist His plan. Believe that God is going to help.

The drought from the previous winter threatened the crops in a village in Crete. The priest told his flock: "There isn't anything that will save us, except a litany for rain. Go to your homes, fast during the week, believe, and come on Sunday for the litany of rain." The villagers obeyed their priest. They fasted during the week and returned to church on Sunday morning. But as soon as the priest saw them, he became furious. He said, "Go away! I will not do the litany. You do not believe!" "But Father," they protested, "we fasted and we believe." "If you believe," said the priest, "where are your umbrellas?"

> *The goal of truth requires faith.*
> *Faith is implicit in the acceptance of the Holy Spirit's purpose,*
> *and this faith is all-inclusive.*
> *Where the goal of truth is set, there faith must be.*

T-17.VI.6:1–3

We can place our faith in the ego and its ability to manipulate its way through the world, or we can place our faith in the Holy Spirit. The choice is obvious! Place faith in the ego and run into trouble. Placing faith in the Holy Spirit, we enjoy an optimistic outlook and recognize all that is holy in our brothers.

Rose Kennedy, the mother of John, Robert, Ted, and six other children, suffered greatly with much loss in her life. When asked what kept her going in light of so much tragedy, she answered, "my faith." She was talking about her faith as a Catholic. No matter the tradition, what matters is faith. While Mother Teresa spoke of Jesus very differently from the Jesus we met in the Course, only the theology is different and difference doesn't matter. We keep learning this lesson over and over again in all our relationships. A universal theology is impossible. A universal experience is not only possible but necessary (CIn.2:5). What matters is to have faith. Because He always has, God will see us through. Holiness cannot be seen except through faith (T-17.VIII.4:3). With faith, regardless of how dire any situation seems to be, faith can carry us through the toughest assignments.

> *Faith and desire go hand in hand*
> *for everyone believes in what he wants.*

T-21.II.8:6

Realistic Optimism

Optimism is not a word used in the Course. *Faith* is a better term. When a scientist performs an experiment, she begins with a vision of what she expects to find. Psychologist Erich Fromm talked about what he called "rational vision." The history of science is full of examples of people of faith and vision who placed their faith in an outcome they knew to be true, even if they were lacking proof.

Bruno, Copernicus, Kepler, and Galileo all held to their vision that the sun—not the earth—was the center of the solar system. They maintained their faith, knowing they were right, even though the Church burned Bruno at the stake, refused to allow Copernicus's works to be published, and forced Galileo to recant his teachings.

Saying it the way it really is helps to make it real. This is one of the reasons for the workbook of the Course. The way it really is is the way it is in Heaven. Nothing else exists. Living life in accordance with God's will, we manifest God's will.

> *I am a man of faith. My reliance is solely on God.*
>
> INDIAN CIVIL RIGHTS LEADER
> MAHATMA GANDHI (1869–1948)

Faithlessness

When we see the world as fearful and threatening, we place our faith in lawyers, insurance policies, copyrights, patents, money, financial markets, stocks and bonds, doctors, guard dogs, surveillance cameras, guns, nuclear arms, and more. I'm not saying we shouldn't have insurance, lock our doors, or save money. None of these things, however, provide lasting security. The only true security comes in knowing the truth of God.

Faithlessness is not a lack of faith, but faith in nothing.

T-21.III.5:2

To place faith in the ego is to place faith in nothing. The greatest expression of faithlessness we can have is to affirm the ego and deny God.

Faithlessness is the servant of illusion (T-17.VII.5:5).

Faithlessness is sickness. It is sadness. It is pain.

Faithlessness is seeing a brother as a body.

Faithlessness is a lack of vision.

Faithlessness is depressing.

There is no problem in any situation that faith will not solve.

T-17.VII.2:1

Faith makes miracles possible. Miracles are "born" of faith. At the end of each of his healings, Jesus would say, "Your faith has made you whole." The first principle of the Course is that there is no order of difficulty among miracles. In faithlessness the mind is seen as impotent. The fact that miracles do not occur is unnatural. It is *natural* to be happy. It is *natural* for things to work out for the best.

There is no cause for faithlessness, but there "is" cause for faith.

T-17.VII.8:7

When we solve a problem that needs solving, it's best to do it with God. Failure often follows faithlessness.

Faithlessness brought to faith will never interfere with truth.
But faithlessness used "against" truth will always destroy faith.

T-17.VIII.3:9–10

Faith is the opposite of fear,
as much a part of love as fear is of attack.

T-19.I.10:1

Fostering Faith

During the 1970s, I had the opportunity to work with a wise guide and teacher—Salvador Roquet, MD (1920–1995), a Mexican psychiatrist. Salvador gained his wisdom from studying Western medicine, along with the shamanism of his native Mexico. On two different occasions my friend Shanti Rica Josephs and I ventured to Mexico to work with him and on two occasions he came to New York to work with a group of active seekers.

I once went to Salvador to talk about a problem that I struggling with. He looked at me confidently and said, "You will let it go." I was struck by his simple faith, and I wanted to believe him. It took some time but I later let go of my struggle with that particular issue. In a similar way, whenever I was a bit down or disheartened, Helen Schucman would encourage my faith, assuring me that on a deeper level all things happen for a right reason and she was sure I would make the right decision. As it says at the end of the movie *The Best Exotic Marigold Hotel:* "Everything will be all right in the end. . . . If it's not all right, it's not the end."

Placing our faith and trust in God and going forward, faith grows ever more deeply. As Mahatma Gandhi said, "Faith is not something to grasp; it is a state to grow into." Just as Salvador and Helen placed their faith in me, so too is it to my pleasant task to foster faith in those who come to me for guidance. When someone comes to me struggling with an an addiction, and he believes he will not be able to overcome that addiction, I tell him that I believe he will overcome the addiction. Because he will. God also has complete faith in us, and as we trust Him and place our faith in Him, we are healed and led home. Everyone is destined to become enlightened, so let's get on with it!

> *When a brother behaves insanely,*
> *you can heal him only by perceiving the sanity in him.*
> *If you perceive his errors and accept them,*
> *you are accepting yours.*
>
> T-9.III.5:1—2

The epileptic boy was thought to be possessed by a demon. He must have heard other people saying he was possessed. Having heard it, he must have believed it himself. He had these seizures where he would fall down, sometimes into fire or water, and he seemed to be possessed. How did Jesus heal him?

> *The mind can make the belief in separation very real*
> *and very fearful, and this belief "is" the "devil."*
>
> T-3.VII.5:1

Jesus looked at him with love, and the boy realized that he could be whole. It was not the devil that was dispelled from him; it was fear. The disciples were unable to see the boy as whole. They must have been afraid and they questioned their ability to effect a cure. Only someone who saw the boy as whole could help him. God sees us as whole because He knows we are whole. He sees us as His children, not helpless sleeping ego-bound bodies of flesh. Remember, "God creates only mind awake" (W-167.8:1). In God's eyes we are perfect because we always have been perfect. The message of the Course is that it is possible for us to see ourselves as God does. It is then, and only then, that we will be completely healed and whole.

There is nothing faith cannot forgive.

T-19.I.14:4

Faith and Forgiveness

Faith and forgiveness go hand in hand. In faith there is no fear, no need to hold on to the unessential. Faith is a tool for the hero on the journey. It is a key to the Kingdom, the password that grants admission to eternal life. The more we rest in faith and rely on the guidance of the Holy Spirit, the more our vision is transformed, the more we experience the peace of God.

The mind can serve ego or Spirit. We can, however, only serve one master. Only from the realm of Spirit can we create. To be lacking in faith is depressing. To be lacking in faith is to believe in chains. In faith we abandon deprivation in favor of the abundance that belongs to us (T-1.IV.4:8). Faith is rational vision. It is realistic optimism. It is seeing the good. It is expecting the good. It is experiencing the good.

What is dedicated to truth as its only goal
is brought to truth by faith.

T-19.I.1:3

Faithlessness is dedicated to illusion, but faith is dedicated to truth. Faith, thus, carries us past illusion.

Where Is Your Faith?

Are we going to place our faith in the ego, which will fail, or will we let go and trust the guidance of the Holy Spirit? We can trust the power of our right mind or choose to believe that we will never be whole. Jesus tells us we can do even greater works than He, so why don't we? We are all children of God, all capable of the expression and experience of the Kingdom of Heaven. Faithlessness is trusting in the ego and the ego is nothing. God is the all. He is everything. As we place faith in Him, we discover richness beyond measure, abundance, and eternal life.

> *What He [the Holy Spirit] enables you to do*
> *is clearly not of this world, for miracles violate*
> *every law of reality as this world judges it.*
> *Every law of time and space, of magnitude and mass is transcended,*
> *for what the Holy Spirit enables you to do is clearly beyond all of them.*
> *Perceiving His results, you will understand*
> *where He must be, and finally know what He is.*

T-12.VII.3:2—4

> *There is no problem in any situation that faith will not solve.*

T-17.VII.2:1

CHAPTER 21

The Centrality of Open-Mindedness

The centrality of open-mindedness,
perhaps the last of the attributes the teacher of God acquires,
is easily understood
when its relation to forgiveness is recognized.

M-4.X.1:1

Open-mindedness is "perhaps the last of the attributes a teacher of God acquires." Why the last? If it is so central, why is it not the first? Open-mindedness is the last because we have to hone our way down to the central core of perfect clarity that total open-mindedness provides, and we need tools like trust, honesty, tolerance, patience, and the other attributes of a teacher of God as the means for reaching that perfect vision found only in complete open-mindedness.

Open-mindedness is fundamental to the teaching of Hinduism, Buddhism, and Taoism. The Indian sage Ramakrishna (1836–1886), who explored in depth the teachings of Islam, Christianity, and Hinduism, taught that in spite of their differences, all religions are valid and true. They all ultimately lead to God. Buddhism and Taoism, in particular, speak of the importance of a still, quiet, lucid—that is, an uncluttered—mind.

Try then, today, to begin to learn how to look on all things
with love, appreciation and open-mindedness.

W-29.3:1

What if it were possible to look upon "all things," with nothing but *love, appreciation, and open-mindedness?* The ego-mind is, by definition, closed, limited, restricted to a little space within itself. It sees only itself. Knowing only its own judgments and projections, it knows nothing else. The following quote from American transcendentalist Ralph Waldo Emerson (1803–1882) is an almost perfect description of a mystical experience. It is also a description of complete open-mindedness.

> *Standing on the bare ground,*
> *my head bathed by the blithe air*
> *and uplifted into infinite space—*
> *all mean egotism vanishes.*
> *I become a transparent eyeball.*
> **I am nothing. I see all.**
> *The currents of the Universal Being circulate through me.*
> *I am part and parcel of God.*

Open-mindedness has no investment in how the world is supposed to look. Open-mindedness has no predetermined, expected, or required outcome. Picture open-mindedness as a vast, open, empty space and yourself as a point of centrality in the heart of this vastness. Perfect clarity is only possible when there are *no blocks* to the awareness of love's presence—no clouds, no fog, no haze obscure true perception. Being completely open-minded, there are no complexes, no hang-ups, no knots within one's psyche.

One of the lines I quote most often from the Course is: "Let him be

what he is, and seek not to make of love an enemy" (T-19.IV.D.13:8). Let
her be who she is. Let "it" (the situation) be what it is. Let the world be
what it is. Letting the world be what it is brings infinite peace.

> *Eternity is one time, its only dimension being "always."*
> *This cannot mean anything to you until you remember*
> *God's open Arms, and finally know His open Mind.*
> *Like Him, "you" are "always";*
> *in His Mind and with a mind like His.*
> *In your open mind are your creations,*
> *in perfect communication born of perfect understanding.*

> T-9.VI.7:1–4

Private Thoughts and Perfect Communication

Private thoughts are blocks to the awareness of Love's presence. They
are "my" thoughts related to guilt, feelings of superiority and inferiority,
fantasies, and "dreaming of the world." Private thoughts (secret sins
and hidden hates) block perfect communication. Abandoning private
thoughts does not mean we need to go around boring the world with our
private thoughts. Abandoning private thoughts means that there are no
thoughts we *need* to keep hidden.

> *The quiet light in which the Holy Spirit dwells within you*
> *is merely perfect openness, in which nothing is hidden*
> *and therefore nothing is fearful.*

> T-14.VI.2:1

Perfect Alignment

To get to perfect happiness, we need to establish perfect communication. We need to be focused on following GPS at all times and not wander off into ego distractions.

> *This convergence seems to be far in the future*
> *only because your mind is not in perfect alignment with the*
> *idea, and therefore does not want it now.*
>
> T-6.II.9.8

Perfect happiness can only come to a mind completely open and transparent. If my mind is completely open, I don't have to think about what to say; it is "given."

> *As condemnation judges the Son of God as evil,*
> *so open-mindedness permits him to be judged*
> *by the Voice for God on His behalf.*
>
> M-101:4

Acceptance Is Open-Mindedness

Nothing need upset you. Nothing need disgust you. Things are what they are. Are baby's diapers disgusting? As a farm boy, I learned to accept many things as they were, like a cow defecating while I was trying to milk her. Complete open-mindedness is perhaps the last attribute the teacher of God acquires. Total open-mindedness means freedom from all judgment. Open-mindedness invites God in. Complete open-mindedness means total acceptance of the role God would have us fill.

> *You are very fearful of everything you have*
> *perceived but have refused to accept.*

You believe that, because you have refused to accept it,
you have lost control over it.
This is why you see it in nightmares, or in pleasant
disguises in what seem to be your happier dreams.
Nothing that you have refused to accept
can be brought into awareness.
It is not dangerous in itself,
but you have made it seem dangerous to you.

T-3.VI.4:1–5

As minds open and we give up on fantasy stories and become progressively more receptive, we experience increasing inspiration. We cannot have perfect communication if we harbor private thoughts. The holy instant is a moment of perfect communication and total open-mindedness enables perfect happiness.

Judgment Closes the Mind

Just as judgment shuts the mind, open-mindedness invites inspiration and revelation (M-4.X.1:3). If there is anything that keeps me from God, it is judgment. God has created us as immaculate. To know God, I must see the immaculate nature of every brother and sister. We are asked to attain to the vision of Christ. We do it through forgiveness—through a complete letting go of everything, through not bringing into the present one thought the past has taught, nor one belief ever learned before from anything (W-189.7:4). Condemnation judges the Son of God as evil. Open-mindedness permits him to be judged by God, who judges perfectly.

The ego never looks on anything with perfect honesty. Without perfect honesty, the mind remains closed. When other people "hide" their thoughts from us, or we "hide" from them, we "feel" as though something is amiss. We do not know what is amiss, but our sense is that something is "not quite right."

Complete open-mindedness invites true perception and perfect communication. During the late 1960s, I used to make retreats at New Mellcray Abbey, a Trappist's Monastery, near Dubuque, Iowa. The monks there developed an ability to communicate telepathically. One day, I was sitting in the yard reading while two monks were repairing a stone wall. A bird was singing prettily in an adjacent tree. One monk stopped and looked up at the bird. Then the other monk looked up as well. They then looked at each other and smiled as though they had just said, "How nice" to each other. Then they went back to working on the wall. No words had been exchanged, yet they had clearly communicated. I noticed many similar instances of nonverbal communication at New Melleray. Language is acquired and in that sense it is artificial and not native to the heart.

Never forget that the Holy Spirit
does not depend on your words.
He understands the requests of your heart, and answers them.

M-296:1

God knows us in our purity and innocence. Sensitivity to inner guidance (that is, perfect communication) requires the quietness of open-mindedness. The more we keep hidden, the more we want to hide our thoughts, the more terrified we become of the world and of God. If we have nothing to hide, it doesn't matter if someone else knows what we are thinking.

Every thought you would keep hidden
shuts communication off, because you would have it so.
It is impossible to recognize perfect communication

while breaking communication holds value to you.
Ask yourself honestly,
"Would I want to have perfect communication,
and am I wholly willing to let everything
that interferes with it go forever?"

T-15.IV.8:1–3

In her book *Mutant Message Down Under,* Marlo Morgan (1937–present) said that, according to the Aborigines, "Westerners" cannot read each other's minds because they do so much hiding. The ego's whole thought system blocks love and therefore our ability to experience joy. Hiding in this way keeps us feeling unfulfilled (T-7.IX.3.5).

Salvation, according to the ego, consists in keeping our thoughts to ourselves. This bolsters the ego by increasing feelings of isolation, aloneness, fear, and the sense of being broken off from the whole. Those who feel broken off from the whole often become withdrawn, and in this reclusiveness lies the potential for mental illness and antisocial behavior. Those who are very fragmented often see themselves as victims of the world and seek to lash out at the world. We see such violence in the lives of serial killers, young men who set off bombs or go on indiscriminate killing sprees, tyrants who engage in genocide, and charismatic sociopaths who (in service of the ego) are charming and skilled in manipulation.

How Do We Find Peace of Mind?

In the early 1820s the Quakers lobbied the Pennsylvania legislature to build a prison based on the idea of reform through solitude and inner reflection. The Quakers assumed that an inmate's conscience, given enough time alone, would make him penitent (hence the new word *penitentiary*). Prisoners were placed in cells with nothing to do—no work, no reading materials, nothing. They were not allowed to sing, whistle, have visitors, see a newspaper, or hear from any source about the outside world. If prisoners were caught communicating with other inmates by, for example, tapping on a pipe, they were denied food and blankets and secluded in a dark, completely empty cell. Hoods were placed over inmates' heads when they were out of their prison cells so they could not see other inmates.

If you were a prisoner at Eastern State Penitentiary in Philadelphia, you went into your cell and you stayed there. You saw no one and you spoke to no one. No love or compassion was to be given to the prisoners. Being treated so inhumanely, they didn't find the Mind; they lost their minds. If the Son of God "is lost in guilt, alone in a dark world where pain is pressing everywhere upon him from without" (T-13.X.8:3), we should not be surprised that the result is madness.

> *The belief in guilt must lead to the belief in hell,*
> *and always does. . . .*
> *For no one who considers himself as deserving of hell*
> *can believe that punishment will end in peace.*
>
> T-15.I.6:5&7

The Quakers thought that by being placed in isolation an inmate would go within and find his soul nature. That might work well for a monk who voluntarily sought silence or for the Quakers themselves; however, for the prisoners at Eastern State Penitentiary, already riddled with guilt, the result of living in hell and seeing no way out was insanity.

> *Truth does not struggle against ignorance,*
> *and love does not attack fear.*
>
> T-14.VII.5:2

Traditional religion is riddled with rights and wrongs and damnation to hell if you do it wrong. Even as a child, I could not understand the teaching of my then-Baptist church—why people should be condemned to the eternal fires of hell because they were deficient in decision making.

Eskimo: "If I did not know about sin, would I still go to hell?"

Missionary priest: "No, not if you did not know."

Eskimo: "Then why did you tell me?"

A divided, closed mind is defensive. An open mind is receptive. When we are angry, we shut ourselves off from others. We cross our arms and we close our fists. Just as open-mindedness is a freeing experience, closing the mind locks us within. Open-mindedness allows the Holy Spirit to work through us. The divided, closed mind establishes that the ego is in charge. Open-mindedness embraces truth, love, and awareness of God and the Holy Spirit.

As the projection of guilt upon him would send him to hell,
so open-mindedness lets Christ's image be extended to him.
Only the open-minded can be at peace,
for they alone see reason for it.

M-4.X.1:5–6

As God loves everyone without judgment, the open mind accepts everything. Accepting everything, we love everything. If I project my guilt onto you and damn you to hell, all I see is hell. When I choose to let go of my judgments, the image and awareness of Christ comes through.

How do the open-minded forgive?
They have let go all things that would prevent forgiveness.

M-4.X.2:1

Forgiveness or Undoing

"Forgiveness does not do anything! It merely looks, and waits, and judges not" (W-pii.1.4:1). It undoes. It clears away the mess. It opens the mind. Forgiveness removes "mind clutter" and what interferes with our awareness of Love's presence. Just looking and "seeing"—truly seeing— opens the door. It is not necessary to seek what is true. It is necessary to recognize what is false (T-16.IV.6:1–2).

The ego knows a lot more about what is false than about what is true. We have been living with the false for so long, we think it *is* true. We do not have to "figure out" what is true. All we have to do is to join with the Holy Spirit in our right mind, and allow His love, through forgiveness, to undo what is not true.

The false is what we feel guilty about. The false is whatever is bothering us. It is the thing we are afraid to talk about. Removing the interference (of lies and guilt) through forgiveness is all that is needed. Once the lie is set aside, the love that is already there can come to the fore. Judging, evaluating, blaming, and accusing—our attacking, our aggression, and our guilt—all keep us from the truth.

> They "the open-minded" have in truth abandoned the world,
> and let it be restored to them in newness and in joy so glorious
> they could never have conceived of such a change.
>
> M-4.X.2:3

Perfect Vision, Perfect Innocence

My friend Tom Baker (1950–present), a Course leader in Virginia Beach, was as a young man a brother in a Trappist monastery, where silence is observed and a great deal of time is spent in chanting prayers. One morning, after some four hours of continual chanting, Tom was walking down a path on the monastery grounds just looking at the ground. All of a sudden, he said, the grass filled with light! He looked up, and the trees were also full of light. He looked over and saw a barn, and that, too, was full of light. In that moment, he said, everything he saw communicated to him, and the message was "We're happy!" Just being grass and a tree and a barn!

> *The Atonement itself radiates nothing but truth.*
> *It therefore epitomizes harmlessness and sheds only blessing.*
> *It could not do this if it arose from anything*
> *but perfect innocence.*
> *Innocence is wisdom because it is unaware of evil,*
> *and evil does not exist.*
>
> T-3.I.7:1–4

Letting It Go!

Lesson 193 from the Course says, "All things are lessons God would have me learn." With an open mind, all things are welcome because all things *are my lessons* in the life-journey process. Oftentimes, when people bring me a difficult problem I advise them to "let it go." It may be the last thing they want to hear if they are grappling with the problem, but it is so often exactly the right advice. Given some time, they can usually see that "letting it go" is the only answer.

Jesus was betrayed, beaten, abandoned, and crucified. Yet, He never saw himself as persecuted. He never got upset or angry with the disciples when they failed to understand what He had to teach. Believing that something can hurt us does not make it true. "Letting it go" is a function of open-mindedness.

> *No clouds remain to hide the face of Christ.*
> *Now is the goal achieved.*
>
> M-4.X.2:7–8

Clouds are symbols of ego illusions that block our vision. The face of Christ is a symbol of forgiveness. "Seeing the face of Christ" in our brothers or sisters doesn't mean we try to see an image of what we think Jesus looked like imprinted on someone else's face. It does mean, however, that when we look into her eyes, we see only innocence. Forgiveness changes nothing in the world of form. When we look at the world through the eyes of innocence, we see no sin in our brothers and sisters—or in ourselves.

The Course is a curriculum of undoing, and forgiveness undoes all the things the ego placed in the mind. Once the blocks to the awareness of Love's presence are undone, what is left is the love of God. This love is not learned, but remembered. Once everything that would hurt and harm us is undone, our minds are open. An open mind holds no hostility, no animosity, no bitterness. There are no attack thoughts, no feeling sorry for oneself, no clutter. Once the mind is open, once there is nothing to hide and no judgments to be made, nothing remains but peace of mind.

Our Natural Inheritance

The characteristics of a teacher of God reflect a guidance system that enables us to live in the world without reliance on the ego's thought system. When the ego's thought system is undone, what is left are the reflections of Heaven.

> It is the function of God's teachers
> to bring true learning to the world.
> Properly speaking it is unlearning that they bring,
> for that is "true learning" in the world.
>
> M-4.X.3:6–7

It is easy to choose the ego because we have so frequently chosen the ego. The ego is a sad addiction. The ego is out there in the world; it is obvious; it is involved; it does not look inside. The ego does not want to see God. To the ego God is scary. "If God wins, I lose," or so the ego thinks. Following the ego's lead, we fear that, if we turn our thoughts over to God, we will be destroyed. On an ego level this is true—the ego disappears before the face of God. What we are left with, however, is not nothing but everything—open-mindedness, oneness, and awareness of God and the Thinking of the Universe (W-52.5:7).

> *If you will lay aside the ego's voice,*
> *however loudly it may seem to call;*
> *if you will not accept its petty gifts*
> *that give you nothing that you really want;*
> *if you will listen with an open mind,*
> *that has not told you what salvation is;*
> *then you will hear the mighty Voice of truth,*
> *quiet in power, strong in stillness,*
> *and completely certain in Its messages.*
>
> W-106.1:1

When the world of sin, guilt, sickness, and sorrow disappears, we are left with peace. The Real World is Oneness. In Heaven, in reality, there is no division; there is no "good and evil." There is only Oneness.

> *Nothing is now as it was formerly.*
> *Nothing but sparkles now*
> *which seemed so dull and lifeless before.*
> *And above all are all things welcoming, for threat is gone.*
>
> M-4.X.2:4–6

True Perception Meditation

Relax for a moment.

There is nothing you need to think about—nothing.

Let the mind be completely open.

There is nothing that possesses it.

There is nothing to worry about.

There are no judgments to be made.

There is no reason to be upset or worried about anything.

Accept everything just the way it is.

Let your mind be completely open—certain, clear, and sure.

Let nothing come to disturb your peace of mind.

Open-mindedness is peace because it is uncluttered.

Say, "There is no one against whom I hold any anger."

"There is no one I would attack in any way."

When these statements are true—when the mind is completely open—we are completely free.

PART V

PRACTICING
THE PRINCIPLES

CHAPTER 22

Engaging Right-Minded Thinking

A Course in Miracles is a symbol of right-minded thinking.
Right-minded thinking helps us to be free of illusion.

DR. KEN WAPNICK

My mission was simply to unite the will of the Sonship with
the Will of the Father
by being aware of the Father's Will myself.
This is the awareness I came to give you, and
your problem in accepting it is the problem of this world.

T-8.IV.3:4–5

T his is a "course" in mind training. In the earlier exercises of the
Workbook, we find repeated use of the phrase *search your mind.*
Nearly six hundred times, the Course asks us to think. We are not
thinking; we're dreaming. Pitiful, meaningless, "private" thoughts are
not thinking. They are fantasies.

The glass in which the ego seeks to see its face is dark indeed.
How can it maintain the trick of its existence except with
mirrors? But where you look to find yourself is up to you.

T-4.IV.1:6

Fantasies and Visions

The opposite of seeing through the body's eyes (or dreaming) is knowledge. True vision (or spiritual sight) is a state free of darkness. Dreaming occurs not only in the dark, when our eyes are closed, but during the day, when our eyes are open. Truth can be revealed only in the light. Fantasy is a distorted form of vision, a consensual reality subtly maintained with smoke and mirrors—not out of any mean-spirited intent; rather, out of simple ignorance.

When we see our body's image in a mirror, it does not occur to us that we are seeing ourselves backwards, unless we're wearing a nametag. Similarly, when we look out on the world, it does not occur to us that we are seeing everything backwards. We think that what the ego sees—hostility, attacks, anger, and defensiveness—is real and our judgment is "proof" of the world's reality.

Anger attacks and defensiveness do not exist in Heaven. Heaven is reality. Everything else is a dream. Our day-to-day life—what we believe is reality—is an illusion from which we will one day awaken. When we awaken, the dream will no longer hold any meaning. It never did.

The mind should be carefully searched
for the thoughts it contains.

W-19.III.3

The mind can become the medium by which spirit creates along
the line of its own creation. If it does not freely elect to do so,
it retains its creative potential but places itself under tyrannous
rather than Authoritative control. As a result it imprisons,
because such are the dictates of tyrants.
To change your mind means to place it
at the disposal of "true" Authority.

T-1.V.5:4–7

We are to recognize erroneous thinking and find a more reasonable and loving voice—a higher, better way of seeing—above the battleground and outside the realm of the ego. As Jonathan Livingston Seagull's teacher, Sullivan, says, "The gull that sees farthest flies highest."

> *Think honestly*
> *what you have thought that God would not have*
> *thought, and what you have not thought*
> *that God would have you think.*
> *Search sincerely*
> *for what you have done and left*
> *undone accordingly, and then change your mind to think with God's.*
> *This may seem hard to do,*
> *but it is much easier than trying to think against it.*
>
> T-4.IV.2:4—7

Everything eventually fails, which goes against the will of God. Eventually, every mind gets tired of trying to go against the "One Mind." Enormous energy is wasted in trying to deny the truth. Trying to make fantasies come true is being at odds with perfection.

Miracle-Mindedness Is Right-Mindedness

We depreciate the mind when we allow the ego to run our lives. We think we are the effect of the world, but we are at all times actually the cause of the world. This makes us unhappy, because things seem to happen to us that are beyond our control. We do not acknowledge the incredible power of the mind and our ability to be happy by simply changing our thoughts. The power of the mind to make the right choice is the only power that can genuinely help us. We all have egos, but we also have the ability to choose the guidance of Spirit.

Installing a Mental Trip-Switch

A trip-switch is a device in a mechanical or electrical system that causes the system to shut down when a problem occurs. When the trip-switch "trips," it renders the system temporarily inoperative until the problem is rectified. The body's trip-switch is often pain. Pain tells us that something is wrong (that is, out of balance) and in need of attention. Little children are sent for a "time-out" when they repeatedly misbehave. Sometimes prisoners or those in mental hospitals have to be put in a padded cell where they cannot hurt themselves or others. They must be watched carefully for a time until they literally "cool down." After a trip-switch trips, a solution to the problem can be found. The system can then be repaired and restarted without damage.

We can install a trip-switch in our minds that can act as an alarm, identifying a faulty choice in thinking and, thus, stopping the mind's miscreations. Thinking can then be properly redirected. It is possible to stop the ego—to stop irrational, unnatural, or unreasonable thinking; reverse the direction of the projective egoistic mind; and go the other way. How simple is the obvious! The ego is always on the defensive; always ready to judge, hide, defend, or attack. The use of defense mechanisms happens so quickly that we do not think about what we are doing. We thoughtlessly react, an explosion occurs, and we experience the often-negative consequences.

The Thought Catcher

Teachers of God learn to catch irrational thoughts. The moment an irrational, judgmental, unkind, or attacking thought comes to mind, a trip-switch initiates a "thought-catcher." Think of a thought-catcher as a net thrown over a thought, keeping the thought from following the ego down the path of madness. As with a trip-switch, a thought-catcher delays action until a more reasonable (that is, peaceful) state of mind can be achieved.

Remember that the ego always speaks first, so, when a problem arises, wait. See what the ego's answer is and then ask for the "reasonable and loving" response. When a trip-switch trips within the everyday world, alerting us to a problem, we may bring in a troubleshooter, a computer geek, a psychologist, a doctor, a plumber, or a problem solver. The "Problem Solver" of all problem solvers is the Holy Spirit. The Holy Spirit corrects the mind by placing the mind under "proper authority," which gives us a better way of perceiving what we might have formerly seen as an "attack."

> *If you cannot hear the Voice for God,*
> *it is because you do not choose to listen.*
> *That you do listen to the voice of your ego is demonstrated*
> *by your attitudes, your feelings and your behavior.*
>
> T-4.IV.1:1–2

Attitude and Altitude: Above the Battleground

Our attitudes reflect our values, likes, dislikes, wants, and needs. An attitude is a "point of view" and a reflection of the way we choose to see the world. Attitudes are also judgments and, as such, they can be blinding. Attitudes are the opinions we hold about people, places, things, and events. Optimistic, pessimistic, liberal, and conservative are points of view that reflect attitudes. We sometimes say of teenagers (or others) that we "can't seem to get through to them," because they have "an attitude," meaning there is a block in our communication and, thus, an impediment to an awareness of Love's presence.

> *Your attitudes . . . are necessarily conflicted,*
> *because all attitudes are ego-based.*
>
> T-4.II.5:6

What Drives Attitudes?

Every thought we have brings either peace or war, love or fear (W-16.3:1). Attitudes are controlled by the mind. They can be changed from fearful to loving, from harmful to helpful. The attitude we choose determines the world we see. Attitudes are also habits. Like all habits, they can be changed. Life is determined not by what life brings to us, but by what we bring to life!

> *We awaken in others*
> *the same attitude of mind we hold toward them.*
>
> AMERICAN WRITER AND ARTIST
> ELBERT HUBBARD (1856–1915)

If the attitude we hold toward a sister or brother is hostile, it is felt, even if nothing is said. If the attitude we hold toward another is loving, it, too, is felt, even if nothing is said.

> *Healing is a thought by which two minds*
> *perceive their oneness and become glad.*
>
> T-5.I.1:1

Comparison must be an ego device, for love makes none.
Specialness always makes comparisons.

T-24.II.1:1—2

Have you ever found yourself wondering why you're having a particular thought? Look at it and "think" about where it came from. Is it peaceful? Is it sane? If it is not peaceful, if it is not sane, it is coming from the ego. And there must be another way of seeing. The greatest difficulty in learning the Course is not in understanding the metaphysics. The greatest difficulty is in putting into practice what it asks us to do.

Irrational thought is disordered thought.
God Himself orders your thought because your thought
was created by Him. Guilt feelings are always a sign
that you do not know this. They also show that you
believe you can think apart from God, and want to.

T-5.V.7:1—4

Trip-Switches

1. GUILT FEELINGS

Guilt Feelings, no matter what their seeming source, are a sure sign of a trip-switch—a signal that a particular thought needs readjusting. Guilt is a result of unnatural, erroneous thinking. Guilt arises when we think that we can think apart from God following the ego's thought system of separation), or when we think we can do something in opposition to God. Ultimately, our ongoing determination to remain separated from God is the only reason we experience guilt feelings.

My friend John Nagy (1941–present), a most perceptive Course student/teacher from the Boston area, tells a story from many years ago. John lives in a secluded area near the ocean. One day he was sitting on the steps of his front porch feeling frustrated about his inability to understand the Course's idea of loving oneself. He was so blocked and frustrated that he started yelling out loud at Jesus. When he finally stopped yelling, an inner voice said, "Well, if you don't want to love yourself, that is okay. But is it okay if I love you?" Within minutes he started to feel loved inside. From then on, he felt love and self-contentment, and now he is one happy guy.

As my friend Terry Badgett (1951–present) from Tennessee says, "You don't have to get God's approval." We already have God's approval. God knows only the timeless truth of our Being. Guilt feelings are the preservers of the illusion of time and separation. They bring fear of reprisal and thus confirm that the future will be like the past. If we want to be happy, we only have to do what God (our Inner Teacher, the Holy Spirit) is asking us to do.

> Watch your mind carefully for any beliefs that hinder
> its accomplishment, and step away from them.
> Judge how well you have done this by your own feelings,
> for this is the one right use of judgment.
>
> T-4.IV.8:6-7

When we experience a guilty feeling, it indicates that something has gone wrong in our thinking. We can examine the source of the feeling and decide to make a more loving choice, acknowledging that we have chosen incorrectly and bought into the ego's thought system of separation. Acknowledging our error—rather than engaging in defensiveness or projection and attack—is refreshing. We may ask for forgiveness, or we may simply acknowledge that we "have to do nothing." It is "doing" that gets us into trouble!

2. DEBILITATING BEHAVIORS

An obvious indication of a trip-switch (that something has gone awry and needs correction) is engaging in any behavior that has debilitating effects on our well-being, such as overindulging in eating, drinking, or drugs. Or perhaps our being involved in some selfish act that irresponsibly results in an accident, being fired from a job, or possibly being arrested. If we are engaging in selfish behavior, we should stop and ask ourselves: Do we want to go on this way? What are we afraid of? Who is in charge here? We can make another choice to see and respond differently.

> *"Lead us not into temptation" means "Recognize your errors*
> *and choose to abandon them by following my guidance."*
>
> T-1.II.4:7

> *Do not see error. Do not make it real.*
>
> S-2.I.3:3–4

3. UNKIND THOUGHTS

Unkind thoughts are attitudes and clear signs of a trip-switch, signaling that some thought needs to be corrected. If you find yourself having an unkind thought, stop it right there. Ask yourself: "What am I thinking?! Why am I having this thought? Can I let it go?"

4. ANGER, ANNOYANCE, AND IRRITATIONS

Anger is never justified (T-30.VI.1:1). That does not mean we should never get angry. It just means that if we do, we need to recognize that something has gone wrong with our thinking process; otherwise, we would not be angry. So, if you're feeling even the slightest irritation, stop and examine the source of your irritation. Where is it coming from? Before insanity takes over, let it go. Anger always involves projection of separation. As such, it is "my" responsibility. It cannot be attributed on anyone else.

The Holy Spirit asks only this little help of you:
Whenever your thoughts wander to a special relationship
which still attracts you, enter with Him into a holy instant,
and there let Him release you.

T-16.VI.12:1

When we get angry, where do we focus our attention? According to neuroanatomist Jill Bolte Taylor, author of *My Stroke of Insight* (2006), research has shown that it takes ninety seconds to stop our insanity and refocus attention in another direction. Let's say you have a child who is throwing a temper tantrum. If you can take that child and just quietly hold him for ninety seconds, the temper tantrum will stop. In the same way, when we notice a judgment or an attack thought forming in our mind, if we can wait ninety seconds the angry feeling can dissipate. If we "feed it," however, it will not go away.

You are responsible for the energy that you bring . . .

FROM *MY STROKE OF INSIGHT,* BY NEUROANATOMIST
AND AUTHOR DR. JILL BOLTE TAYLOR (1959–PRESENT)

It is imperative that we heal our own projections first. Freud said that all projections come from repression. Let's look carefully at what we may be repressing. Remember:

We do not project what we are aware of.
We project what we are not aware of.

The Course is trying to help us consistently raise our level of awareness. If we were fully aware, we would not be projective. If we're engaged in any form of condemnation, we need to look carefully at our own thinking process. Ask, "What am I thinking? What am I afraid of?"

Maybe the person we're upset with has done something selfish. Maybe that same selfishness lies in me. Look at it carefully. This is the real meaning of "Do unto others as we would have them do unto us."

> *Anger may take the form of any reaction ranging from mild*
> *irritation to rage. The degree of the emotion you experience*
> *does not matter. You will become increasingly aware*
> *that a slight twinge of annoyance is nothing but*
> *a veil drawn over intense fury.*
>
> W-21.2:3–5

If there is something that irritates us about someone else, it is a key to understanding where we need to be doing our own spiritual work. The first step is not to attack the other. The other is not the source, or cause, of annoyance and needs no "fixing." Next, look within (to the projected source) for the cause of the irritation. Even a little annoyance is a cover for wrath, fury, and rage. We want to be vigilant, looking under every rock within our psyche for whatever darkness may lurk there and exposing it to fresh air and light.

If you are upset in any way, for any reason, no matter how large, no matter how small, stop and look. You put this experience here, and you are responsible for how you perceive it.

> *Our task is but to continue, as fast as possible,*
> *the necessary process of looking straight at all the interference*
> *and seeing it exactly as it is.*
>
> T-15.IX.2:1

Word-Fasting

A student kept talking about how much he "hated" a certain situation he was involved in at work. When I pointed out his repeated use of the word *hate*, he said he had no idea he'd used the word even once. Words like *hate* are obvious trip-switches. Such words tell us there is something wrong with our thinking. Hate is a reactionary response that comes from fear. This is exactly the kind of response we can become aware of and observe. Look at the hate response, but don't judge it. Just stop! God does not condemn; neither can we. The Holy Spirit (who speaks for God) does not condemn, and when we are in our right mind, we are in alignment with the Holy Spirit.

Watch the words that come out of your mouth, remembering that projection makes perception. The words we use reveal our projections as well as our perceptions. Why would we want to use words that fall under the following categories?

1. Profanity and vulgarity.

   Do we want to condemn someone to hell?

   Dolores tells the story of a parent who came into the school where she works to see the principal. The principal was busy with another parent, so the parent had to wait. During this time she used the phrase *pissed-off* dozens of times. Finally, she got to go in to see the principal. After she left, the principal came into the office, shaking his head, and said, "Boy, was she ever 'pissed-off.'"

2. Name calling—including words such as *stupid, insane, idiotic, ludicrous, absurd*, and more.

3. Judgmental words. *Disgusting* and *irked* represent something that comes up from the gut and makes us sick. *Despicable,* from the same root as the word *spectacle*, literally means "something that is unpleasant to the eye." Why would we call anything despicable? What is it in us that is disgusted, irked, or infuriated?

We can only say we're *disappointed* when we've made an appointment. That is, when we have some expectation or anticipation about the way a situation is supposed to be. If it doesn't work out that way, then we are disappointed. *Upset* and *offend* represent our minds being out of balance. We can only be upset if we have a "setup." If something "off-ends" me, it knocks us off the end.

Outraged comes from the Anglo-French *ut-rage*, meaning "outer" or "other." The word outrage suggests that the problem is not with us; it is in the other!

Reversing Thinking and Going the Other Way

> *Today we go beyond the grievances,*
> *to look upon the miracle instead.*
> *We will reverse the way you see*
> *by not allowing sight to stop before it sees.*

W-78.2:1–2

When I was a kid in the 1950s, I loved going to the Audrain Country Fair in Mexico, Missouri. My great-grandfather, Jonathan Mundy, raised saddle horses, and Mexico was, at one time, the "Saddle Horse Capital of the World." Saddle horses are known as the "peacocks" of the horse show world. There were wonderful horse shows and contests going on in front of the grandstands, day and night, during the last two weeks of August every year. We would go and visit some of the horses in their stalls, and what wonderful fun it was.

During a horse show, one of the commands the judge behind the mike used to give to the riders was "Reverse and walk your horse." The riders would then turn their horses in the opposite direction and parade them back in front of the grandstand in a slow, beautiful, measured gait. The horses lifted their legs high and walked slowly. They were quite pretty. To this day, if I see a thought beginning to go down a wrong path, I sometimes say to myself, "Reverse and walk your horses." Whenever you notice an unloving or mean-spirited thought, stop! Slow down, turn around, and come back slowly, lightly, and lovingly.

> *Progress [in psychotherapy] becomes impossible until the*
> *patient is persuaded to reverse his twisted way*
> *of looking at the world;*
> *his twisted way of looking at himself.*
>
> P-2.V.2:3

The Undoing Process

Lesson 11 from the *Workbook* says, "My meaningless thoughts are showing me a meaningless world." This realization is a beginning step in the reversal of thinking. It may seem as though the world determines what we perceive, but it's the other way around: Our thoughts determine the world we perceive.

To reverse thinking, we recognize that, regardless of what is happening, "This is not done to me, but I am doing this" (T-28.II.12:5). We made up the ego, and the ego can be undone by relinquishing belief in it. What we perceive as an effect (our ego-based thought) is really a cause (of what we perceive). We are not victims of the world we see. Accepting responsibility for what we perceive as the effect, we change the cause (to that of the mind), and everything changes in response.

"The miracle does nothing." The miracle, or shift in perception, simply wipes away illusion and allows us to see things the way they are, rather than the way we have made them up in our "dreaming of the world." A miracle is a correction in misperception. This correction (miracle) is accomplished by dropping all projections, judgments, definitions, classifications, and characterizations. To accomplish this reversal in perception, the Course asks us to look for the truth in our brothers and sisters, no matter how deeply it may appear to be buried.

Do not allow your brother to be sick, for if he is, have
you abandoned him to his own dream by sharing it with him.

T-28.III.3:3

If we say that a person has done or said something *disgusting* or *repulsive,* we're projecting our own revulsion upon her. What we see is not the truth. God has no favorite children. "The sun rises on the evil and the good and the rain falls on the just and the unjust" (Matthew 5:45).

Look for the Good in Everything You See

If we are not aware of how projective we are, how can we drop our projections? No matter how dark a brother's soul may seem, there remains a light the ego does not see. More precisely, there is a light inside of ourselves that we are not aware of, as darkness blocks perception of the light in our brother. It is that light we seek to see in our brother—not the darkness. As my friend Jeannine Caryl says over and over again, "Look for the good in everything you see." Look for the good because it is there. If we place emphasis on darkness, we're looking through the eyes of the ego, and the ego is blind. The ego knows only darkness, yet there is no place that God is not.

Conflict is the root of all evil,
for being blind it does not see whom it attacks.
Yet it always attacks the Son of God, and the Son of God is you.

T-11:III.1:7–8

If what we see in a brother or sister angers, disgusts or even annoys us, then we give way to the demands of the ego and, thus, to an illusion. A student sent me an e-mail, saying he was struggling to understand how he was "at cause" for his wife's health issues. I wrote back saying, "You are *not* 'at cause' for your wife's health issues. We are not responsible for another's choices. We *are* responsible for our 'reaction' to someone else choices." When we react to the decisions of others, we reinforce those decisions in ourselves and others.

Let's say you have a friend who smokes and you point out to that friend the negative consequences of smoking. No one needs to be told that smoking is detrimental to health. We are bombarded daily with that information. If we try to correct a brother by pointing out how sick he is, we project our own guilt onto him and make ourselves sick. Projecting guilt is the root of all sickness. We do not see our brother as he truly is; we see an illusion. If we imbue that illusion with power, we condemn us both to hell.

> *Would God condemn Himself to hell and to damnation?*
> *And do you will that this be done unto your savior?*
>
> T-24.II.8:3–4

> *Illusions carry only guilt and suffering,*
> *sickness and death, to their believers.*
>
> T-22.II.3:1

> *Reason will tell you that the only way to escape*
> *from misery is to recognize it and go the other way.*
>
> T-22.II.4:1

Going the Other Way

Reversing cause and effect (acknowledging thought as "cause" and seemingly "outside" projection/perception as "effect") enables us to go the other way, retreating from "misery" and error to peace and truth. Lesson 12 from the Workbook of the Course says, "You think that what upsets you is a frightening world, or a sad world, or a violent world, or an insane world. All these attributes are given it by you." Until we can learn to look at "all things" through eyes of love, we're stuck in judgment, and we cannot know perfect happiness.

> *This is the separation's final step,*
> *with which salvation, which proceeds to go the other way,*
> *begins. This final step is an effect of what has gone before,*
> *appearing as a cause. The miracle is the first step in giving*
> *back to cause the function of causation, not effect.*
>
> T-28.II.9:1–3

> *If everybody minded their own business,*
> *the world would go around a great deal faster than it does.*
>
> ALICE, FROM *ALICE IN WONDERLAND*, BY LEWIS CARROLL

> *Everyone thinks of changing the world,*
> *but no one thinks of changing himself.*
>
> RUSSIAN WRITER LEO TOLSTOY (1828–1910)

To perceive error in a sister or a brother, and then point out that error, amplifies the error. When we attack a brother or sister, we attack ourselves. An insane (ego-bound) mind will always perceive correction as attack. Yet a sane mind can neither attack nor be attacked. Jesus remained calm in the presence of the insanity that surrounded him.

The ego is wholly mistrustful of everything it perceives.
Because of its misperceptions it is capable of suspiciousness
at best and viciousness at worst.

T-9.VII.3:7

Forsaking Ourselves

The Course asks us repeatedly to watch our minds for scraps of fear.

I will never forsake you any more than God will,
but I must wait as long as you choose to forsake yourself.
Because I wait in love and not in impatience,
you will surely ask me truly.
I will come in response to a single unequivocal call.

T-4.III.7:5–10

A conflicted mind cannot learn with consistency. If we project conflict, we are not experiencing consistency. Aware of the ego in ourselves and responding to the ego in others, we are blinded to the truth.

Engaging in Right-Minded Thinking

1. Install trip-switches.
2. Watch your thoughts.
3. Watch the words that come out of your mouth.
4. Stop the negative thought.
5. Stop the mood. Stop the attitude. Cool down. Do nothing!
6. Let it be. Peace comes to the quiet mind.
7. Experience the feeling. Do not analyze it.
8. Acknowledge that an error in thinking has occurred.

9. See how incredibly projective we are!

10. The fourth time a new student came to our Miracles group, she said, "I'm beginning to realize how incredibly judgmental I am." And I replied, "That's great! You're getting it."

11. Reverse your thinking! Go the other way.

12. If necessary, let off steam in a quiet way.

13. Go for a walk or a swim, or just go into another room.

14. Offer healing, instead of hurt.

15. Say, "No, thank you" to temptation.

16. Turn all seeing over to the Holy Spirit. Look through His eyes.

Christ's vision does not use your eyes,
but you can look through His and learn to see like Him.

S-2.I.6:4

If there is an effect, there must have been a cause. That cause is always in the mind; thus, the emphasis in the Course on our need to see differently. The mind is the determiner of everything we see. Once we decide with God, ". . . all decisions become as easy and as right as breathing. There is no effort, and you will be led as gently as if you were being carried down a quiet path in summer" (T-14.IV.6:1–3). Eventually, everyone realizes it's better to let God win. After all, that is what happens when the illusion ends.

Letting something that seems great or small take the peace of God away is a waste of time. The way in which we see things makes all the difference in the world—literally. Our path to Heaven leads us exactly where we are supposed to go. The further we move along our appointed path, the easier it is to look back and see how perfect that path has been and we can laugh at the absurdity of thinking it should have been different!

Destiny unfolds at its own unhurried gait. The process of awakening is highly individualized and, in that sense, it is also perfect. With patience, we understand that regardless of what is going on in the world, we have a choice. We can always choose love instead of fear, forgiveness instead of anger, God instead of the ego. When we forgive, the past no longer matters.

Salvation is a paradox indeed!
What could it be except a happy dream?
It asks you but that you forgive all things that no one ever did;
to overlook what is not there, and not to look upon the unreal
as reality. You are but asked to let your will be done,
and seek no longer for the things you do not want.
And you are asked to let yourself be free of all the dreams
of what you never were, and seek no more to substitute
the strength of idle wishes for the Will of God.

T-30.IV.7:1–5

CHAPTER 23

Sacred Contracts

THE SCRIPT IS WRITTEN

God's Perfect Plan

There is a plan of redemption behind the facades of the world. I become increasingly happy to the extent that I understand and follow God's perfect plan. In Lesson 113, which is a review of Lesson 96 (*Salvation comes from my one Self*), we read,

> . . . *I see God's perfect plan for my salvation perfectly fulfilled.*

> W-113.2(96).2

We can have a complete assurance that we will all find our way back home. Actually, we already have. It's just a matter of our remembering the truth.

> *There is a plan behind appearances that does not change.*
> **The script is written.**
> *When experience will come to end your doubting has been set.*
> *For we but see the journey from the point at which it ended,*
> *looking back on it, imagining we make it once again;*
> *reviewing mentally what has gone by.*

> W-158.2.2–5

Contemporary author Carolyn Myss (1952–present) refers to this script as our Sacred Contract, an agreement to learn certain lessons and develop wisdom in our life. Everyone is on the path home and we are all struggling in our own way to awaken. The more awake we are, the more conscious we are, the fewer "unconscious"-type things "seem" to happen to us. Even when unexplainable and unwelcome experiences come our way, we are more capable of handling these difficulties when we see that even these experiences are part of a greater plan of our awakening.

> *Your passage through time and space is not at random.*
> *You cannot but be in the right place at the right time.*
>
> W-42.2:2–4

Life always gives us what is most helpful for our spiritual development. Even if we go off course, Spirit is ever present to help us recalculate and find our way home.

The lessons we face in life are part of the script I (you) (we) wrote. I may be looking at cancer, a divorce, bankruptcy, or something I would prefer to bypass. In 2001–2002, I had colon cancer and a tumor the size of a lemon was removed from my insides. At the time of the operation, they found that the cancer had spread into my lymphatic system, requiring thirty weeks of chemo. After the experience, I wrote a chapter in my earlier book, *Missouri Mystics,* called "The Classroom Called Cancer." It was a classroom because I was given the opportunity to look at death up close and carefully, and surprisingly it led me into a deeper experience of the immediacy of life.

> *The kind of brain and body you have, the family and society,*
> *the time in history you were born into, all these and more were*
> *determined by you yourself, by your degree of expansion,*

by your willingness to love. No one did anything to you.
No one forced you. There is absolute justice in the experience
that each of us is having every second of the day.
In one sense we can all relax, because nothing is secret,
nothing is lost, nothing is forgotten, no one is abandoned.

FROM *THE LAZY MAN'S GUIDE TO ENLIGHTENMENT*
(1983), BY THADDEUS GOLAS

Ask for Help

As with any good GPS system, we are consistently and persistently being
given exactly the right information to guide our decision making. We
have to be "willing" to be led, however. We all know the jokes about
men not being willing to stop to ask for directions. To admit to being
lost implies helplessness. Asking for directions, means recognizing
our dependence on God's Plan for Salvation. Not following GPS is
pure foolishness. Alcoholics Anonymous will not help folks until they
are willing to admit that they need help. We must admit that we are
miserable before we can change. Once we ask for help, help is available,
but we must ask for it.

God did not make the body, because it is destructible,
and therefore not of the Kingdom.

T-6.V.A.2:1

According to his biography, former president Richard Nixon worried
a great deal during his later years about how he would be remembered.
We live on not in memories. We live on always in that which has always
been alive and eternal. Ego-based plans always fail, as they contain
within them the seeds of their own destruction. There is a built-in
implode mechanism in every ego. And, because all bodies are physical,

they, too, have a built-in implode mechanism. All bodies die.

As I write these words, the oldest person in the world is 116. The oldest person on record lived to 122. Life expectancy is slowly getting longer, but it is not infinite. Anything that is destructible cannot be real (T-6.I.4:3). Even mountains are slowly crumbling and one day, billions of years from now, our sun will burn out. Spirit takes whatever we have built and, after our worldly endeavors fail, turns these experiences into spiritual lessons. The ego-body is doomed, but Spirit is eternal and in the body's loss (purification), we see our way more clearly home.

> The Holy Spirit, as always,
> takes what you have made and translates it into a learning
> device. Again as always, He reinterprets what the ego uses as
> an argument for separation into a demonstration against it.
>
> T-6.V.A.2:4–5

The Easy Pass

A miracle works like an E-ZPass. It can whisk us right around any potential slowdown. You don't need to stop and pay a toll taker. Someone who looks like a doctor, a lawyer, a judge, or a therapist need not take your money away from you.

God does not know the details of our soap opera dreams because they are dreams. He knows His children are sleeping and He has a plan by which we might awaken and find our way home. Time is kind and if we use it on behalf of reality, it will keep gentle pace with our transition (T-16.VI.8:2). A clear highway home is laid out for us, if we choose to follow it. Giving up on arrogance and following GPS, we all soon return home.

I Could Go Home

We all come into this world with a variety of talents and treasures.
The Prodigal Son wastes his inheritance and becomes impoverished.
He repents and then there comes a revelation: "I could go home!"
Acceptance of the curriculum of the atonement and the "undoing" of the
ego eventually brings us home. Our task is easy. We are to assume full
responsibility for everything that comes our way. It may not sound easy,
but it is the smoothest way.

Lesson 25 from the Course is: "I do not know what anything is for."
This idea explains why nothing we see means anything. How many
times have you been through some experience and said, "I do not know
what this is for," only to realize years later "exactly" why you wrote
the script that way? As I accept responsibility for my script and grow
in trust, fear subsides and life becomes increasingly purposeful and
meaningful. Once I quit trying to do it my way, once I begin to follow
GPS, I can move with purpose. The fulfillment of the son's role is to
return to the father, as does the Prodigal Son. Luke, in the movie *Star
Wars*, opens up to his true Self and is thereby able to bring about his
own salvation. And, in the end, he redeems his father, Darth Vader.

How Long Has This Been Going On?

Once the response is made, the results are wonderful. Doing what
were called to do means living an inspired life. American actor Tony
Randall (1920–2004) tells of his discovery of opera at the age of thirty.
He was taking voice lessons, and his teacher asked him to go listen to
a particular male opera singer. Randall was resistant, not the least bit
interested. He had avoided opera all his life. Now, at the urging of his
teacher, he went. He was enthralled, enchanted, indeed entranced. A
new world suddenly opened up for him. At the end of the performance,
he came out saying, "How long has this been going on?"

There is no need to live in bondage. There is no addiction, no special relationship, nothing that has the power to take the peace of God from me unless I give it that power. All I need to do is do God's will. The quieter I get, the more clearly God's voice can be heard. Then it is that we say, "Let me not try to make another will, for it is senseless and will cause me pain" (W-307.2). Doing God's will brings perfect happiness. Nothing else will ever work. When we respond, when we do what God is asking us to do, we say, "How long has this been going on?" Perfection awaits us, not at the end of the rainbow, but just inside the doorway of Heaven—very close to the heart of God.

> *Look up and find your certain destiny*
> *the world would hide but God would have you see.*
>
> C-EP.3:7

How It All Ends: There is No "I" in Heaven

Italian Renaissance sculptor Michelangelo (1475–1564) said of his masterwork, the statue of David, that he simply removed from the huge slab of marble everything that was not David. Spanish mystic Saint John of the Cross described the spiritual path as *via negativa* (the negative way). We are to remove from our lives, he said, everything that is not of God and what is left is God. If I remove from my life everything that is not of God, what I find is my Self, in all its purity and wholeness.

I am either God-created or self-created. If I am God-created, I am of God and ultimately all I know is God. Then there is no fear, no doubt of eternal life. The ego looks real, big, and important. It looks like who we think we are. Moving beyond this false self is the end-game message in the Course and all deeply committed spiritual traditions. When concepts of the self are set aside, truth is revealed (T-31.V.17:4).

It's the destiny of everybody to be nobody,
and thus, something eternal though nobody special.

Losing an illusion, we go from identification with ego-body to Mind – Spirit = Self. The ego falls away as it is seen for what it is—nothing, nonexistent, not a problem. We are left with Oneness. There is no "me" and God. In God there is no other, no body, and no separate self. We move to an experience of God beyond ideas about God. It is a matter of acceptance, a matter of experience.

Our choices . . . show what we truly are,
far more than our abilities.

Albus Dumbledore, in *Harry Potter and the Chamber of Secrets*
(2000), by J. K. Rowling (1965–present)

Once the right choice is made, there is no other choice to be made. There is no subject-object. There is no self and other. There is only God, only Oneness. The final decision for God awakens us from dreaming. Why does a bird sing? Why does a kitten mew? Why does a dancer dance? Why did Helen Schucman scribe the Course? There was no other choice. Someone was needed who could shut the ego out and let the voice of God come through. Going all the way to no-self is freedom from aloneness. In the end, it means identity with Christ and, through the Christ, to the oneness that is of God.

When I said "I am with you always," I meant it literally.
I am not absent to anyone in any situation.
Because I am always with you,
"you" are the way, the truth and the life.
You did not make this power, any more than I did.
It was created to be shared, and therefore cannot be meaningfully perceived as

belonging to anyone
at the expense of another.

T-7.III.1:7–11

The more I see myself as separate and special, the more I experience aloneness, the more illusion creates me. Awakening from the dream of specialness, true identity is restored. Perfect happiness, self, eternity, oneness, life, love, Christ, and God are reclaimed.

Being is perfect.

Being is timeless.

Being is changeless.

Being is never threatened.

Being is without distinction.

Being is the opposite of aloneness.

Being is in communication with everything that is.

Being is incredible.

Being simply is.

Freedom from specialness means knowing Heaven now. We have "present memory." It's not about the past—never. It not about the future. How could it be? Present memory means knowing now. Our relationship with God is vertical, not horizontal. There is no past and no future. Always must be now. Alpha and omega is where it all begins and ends.

Henceforth, hear but the Voice for God
and for your Self when you retire from the world,
to seek reality instead.
He will direct your efforts, telling you exactly what to do,
how to direct your mind, and when to come to Him in silence,
asking for His sure direction and His certain Word.
His is the Word that God has given you.

His is the Word you chose to be your own.

W-EP.III.2–5

Sawing Wood and Drinking Water

In October 2012, Hurricane Sandy blew through our backyard, bringing down an ancient oak tree. A seventy-six-year-old man named Lester came to cut up a tree twice as old as he was. As he was sawing, I was busy carrying away limbs. When he stopped sawing wood to take a drink of water and rest for a moment, we talked for a bit. "I absolutely love sawing wood," he said. "I always have." Sawing wood was Lester's form of meditation. If we love the way we are living, if we are listening to and following the voice for God in our lives, we are always meditating, and we are always happy.

> *My mother always told me that happiness was the key to life.*
> *When I went to school, they asked me what I wanted to be*
> *when I grew up. I wrote down "happy."*
> *They told me I didn't understand the assignment,*
> *and I told them they didn't understand life.*

BRITISH MUSICIAN JOHN LENNON

Ultimately, if we are not happy in the world, it is "never" because of outside circumstances. If we are not happy, it is because we have *chosen* not to be happy. What we possess, where we live, or what we do does not make us happy or unhappy. If we can't be happy where we are, we definitely cannot be happy where we are not. Everything depends on how we perceive the world because, in the final analysis, the world is our "dream." Projection makes perception, and perception is a matter of choice. The world we see is what we make it—nothing more than that. If we are content with what we have and rejoice in the way things are, we lack nothing.

Everything is in the mind. Awakening from dreaming means recognizing that "we were dreaming." Alice in *Alice in Wonderland* is lying under a tree, sleeping, with her head on her sister's lap. When the boy in the modern fairy tale *The Polar Express* awakens, he is safe at home in his bed and it is Christmas morning. Dorothy of *The Wizard of Oz* is safely asleep in her bed.

Real Happiness

Real happiness comes from:

- The successful resistance of temptation.
- Knowing that our actions come from love.
- Letting annoyances go.
- The joy of having truly forgiven.
- The restoration of full communication with God.

Am I God-created or self-created? If I am God-created, then I am of God and ultimately all I will know is God. Either love is real and fear is not, or fear is real and love is not. Either there is perfection or there is no perfection. I'm betting on perfection. I'm betting on God. I'm betting on love. I'm betting on eternity. This is what trust is all about. God comes in where time ends and eternity begins. Time is an illusion—past or in the future, but never here, never now. How could the will of God be in the past or yet to happen? What God wills is forever now (W-131.6:1–6). Focusing our attention on the voice for God and no other means finding perfect happiness now. We need only hold to the truth with consistency. As the Course expresses it, "The Kingdom of Heaven '*is*' you" (T-4.III.1:4).

Fantasy (the ego's dreaming of the world) is a distorted form of vision (T-1.VII.3:1). For Peter Pan there never was a Never-Never-Land. In every Jesus there is an eternal Christ, in every Siddhartha an everlasting Buddha, in every Cinderella a princess, in every Pinocchio a real boy, and you are the light of the world. Amen.

Postscript

IS PERFECT HAPPINESS POSSIBLE?

Perfect happiness is not only possible, it is the only thing there is. All else is illusion, a dream, a fantasy. The Course is trying to help us awaken from the dream of separation and division, a dream in which the ego seems very real and God seems like a nice idea. In truth only God is real and perfect happiness is our eternal state.

> *Whatever is true is eternal, and cannot change or be changed.*
> *Spirit is therefore unalterable because it is already perfect...*
>
> T-1.V.5:2

As long as we are working our way home we might as well have fun along the way. The fun comes in doing God's will and sharing the path with every soul we meet.

> *Then one day Jonathan, standing on the shore,*
> *closing his eyes, concentrating, all in a flash knew what Chaing*
> *had been telling him. "Why, that's true! I am a perfect,*
> *unlimited gull!" He felt a great shock of joy.*
>
> —FROM *JONATHAN LIVINGSTON SEAGULL,*
> BY RICHARD BACH

Acknowledgments

Dr. Helen Schucman, Dr. William Thetford, and Dr. Kenneth Wapnick formally introduced me to *A Course in Miracles* in April 1975. Ever since, Ken has been a consistent wise older brother and a gentle guide in my understanding of the Course. Ken is the mountain. Go visit the mountain. I wrote an article about Ken in 1991, titled "Impeccably on the Path." Ken is as impeccable as ever. We are all indebted to Ken and his wife Gloria for the example they set as guides on the path to perfect happiness.

My thanks to Judy Whitson of the Foundation for Inner Peace for her friendship of over forty-five years; it was Judy who helped with the connections that made this book possible. My assistant Fran Cosentino helped in every stage of development. I am grateful to her for her editorial skills, diligence, and patience. I'm very appreciative for the help of four *Course in Miracles* student/teachers: Lynne Matous, David Brown, Dorothy Gaydos, and Sonja Spahn, each of whom read through the entire text and offered their suggestions for corrections and improvements.

My friend Shanti Rica Josephs has, since 1972, been my steady rock—the one to whom I've been able to pour out my soul, the one who has consistently known the right answer.

I am grateful for the consistent, kind guidance of my agent, Ivor Whitson, his wife Ronnie, and my editors at Sterling Publishing, Michael Fragnito and Kate Zimmermann.

At the top of the list goes my thanks to my partner in life, my darling Dolores, who is ever-present in love and devotion to the life we share. I am a very lucky man. The day I met Dolores was the best day of my life. She brought me my daughter Sarah—a shining light in my life.

Index

About the Author

Jon Mundy, PhD, is an author, lecturer, and the executive director of All Faiths Seminary International in New York City. He taught university courses in philosophy and religion from 1967 to 2009. He is the publisher of *Miracles* magazine, the author of nine books, and senior minister emeritus of Interfaith Fellowship in New York City. He met Dr. Helen Schucman, the scribe of *A Course in Miracles*, in 1973. Helen introduced Jon to the Course and served as his counselor and guide until she became ill in 1980. Jon also appears on occasion as *Dr. Baba Jon Mundane*, a stand-up philosopher comedian.

If you enjoyed this book, you might enjoy a subscription to *Miracles* magazine. It's $34 a year for a regular subscription or $29 a year if you are a senior citizen. Visit:

www.miraclesmagazine.org
Box 1000, Washingtonville, NY 10992
Or, call 212-866-3795 or 845-496-9089